HIDDEN IN GENESIS

HIDDEN IN GENESIS

Delving deeply into Scripture to discover the veiled truths about our ancient history, fallen angels and Nephilim

Advantage BOOKS

Paul Knauber

Hidden in Genesis by Paul Knauber
Copyright © 2021 by Paul Knauber
All Rights Reserved.
ISBN: 978-1-59755-636-1

Published by: ADVANTAGE BOOKS™
　　　　　　　　Longwood, FL
　　　　　　　　www.advbookstore.com

This book and parts thereof may not be reproduced in any form, stored in a retrieval system or transmitted in any form by any means (electronic, mechanical, photocopy, recording or otherwise) without prior written permission of the author, except as provided by United States of America copyright law.

All material contained herein that is not original is reprinted with authorized permission or license from the authors, artists, and/or publishers with appropriate attributions, or are in the public domain, or within the publishers' gratis use guidelines.

Library of Congress Catalog Number: 2021940855

Names:	Knauber, Paul, Author
Title:	Hidden in Genesis / Paul Knauber
Description	Longwood: Advantage Books, 2021
Identifiers:	ISBN (print): 9781597556361, (mobi, epub): 9781597556484
Catgory:	RELIGION: Christian Theology - Creationism
Subjects:	Nephilim in Genesis; Nephilim; Nephilim Giant; Nephilim in the Book of Enoch; Giants in the earth; Giants Fallen Angels and the Return of the Nephilim; Giants on the earth; The Book of Enoch fallen Angels; Enoch watchers; Preadamites; The pre-Adamite world; The pre-Adamite world and the origin of Satan aka Lucifer; Preadamite existence; The creation of the world according to the Bible; When was the world made

First Printing: June 2021
21 22 23 24 25 26   10 9 8 7 6 5 4 3 2 1

Table of Contents

ACKNOWLEDGEMENTS 5

PREFACE: THE IMPORTANCE OF THIS INVESTIGATION 7

INTRODUCTION 13

    THE BIBLE 14
    THE BOOK OF JASHER 14
    THE BOOKS OF ENOCH 15
    THE ANTIQUITIES OF THE JEWS 15
    THE BOOK OF JUBILEES 17
    SEDER OLAM 17
    THE ANNALS OF THE WORLD, BY JAMES USSHER 18
    GENESIS 6 GIANTS, MASTER BUILDERS OF PREHISTORIC AND ANCIENT CIVILIZATIONS, BY STEPHEN QUAYLE 19
    THE CHRONOLOGY OF ANCIENT KINGDOMS AMENDED. TO WHICH IS PREFIX'D, A SHORT CHRONICLE FROM THE FIRST MEMORY OF THINGS IN EUROPE, TO THE CONQUEST OF PERSIA BY ALEXANDER THE GREAT, BY SIR ISAAC NEWTON (1728). 19
    OBSERVATIONS UPON THE PROPHECIES OF DANIEL, AND THE APOCALYPSE OF ST. JOHN: FULL AND FINE TEXT OF 1773 EDITION, BY SIR ISAAC NEWTON 20

CHAPTER 1: DO WE KNOW WHAT YEAR THIS REALLY IS? 21

CHAPTER 2: CREATION, SUPERCONTINENT, AND TALKING ANIMALS (GEN1) 25

    PRELUDE: EVIDENCE SUPPORTING A YOUNG EARTH 25
    THE BEGINNING 25
    DARK MATTER? 28
    IS THE EARTH FLAT? 30

CHAPTER 3: THE GARDEN OF EDEN (GEN 2) 33

    THE SUPERCONTINENT 36
    THE PIRI REIS MAP 38
    DRAGONS WERE REAL 41

CHAPTER 4: THE FALL OF MAN (GEN 3) 45

CHAPTER 5: THE SECOND GENERATION (GEN 4) 49

CHAPTER 6: THE COMING BIBLICAL DELUGE (GEN 5) 51

CHAPTER 7: ANCIENT ALIENS (GEN 6) 55

    ANGELS IN THE OUTFIELD 61
    PETROGLYPHS OF ANGELS 64
    MAGIC IS REAL 73
    THE FIRST, SECOND, AND THIRD FALLS OF ANGELS 83
    THE FALLEN ONES 84
    SKELETAL REMAINS OF GIANTS AND ELONGATED SKULLS 88

CHAPTER 8: EGYPT AND THE PYRAMIDS 97
- The First Rabbit Hole 104
- A Brief Departure on the Hyksos Dynasty 110

CHAPTER 9: THE DELUGE (GEN 7) 115

CHAPTER 10: ORIGIN OF NATIONS AND LANGUAGES (GEN 10-11) 118
- The Tower of Babel 118
- The Dispersion of Nations 121
- The Descendants of Ham 123
- The Descendants of Shem 130
- The Descendants of Japheth..131

CHAPTER 11: MYTHOLOGY 135

CHAPTER 12: THE LOST CITY OF ATLANTIS... 139

APPENDIX A: CHRONOLOGY OF BIBLICAL HISTORY 143
- The Enigma of the Period of the Judges 145
- The Mysterious Numbers of the Hebrew Kings 157
- Complete Biblical Chronology to the Time of Christ 166
- Chronology of the Patriarchs – from 1 - 2047 AM 171
- Chronology of the Patriarchs – from 2047 - 2531 AM 172
- Chronology of the Judges and Monarchs..173
- The Chronology of the Divided Kingdom to the Siege of Jerusalem..175
- Chronology from the End of the 70-Year Desolation to the Crucifixion of Christ 177

ABOUT THE AUTHOR 179

Acknowledgements

I want first and foremost to acknowledge Jesus Christ for my salvation. I believe in the truth of *all* Scripture, and my quintessential verse is Isa 64:6a (NIV) which reads, "*All of us have become like one who is unclean, and all our righteous acts are like filthy rags....*" The extent of our unrighteousness is herein expressed (and indeed is self-evident), as is our *continuing* need for salvation…every day, every hour, every minute and second of our existence. For no matter what I could even conceive to do in my own strength, it would fall so far short of genuine goodness, that without Christ's intercession I would be most certainly damned to the second death. From the days before I accepted the salvation that He secured for me by the voluntary forfeiture of His very life, I prayed to know the truth, and I believe that The Holy Spirit has since revealed some of that truth to me. So while I would like to take credit for the work herein, I cannot, as God opened my eyes to it. My worst fear is that people might praise me for this work, and that I might start to believe that I actually had something to do with it. Indeed, I invested the time, but the Holy Spirit did the rest. There is a passage in Josephus' *Antiquities of the Jews* (XI:III:9) that he reports were words of thanks to God by Zerubbabel, "*I had not been thought worthy of these advantages, O Lord, unless thou had been favorable to me.*" I read this as the completion of this book was imminent, and felt as he did, which brought me to tears.

I thank my wife, Neli, for her unwavering love and support. She is the one who showed me what *agape* love is, before and since my salvation. I did not understand the nature of true love until we had been married for seven years, and when my eyes were opened, it was her devotion that I, only then, fully appreciated. I will also thank Neli's sister Alice, who, after telling Neli not to date or marry me, prayed for my salvation for almost 20 years.

My sincere gratitude goes out to Albert ("A.B.") Edwards and his dear wife Virginia ("Ginny") for leading me to salvation.

Jeff Bracken has been a staunch supporter and critic, and has helped me greatly in reviewing and correcting this work. I also extend thanks to Barbara Ayers for her help and encouragement.

I would be remiss if I were not to extend thanks to my pastor, Robert Furrow, for helping to equip me for the daily challenges in and of the world. And I cannot neglect my most encouraging brother and sister in Christ, Bob and Elma Mangen.

Lastly, I must honor my father, Charles, and my mother, Joyce, here and now, for I did not do so while they were alive. I was callous and ungrateful to them while they were alive, and even after they passed. For most of my life I failed to recognize their sacrifice or their love for me. For this, and so much more, I am truly sorry.

PREFACE: The Importance of this Investigation

This book is a Bible study…a very different one, as you'll discover. It is not intended to persuade the willful nonbeliever into trust in God, or lead them to salvation through faith in Jesus Christ. ***I believe that its purpose is to bolster the confidence of believers whose faith has been compromised by the atheistic world views of this generation, and to move those who are willing to believe, but whose inclination to such has been thwarted by such synthetic doctrines. Many in this world want to deny, obscure, mock, and invent machinations that require even greater faith, to bury the truth of the God Who created us, sustains the natural laws that support us, and has written our history from beginning to end.*** The intent is to reveal the lost truth of real history hidden in the passages of Scripture…truths that are commonly ignored because they are problematic, or overlooked because they are veiled.

I am a truth seeker. I was born with a curious mind, always keen to understand the moving forces inside the various boxes that surrounded me. As a child, I disassembled many things around the house which, not surprisingly, irritated my parents…especially when neither they nor I could put them back together (they seemed to have less mechanical aptitude than even I in my youth). Later, I became attentive enough to be able to reassemble them. I remember the first time I rebuilt a carburetor; after the first reassembly, I was taken aback that I had several parts left over. I had to disassemble and reassemble it three or four times before I finally got all the parts back in, and confident that they were all in the right places. That learning process, though, gave me a better understanding of how it actually worked. It forced me to reason through each section of the assembly to understand where and why a part was required. As I grew older, that fascination with the mechanical things at home progressed to an interest in how nature worked…that is, the sciences.

I chose to study physics in part because I understood physics to be the pedestal underpinning all the other sciences. I reasoned that if I learned enough in this field, my curiosity would be satisfied and there would be no more questions. But the definitive answers I sought were, and still remain, elusive: not only can we never close the book and say that all is known, but it seems that whenever we discover something new, we end up with a whole new layer of phenomena and an attendant set of new questions. Thus, as we delve more deeply into the realm of things to be known, the more we realize how endlessly deep the extent of the unknown is.

For most of my life, I separated science from religion. While I've always believed in God, I did not want to investigate religion as I feared I might discover something I really did not want to know, be held accountable for something, or be compelled to give my hard-earned money to someone else.

When I was still in elementary school, my parents afforded me the opportunity to make my own decision about religion. I had been raised in Roman Catholicism, but the meaningful aspects of the faith were never properly conveyed to me. So, it did not take me but one minute to develop my response: I was not going to attend church anymore. Now, I rationalized my decision with a hypothetical: I posed the question that if Jesus Christ were walking the earth today, would he be in Rome doing whatever it is that the Pope does? I decided that He would not, and thereby commenced to throw the proverbial baby out with its murky bathwater. The bottom line is that I feared the truth, so I buried it and pursued worldly fulfillment.

It was not until I was about 40 years old that the issue of religion reared its ugly head again. My wife, raised a Baptist but who had also largely disregarded it for many years, suggested that we attend a Bible study at a friend's home. She had, over the previous 17 years or so of our marriage, asked me to go to church a few times, mostly around holidays like Easter and Christmas. I had declined every such opportunity, as my trepidations still swirled within, but only when probed…I was otherwise blissful in my self-inflicted ignorance. Such trepidation was manifest as guilt each time I rejected the opportunity…but why should I feel guilty? Wanting to please my wife, and feeling that a Bible study was somewhat less threatening than a church service, I reluctantly agreed. Well, when we arrived, these folks would read one thing and then talk about what seemed to me things completely disconnected. I started wondering, 'Where in the heck are they getting this…am I missing something?' I wanted to challenge them but found myself so intimidated by my lack of knowledge that I withheld almost all questions. (The Catholic Church had not encouraged us to read and understand the Bible; we were cautioned only to allow the clergy to interpret the Scriptures for us. Thus, much of what we read that evening was actually foreign to me.) I was feeling the actuality of the quote attributed to Abraham Lincoln, "Better to remain silent and be thought a fool, than to speak and to remove all doubt." So, I figured I would go home and read ahead so that I could be sufficiently prepared for the next session to challenge these people and their weird conclusions. Years later, I realized that God had used my own pride against me; He does indeed have a sense of humor.

Over the next year or so, I found myself delving ever more deeply into the subject. We had withdrawn from the Bible study group due to their condescension, and sought out a more personal study with the pastor from their church, who was not a participant in the aforementioned study group. I frustrated him profoundly as I questioned the veracity of every Biblical precept he put forth. About a year later, the fateful evening finally came when he turned my cynicism on its head. He posited to me, "Why not, instead of distrusting the Bible until proven right, trust the Bible until it is proven wrong?" I pondered that as I went home that evening, and finally concluded that it was, if not equally valid, at least a reasonable perspective. While I did not reckon this at the time, I realized later that religion, after all, is not a matter of irrefutable fact, it is a matter of faith in the unseen…in direct contrast with the scientific method. (As an aside, this is not irreconcilable, as religion and science deal with different aspects of truth and reality. But there is some common ground, and that is the heart of what I investigate herein.) I determined to accept the Bible as truth until such time as any disproof might present itself. God had, that very night, given me the gift of faith, as from that day forth, I've neither doubted the authenticity of the Bible, nor have I yet found any evidence that would give me cause to do so…in fact, quite the contrary.

Once understanding that the Bible is a book not only of faith, but also one of history past, present, and future, I became something of a fatalist. The complete span of history in the Bible, even though from a single perspective, has been written in its pages. How else can the myriad Biblical prophecies have come to pass if this were not so? Though we are helpless to change history as a whole, we are still challenged to change the fate of others as part of that written account. The reconciliation of free will and the prophetic nature of Scripture remains something of an unresolved mystery. But, when you realize that God exists outside of the confines of time and space, you realize that it is not so mysterious, since He is able to regard all time past, present, and future concurrently (apologies for the use of a temporal adverb here, applied to a God existing outside of time, but I have no more appropriate language). It is only when you constrain God to exist within the limits of time that the issue becomes irresolvable.

But this book is not written with the intent to persuade you of the spiritual message of the Bible; it is written to provide you with a more complete depiction of our ancient history that I've discovered in its pages through trust only in the historicity of the Bible, and augmenting that with extra-Biblical sources that I later delineate.

I could not help but still wonder at the scientific disconnects that surround us, such as we have with the mystery of evolution, which theory violates the inviolate second law of thermodynamics. Even with all of our scientific knowledge applied under highly controlled conditions, abiogenesis experiments (i.e., creation of living organisms from non-living constituents) have generated only amino acids, and have yet to yield even the simplest protein from these amino acids, much less a complex DNA molecule, and less yet a living organism of any type. Bear in mind that the human genome (DNA molecule) is over 2 meters in length, containing over 3 billion base pairs of nucleotides (~90 billion atoms), and yet these molecules are folded within the nuclei of cells approximately 6×10^{-6} m in diameter. The human genome consists of about 20,000 genes, each gene ranging from about 27,000 to about 2 million base pairs, and these genes encode the various proteins that are critical to our life and makeup. What's really interesting is that for reproduction, our cells are factories with molecular-level machinery to unwind the DNA double helices of the two parents, and then splice the two single strands together with virtually zero errors. (The two indeed become one flesh.) So we are faced with the dilemma of how random processes generate a fully functioning human being from amino acids without design and intervention. Not only that, but we still find no evidence of any "missing links" between man and lower life forms…the evolutionary evidence is still missing. Is this not a critical scientific disconnect?

Evolutionists love to tell the tale of how subspecies 'developed' certain differences based on environmental demands…e.g., as Darwin's finches, variations in beak characteristics 'developed' based upon the accessibility of local food sources. But, while feedback mechanisms (homeostasis) are an intrinsic part of living organisms, there is no feedback mechanism to alter the structure of DNA based on need, desire, or environment. It is indeed evident that multiple subspecies of the finch exist across the Galapagos Islands, but they could not evolve their variations in beak form without such a closed-loop, feedback process. Such a process is even conceptually problematic as stable feedback systems require an ideal for reference…meaning that the system would have to have an intrinsic goal, or perfected DNA, and the feedback would have to process a change in the singular gene that produces the improvement required. Darwin's machination is fantasy. Why would we propagate such an unsupported and whimsical tale?

Without feedback, we are left with a random evolutionary process. If we start with a living organism (in itself an incredible leap of faith), random mutations precipitate changes in the DNA. In the most rudimentary organism conceivable it would seem that a random mutation would, at the very best, have a 50-50 chance of making the organism better. To string together successive improvements becomes decreasingly likely simply on the basis of statistics. This dooms success beyond about 20 beneficial mutations (statistically, ~1:1,000,000). The organism might withstand one or two destructive mutations, as long as the improvements do not end up dependent upon one another. As dependencies increase, however, the likelihood that the whole house of cards collapses becomes inevitable. For example, in the human body, production of blood requires bone marrow, its transport requires arterial and venous systems, its oxygenation requires a pulmonary system, a spleen is necessary to filter it, clotting mechanisms to stop bleeding, and the cardiac system to pump it. If a failure occurs in any one of these systems, the entire organism fails. So, as the organism becomes increasingly complex, the likelihood of improvement becomes exponentially less likely, making advancement beyond even a rudimentary level impossible, dooming virtually all random paths to an advanced lifeform.

I've reflected on other aspects of the origin and development of life. Given that asexual reproduction is so efficient, how did we come to be sexual? How did this alternate, and far more complex, construct develop? Here's food for thought: if I accept the miraculous evolutionary development of two complete male and female counterparts, all otherwise perfect in function but lacking hormones, how do we procreate the species? You cannot rationalize an evolution of hormones...design is implicit.

We also have issues like that of irreducible complexity. Things such as the human eye that have their multiple parts, where they all function together to perform the organ's specific function, and if any one of the multiple parts is missing or imperfect, it does not function at all, rendering it completely useless baggage that actually handicaps further evolution. It's very much like having a box of engine parts, but missing a camshaft. Not only would the evolutionary process have to produce the missing part, but it then must correctly assemble it with all the other parts in the box to produce a working engine. Such developments cannot rationally be considered the result of random events. And in spite of all these and many other issues, evolution is taught as *fact*, not even a theory, in spite of its multiple, critical failings. *This is scientifically disturbing and illustrates that even scientists have biases, and demonstrate a religious 'faith' in theories unsupported by evidence*. It seems that such people will believe the unbelievable in order to avoid the clear conclusion that life forms are created and that there must, therefore, be a Creator. Sir Robert Anderson, in Chapter IV of his book *The Coming Prince* (1894) said, "*Men have come to regard the earth as their own domain, and resent the thought of Divine interference in their affairs.*"

Cyrus H. Gordon was a 20th century college professor who headed the department of Mediterranean Studies during his 18 years at Brandeis University. He wrote over a dozen books in his field, including "*Before Columbus,*" (©1971). In this book, he put forth a then-unorthodox theory of meaningful connections between ancient civilizations and those in the Americas. In spite of the convincing evidences he provides, he seems to anticipate criticisms of his theory, and thus sets out an appeal to the reader that scientific work must be viewed with an open mind, and to avert the temptation to conflate mainstream opinion and truth. He goes on to say that academics with established standing in their respective circles would not dare to jeopardize their positions and reputations by professing truth, if such truth flies in the face of the contrary consensus opinion. (Copyright constraints by the publisher prevent me from quoting Gordon directly, and thus I have summarized and paraphrased his points; I apologize for having hereby compromised his eloquence.)

Shifting to the realm of history, how can the enormous stones used to construct the pyramids and other such monuments around the globe have been engineered, cut, and systematically placed without the aid of precision tools and complex machinery? Even with modern equipment, it would be exceedingly difficult, requiring multi-disciplinary engineers, our best technologies, enormous sums of money, and a lot of time. And why do we have so unique a structure as the pyramid on multiple continents? It cannot be attributed to simple coincidence, but rather points to a common heritage. The method of manipulating such megaliths remains elusive, and historians seem to simply gloss over this critical point, assuming that the Egyptians and other civilizations had engineers that were clever beyond even today's experts. Are we to be satisfied with a shrug of the shoulders and disregard for such appropriate concerns?

How does early man survive without assistance? We have no integral weapons or defenses, as most beasts do…no sharp claws, powerful jaws with great incisors, no great speed, strength, or size, the ability to fly or burrow, thick hides with furry coats to protect us not only from predators, but also from the extremes of weather. How does naked and unaided man support and protect himself to simply survive to a second generation?

We are faced with many such quandaries…disparities between what we are told by 'scientists' and historians, and the reality of the evidence we see. The world is full of theories (unproven postulates), but many are served to us as established fact, as long as it serves a purpose: to deny and obviate the evidence of God. I hold that much of the science taught to us is, in fact, unscientific, with evidence (or the lack thereof) that defies the proclaimed conclusions.

Once believing the Bible, I still struggled to reconcile certain things, as alluded to above: the amount of information early man had, including language, tools, weapons, and a host of megalithic structures across the globe. If Adam and Eve were truly created in Mesopotamia, how did early man get to the other continents? I also had difficulty reconciling the archaeological records of dinosaurs with the story of Noah and the flood. What killed off the dinosaurs…did God not bring to Noah two of *every* creature onto the ark? If there were a global event such as an asteroid strike or massive volcanic eruption that killed all dinosaurs on all continents, would not man also then have met his doom? And what of the petroglyphs of what appear to be ancient alien beings? Why are there pyramidal structures on several continents? And how about the skeletal remains of humanoids with elongated skulls, and those of giants? In my research, the truth of each one of these and other mysteries have become evident through the historical reconciliation I present herein.

God blessed me with a mind to discern patterns in information. I was confronted with a lot of puzzle pieces that others force-fit to suit their various preconceived notions, and I've invested the time and reason (with the counsel of God, through prayer) to assemble these pieces into a more harmonious picture. That does not mean that it's right or even without flaw, and I accept that…it's a theory, or perhaps a collection of theories. Some will argue that I also had preconceived conclusions searching for fitting evidence, and I would counter that I started with the best source of truth that I know, using that only as a framework. In spite of my religious inclinations, I strive always to be faithful to the facts. As I assembled the puzzle pieces, the picture itself was unanticipated; but once I realized that the data fit the theories so well, I was compelled to present these discoveries.

In this book, I start with Gen 1:1 and work through the first eleven chapters of that book. I take many digressions, drawing on later Bible verses and the extra-Biblical sources to present a more complete comprehension of the text. As a result, there will be twists and turns, but we always make our way back to the order of the chapters.

INTRODUCTION

While I and billions more in the world believe that the Bible is the inspired word of God and reveals truths about Him and His love for us, it is, at its most rudimentary level, a history book. You needn't believe that it is the inspired word of God to acknowledge its historicity. It is not an all-encompassing history book, as the intent is to tell of the past and future of man as they relate to the LORD and His chosen people, the Jews, and their Messiah, Jesus Christ. Thus, it was not intended to provide an exhaustive history, but rather a selective history. However, there are other books, extra-Biblical texts, that are not generally esteemed to be Scripture (i.e., the inspired word of God), but are also regarded as historically accurate. For example, the apocryphal Books of the Maccabees are not generally considered to be Scripture, but most scholars accept these as historically accurate books.

In order to augment the Genesis record, to amend the Biblical aspect of history, I reference books that have various degrees of established legitimacy in their own historicity. For the greater part, I refer to the *Antiquities of Jews* (by Flavius Josephus), *The Book of Jasher*, *The Book of Jubilees*, the *Seder Olam*, and the book of *1 Enoch*. Since I believe most fundamentally in the truth of the Bible, if I find any discrepancies among these extra-Biblical sources and the Bible itself, my resolution is to trust in the legitimacy of the Bible foremost, because I believe that God is both the author and the protector of its integrity.

These extra-Biblical texts provide dates for some of the undated events in the Bible, additional happenings, as well as more detailed accounts of many events mutually recorded. When examined collectively, they give us a much clearer picture of ancient history that address many of the questions I've raised…and more. The Bible itself, despite its incomplete historical account, does provide a nearly seamless timeline from the creation of the world through the death of Christ (the first 4 millennia of the world) as well as yet unfulfilled prophecies about the future. *The end result of this process of integration is a reconstruction of our ancient history that has been forgotten, ignored, discounted, or purposely obscured.* This first attempt at such a reconciliation, based on my admittedly limited knowledge of ancient history, reveals some of the hidden truths of time. My own ignorance in the realm of history may raise criticisms that might give rise to future, expanded, and/or improved editions of this book. But I also caution those who might criticize before they read the evidences I present.

In the sections below, I present a brief summary about the principal sources I reference throughout the rest of this book. I should note here that there are seeming discrepancies in the dates of events, even within the Bible itself, that have proven difficult to reconcile...most specifically with the period of the Judges and that of the Hebrew kings (the divided kingdom), as well as with birth years for key figures. In addition, the extra-Biblical sources have their own issues. The dates for events given in the *Book of Jasher* are virtually identical to those in the Bible. Flavius Josephus also has errors, as do the *Book of Jubilees* and the *Seder Olam*. Again, I do not put full faith in these other sources, but have been admittedly selective. Such errors in the dates themselves do not necessarily disqualify the record of the events they chronicle, but underscores the need for ultimate reliance on the most trustworthy record wherever such discrepancies exist. In the Appendix of this book I address and reconcile the apparent temporal disparities within the Bible.

The Bible

The Christian Bible, though generally viewed as a single book, is actually a collection of 66 books written by some 40 authors. It is logically broken into two main sections: the Old Testament (OT), and the New Testament (NT). The Jewish Bible consists only of the Old Testament, which is comprised of three sections: The Law ("Torah" in Hebrew, "Pentateuch" in Greek), The Prophets ("Nevi'im" in Hebrew), and the Writings ("Ketuvim" in Hebrew). If you take the first letters of each of these in the Hebrew, you have the acronym TNK which is then pronounced "Tanakh."

The Christian OT consists of 39 books, the content being identical to that of the Tanakh except that the latter is comprised of fewer books primarily because several are consolidated…specifically Samuel, Kings, Chronicles, and Ezra-Nehemiah. The New Testament can be viewed as comprised of four parts: the Gospels, The Acts of the Apostles, the Epistles (letters), and the Book of Revelation (Apocalypse).

The Old Testament (OT) spans about the first 3900 years of world history, while the New Testament covers less than about 70 years. However, in both OT & NT there are prophecies that include the end of days, most notably the time of the great tribulation which should complete its 7-year duration at the end of the first 6000 years of time.

There are few gaps in the 3900-year chronicle. While some books lack specific years (e.g., Judges), the temporal continuity to the time of Christ is still established by the connection of accounts in the other Biblical books. Nonetheless, we do get more definitive continuity through references in the extra-Biblical source books.

Unless otherwise noted, the citations in this book are from the New King James Version Study Bible, Second Edition, ©1997, 2007 by Thomas Nelson, Inc. Used by permission of Thomas Nelson, www.thomasnelson.com. If not noted in the narrative, the citations reference the translation in brackets following the associated verse, e.g. [Gen 1:24-26, KJV].

The citations herein from the NIV translation are from The NIV Study Bible, ©1985 by the Zondervan Corporation, and used by permission of Zondervan.

The Book of Jasher

The *Ancient Book of Jasher* ("Sepher HaYashar") that we have today has questionable origins…perhaps as late as the 17th century AD. There is no doubt that references made to this book three times in the Bible (both the OT and NT) legitimize the authenticity of "a" *Book of Jasher*. However, there are significant uncertainties that the book by this name in publication today is the same book referenced in the Biblical books of Joshua, 2 Samuel, and 2 Timothy. Thus, we must not weigh too heavily the information provided therein. But even though it may not be Scripture, nor be *the* ancient *Book of Jasher*, its contents may still contain valid foundations from Jewish oral history. Given the possibility of its late authorship, it is not surprising that the dates and times presented in *Jasher* would be in 100% agreement with those in the Bible. By the same reasoning, it should not be surprising that the citations made in Joshua and 2 Samuel would be found therein. It is interesting, though, that these quotes are found within solid context, and do not seem force-fit.

As a point of interest, the word "jasher" is not a person's name; rather it is the Hebrew word for 'straight,' 'upright,' or 'just.' Thus, one translation of the title might be "Book of the Upright."

All references in this book are from the Biblefacts Annotated Edition, 2008, by Ken Johnson, ThD, and re-printed with his permission.

The Books of Enoch

There are three Books of Enoch presented as a single volume in circulation today. As I read all three, I found incongruities in the second and third books. Only parts of the (first) *Book of Enoch* were found among the Dead Sea Scrolls, and this same book was considered, but ultimately rejected, for inclusion in the Septuagint (the original Greek translation of the Tanakh). The only complete, extant version is a Ge'ez (Ethiopic) translation of a Greek translation made in Palestine from the original in Hebrew or Aramaic. The Dead Sea Scrolls were likely written between the first and third centuries BC, thus indicating 1 Enoch's origins *at least* that old. Most scholars date the book to about the time that the Dead Sea Scrolls were authored, and thus that the authors were likely members of the Essenes at Qumran; but we know that most of the other books found there have origins far earlier. Thus, this late dating seems to me a somewhat dismissive position to take.

It is interesting that the *Book of Jubilees* seems to make reference to this book in chapter 4, starting in v 20:

> *And in the twelfth jubilee, in the seventh week thereof, he* [Enoch] *took himself a wife, and her name was Edni, the daughter of Danel, the daughter of his father's brother, and in the sixth year in this week she bare him a son and he called his name Methuselah. And he was moreover with the angels of God these six jubilees of years, and they showed him everything which is on the earth and in the heavens, the rule of the sun, and he wrote down everything.* [Jub 4:20-21]

Because of the more questionable origins of the second and third books of Enoch, as well as their specious content, I do not cite either of these latter books ascribed to Enoch. In addition, I take the position that the elements of 1 Enoch *not* found among the Dead Sea Scrolls (chapters 37-71) may indeed have been authored by someone else and thus added later. As with the *Book of Jasher*, this may not disqualify the content as non-historical, but to avoid any controversy over the debatable content, I have not presented any citations from 1 Enoch after chapter 36.

All citations and references in this book are from *The Books of Enoch: Complete Edition*, ©2012-2019, by Paul C. Schnieders, translated by Robert H. Charles, and re-printed with permission from International Alliance Pro-Publishing, LLC.

The Antiquities of the Jews

Joseph ben Matthias lived between the years 37 AD and sometime after 100 AD, a near contemporary of the Apostle Paul. He was a Jewish priest, a Pharisee, and at one point, a general of Jewish troops during an invasion of Jerusalem by the Roman general Vespasian that began in the year 66 AD. After a siege of several weeks, Joseph surrendered and was taken to Rome as a prisoner. Two years later, when Vespasian became emperor of Rome, Joseph was freed and, owing to his favor with Vespasian, took the Roman name of Flavius Josephus, Flavius being the surname of Vespasian. Josephus then returned to Jerusalem only to witness the resumption of the war with the Romans that concludes with its scripturally prophesied destruction in 70 AD.

Afterwards, Josephus returned to Rome with Vespasian's son Titus, became a Roman citizen, and was commissioned by Vespasian to write a history of the Jews. It is my understanding that this was common practice so that the Romans would have complete documentaries on the history, philosophy, and beliefs of those peoples that they conquered in order to better understand, and consequently, to better rule in those nations.

Josephus wrote his *Antiquities of the Jews* under the commission by Vespasian. After Vespasian dies, his son Titus becomes emperor, and after his death, Domitian. Josephus tells us that all of these rulers regarded him well and continued the pension he had been granted first by the Roman emperor Vespasian. But Josephus was also motivated to simply tell the whole truth of the Jews, as he found that other historians were publishing versions of the then recent wars that were biased or inaccurate. He tells us in his writings that he has no reason to present a biased history, but wanted the world of the Greeks to "understand the Legislator" of the Jewish people.

Now, one of the profound problems I find in his Antiquities is the dating. At the very outset, he claims that the history of the Jews from creation to the twelfth year of Nero's reign spans some 5782 years, as contrasted with the comparable Biblical accounting of just over 4000 years. He has problems with the earliest generations from Adam, systematically adding 100 years to most of the ages at which they had children. The accumulation of these systematic errors totals 1600 years, which accounts for most of the difference. In another place he adds 10 years to the date of birth of Arphaxad (12 years after the flood instead of 2 years), and he puts Isaac's lifespan at 185 years instead of 180 in the Bible and other corresponding histories. In Book X of the *Antiquities* (covering the early captivity of the Jews), he specifies the reign of the Babylonian King Nerglissar as lasting 40 years, but fails to include this in the total for the chapter.

At first, I reasoned these to be the result of his limited understanding of the Greek language, in which these Antiquities were written. However, his subtitle for his first chapter of his Antiquities specifies the time from creation to the death of Isaac at 3833 years, and this tally is the correct summation of the years for the events as he delineates them. This being the case, I later surmised that his problem was more likely one in the reading of the Hebrew. However, he discloses in his Antiquities that he had to learn Greek after his surrender to Vespasian.

During work on my chronologies (see Appendix A), in the Appendix of *The Complete Works of Flavius Josephus*, by William Whiston, I discovered a dissertation on Josephus' chronology. In Dissertation V, Whiston shows that Josephus' figures are identical with those in the Septuagint version of the Bible. So it seems that Josephus was using this secondary source, rather than a primary, Hebrew Tanakh, to build his *Antiquities*, and that the errors therein were copied directly from the Septuagint.

The chronology I developed for the timeline of history to the crucifixion of Christ, includes a column with Josephus' figures as written, and another column that corrects his errors. With corrections, his timeline is in good, general agreement with that of the Biblical chronology. With the issues each identified and corrected, the accounts comprising his Antiquities and other works seem quite trustworthy, being an integration of the Septuagint, oral history of the Jews, and other histories available to him.

All references in this book are from the *Complete Works of Flavius Josephus*, ©1960, 1978, 1981, by William Whiston; published by Kregel Publications, Grand Rapids, MI. All citations from this work quoted herein are reprinted by permission of the publisher. All rights reserved.

The Book of Jubilees

No author is declared within the text of this book, but it is presumed to be a Pharisee. The text claims to be the word of God presented to Moses during his time with God on Mount Sinai, given through the angels. The Book of Jubilees was also found among the Dead Sea Scrolls, and this renders to it authoritative weight. However, it also has issues with numbers and dates. Many of the dates provided are given as the nth year of the mth week of a specific jubilee. A jubilee is by definition a collection of 7 sets of 7 years, or a 49 year span. The "year of Jubilee" was always celebrated in the year after the completion of the jubilee. Thus, for example, the first year of the third jubilee would be 49 + 49 +1 = 99 AM, in which year the completion of the second jubilee would be celebrated. I seem to find more discrepancies than agreements between dates given in the Book of Jubilees and those found in the OT. Consequently, I largely treat the descriptive, historical content of this book as being accurate, but discount the dates for the greater part.

All references in this book are from *The Book of Jubilees*, translated from the Ethiopic text, ®2018, by R. H. Charles, published by The Best Books Publishing.

Seder Olam

The *Seder Olam Rabbah* (translated "The Great Order of the World") is a Hebrew chronicle of the Tanakh up to about 323 BC, with the death of Alexander the Great, written in the second century AD. The author is never declared within the text, but many hold that Rabbi Yosi ben Halafta wrote it. As far as I know, the date of the original work is unknown, but the author closes out the first chapter with the words, "*…and Elijah the prophet…is still living.*" Elijah was born about 900 BC, but this comment might only be an indication of the manner in which Elijah departed this world. Most believe that the work is dated to about 160 AD.

Ken Johnson, who has published an English translation of the *Seder Olam* from a Christian perspective, notes that several quotes from the ancient *Seder Olam* can be found in the Talmud which are deficient in the current Hebrew editions of the *Seder Olam*. This infers that something has been lost or purposely changed.

The main issue with the dates in the *Seder Olam* are associated with the period of the destruction of the first Temple, and consequently the reigns of the Persian kings Cyrus, Artaxerxes, and Darius. In order to accommodate the elimination of about 165 years, it is necessary to conflate these three monarchs into a single personage. It appears that indeed this inaccuracy was introduced purposely to preclude the possibility that Jesus of Nazareth fulfilled the Messianic prophecies of Daniel. Dr. Floyd Nolan Jones in his book *Chronology of the Old Testament* (Copyright© 1993, 2004, 2009, Floyd Jones Ministries, Inc.) wrote an extensive commentary on this, and copyright prevents me from directly quoting his work here, but the synopsis is that the very purpose of corruption of the Jewish calendar was to create a conflict between the seventy-week prophecy of Daniel and the crucifixion of Jesus Christ. With the deletion of some 165 years, Daniel's Messianic prophecy pointed instead to one Simon bar Kokhba, a Jewish leader who led the "Bar Kokhba revolt" against the Romans in 132 AD. This short-lived success led many to believe that Bar Kokhba was, in fact, the Messiah. His Davidic lineage and adoption of the title "prince" rendered Biblical support for this belief.

The consequence of this scheme is that the Jewish calendar is shortened by somewhere between 164 and 168 years, depending upon whose chronology you use. Some refer to these simply as the "missing years." So, if we take this singular issue into proper account, I believe that the rest of the *Seder Olam* can then be regarded as reliable.

All references in this book are from the *Ancient Seder Olam, a Christian translation of the 2000-year-old scroll*, 2006, by Ken Johnson, ThD, and re-printed with his permission.

The Annals of the World, by James Ussher

James Ussher was a noted scholar, church leader, and prolific author of the 17th century. He published over 129 works, of which his *Annals of the World* may be the most recognized and enduring. The complete title of the work (translated from the Latin) is actually "*Annals of the Old Testament, deduced from the first origins of the world, the chronicle of Asiatic and Egyptian matters together produced from the beginning of historical time up to the beginnings of Maccabees.*" Ussher was noted for his use of one of the most extensive collections of manuscripts of his day, as well as his ability to understand the ancient languages in which these were written, not having mentioned his knowledge of astronomy, calendars, and chronology. I found his *Annals* to be precise and well-founded, with one major exception: the birth year of the Biblical patriarch Abram (Abraham). I undertook a review of the *Annals* because of my belief that there must be an error therein, and I thank God that I identified the issue so quickly after I started, since the work is nearly a thousand pages in length.

The most significant miscalculation I discovered is one of sixty years: the Biblical record and other sources consistently place the birth of Abram at the year 1948 AM, while Ussher places it at 2008 AM (AM stands for the Latin '*anno mundi*' or 'year of the world'…meaning 'since creation'). I believe he did this through a failure to realize that Abram was in Haran twice: the first time was when Abram had just left Ur of the Chaldees at age 75; the second was at the death of his father, Terah, who died in Haran at age 205 years. Ussher's failure to distinguish these events results in a conflation that can only be reconciled if Abram were born 60 years later that he actually was. Ussher ultimately concludes that creation took place in 4004 BC. Correcting his error means that 1AM was more nearly in the year 3944 BC, and this is the figure I use in my chronology.

With this singular rectification, I believe that Ussher's account is most thorough and excellent, to the extent that I've investigated, and I regard his effort of comparable order with those of Sir Isaac Newton, whose intellect I regard as perhaps the greatest among all scientists and mathematicians in human history. Newton was a highly regarded historian and theologian, as well.

All references in this book are from an e-book version of *The Annals of the World*, by James Ussher, printed by E. Tyler, 1658 (public domain; no copyright specified).

Genesis 6 Giants, Master Builders of Prehistoric and Ancient Civilizations, by Stephen Quayle

Stephen Quayle's book represents a masterwork of revelation regarding the truth of the existence of giants in both ancient and modern history. I'm certain that many have tried to obscure, deride, and even destroy the evidence of such truth. He presents what amounts to a case-by-case catalogue of these giants in such numbers and with such provenance that their existence is undeniable.

Quayle spends a good portion of the book advocating his theory of a pre-Adamic civilization, and to be clear, I do not subscribe to this. Since the existence of the giants and the theory of such civilization are not dependent upon one another, we can discount the one without consequence to the other.

All references in this book are from *Genesis 6 Giants, Master Builders of Prehistoric and Ancient Civilizations*, 7th Printing, 2011, by Stephen Quayle.

The Chronology of Ancient Kingdoms Amended. To which is Prefix'd, A Short Chronicle from the First Memory of Things in Europe, to the Conquest of Persia by Alexander the Great, by Sir Isaac Newton (1728).

The Short Chronicle section of this book is quite similar in format to Ussher's Annals, providing a chronology of events described in brief summaries, spanning the period of 1125 BC to 331 AD. This chronicle is actually presented as a preface to the rest of the work, which is a collection of dissertations on the histories of several ancient civilizations including those of Greece, Egypt, Assyria, Babylonia and Media, and Persia. There is also a chapter describing the temple of Solomon.

Newton apparently undertook this work in his "vacant" hours, which "...*was to him a diversion, and amusement!*" I cannot help but believe that he was trying to bring an integrated order to the various, disordered, and inconsistent histories extant in his time. The work was unpublished until about a year after his death, and was then presented to the Queen of England (wife to King George II), Caroline of Ansbach. In the introductory letter addressed to her by John Conduitt (Newton's successor as the Master of the Mint, and husband to Newton's half-niece), he presents the work to her as her "just right to his Productions." Herein, Conduitt also makes it clear that the "Short Chronicle" that is preface to the rest of the work, was incorporated by Newton in response to her command.

As myself, Newton believed that various mythologies were founded in fact, and he documents various events of ancient mythologies as factual, and this has brought criticism to this work, and consequently its common classification as one of "Newton's occult studies." I believe that Newton will ultimately be vindicated in some, if not all, of his assertions.

All references in this book are to an e-book version of *The Chronology of Ancient Kingdoms Amended, To which is Prefix'd, A Short Chronicle from the First Memory of Things in Europe, to the Conquest of Persia by Alexander the Great*, by Sir Isaac Newton, 1728 (public domain; no copyright specified).

Observations upon the Prophecies of Daniel, and the Apocalypse of St. John: Full and Fine Text of 1773 Edition, by Sir Isaac Newton

In the first chapter of this book, Newton sets out a history of the books of the Bible, establishing the periods of their writing from inferences in the texts, and the authors from the prosaic styles and other observations. In the second chapter, Newton ascribes symbolic meaning to various occurrences in the celestial and earthly realms.

The balance of Part I of the book renders interpretation of prophesies through Daniel, assigning specific names of countries, kingdoms, and monarchs, not to mention dates. Herein, he mixes English and Latin languages, making the reading tedious for someone like me, lacking a classical education. (I did study Latin for one year in high school, but had no aptitude for it, or any other language, and have now forgotten most of what I did manage to learn.)

Similarly, Part II of the book provides interpretation of the Book of Revelation (called by Newton "The Apocalypse of St. John"). The version I used is amended with a biography of Newton's life.

All references to this book are from an electronic version entitled *Observations Upon the Prophesies of Daniel, and The Apocalypse of St. John, In Two Parts*, by Sir Isaac Newton, 1733 (public domain; no copyright specified).

I do reference more than 30 source books and articles, but those outlined above constitute the material for the majority of the citations herein. When I do reference such others, I provide information on the author, date, and publisher, where available.

CHAPTER 1: Do We Know What Year this Really Is?

An essential part of history is dating, and in Biblical history, critically so. Part of my investigation was to attempt a connection between the BC/AD ("Before Christ"/"Anno Domini") years with AM years (for the Latin *Anno Mundi*, translated "year of the world")…that is, years from Creation forward. Clearly, prior to the establishment of the generally accepted AD dating system (later "CE," abbreviating "Common Era," to purposely remove any connection to Jesus Christ), civilizations were either not using any dating references, or recording years and events in regnal years (i.e., relative to rulers' reigns; e.g., 'In the fifth year of Sennacherib, Assyria waged war on….'). But the Biblical record provides great detail as it relates to the Hebrews and their ancestors. There are certainly references to the years of various Kings' rules, but the continuity and synchrony of the other significant civilizations' timelines have been lost. What I did not realize was that it seems that nobody has even successfully fully reconciled AM with BC. We have estimates, but there are a lot of assumptions involved. And we also have the issues created by different calendar systems, and the cumulative errors arising from false assumptions about the length of a 'year.' In addition, I thought that the Biblical AM timeline was well understood and resolved; but my further investigation, along with my understanding of scriptural metaphor, meant that there was something, and perhaps several things, wrong with that, as well.

So, let me first clarify my reference to the "scriptural metaphor" above. First we need to understand that numbers in the Bible have specific significances. The study of such is referred to as 'Biblical numerology.' You will find that certain numbers appear again and again throughout the Bible, and that these repetitions reinforce the fundamental connotation of each number. For example, the number 7 is contextually deemed to signify Divine completion or Divine perfection. Throughout the Bible, this rendering is consistent in each and every occurrence. God's work of creation was finished in 6 days, and on the 7th day He rested. Taken as a whole, this 'week' of days comprises a closed chapter of work and rest. The number 'seven' occurs 439 times in the Bible, and the word 'seventh' another 119 times. From Genesis through Revelation, it is clearly the most significant symbolic number.

So it is also with other numbers such as 3 (perfection, spiritually), 6 (imperfection, sin), 10 (completeness, in the worldly realm), 12 (governmental totality), 40 (judgment), etc. And the products of the fundamental numbers combine the essences of the constituents: 30 (3x10), 49 (7x7), 70 (7x10), and so on. For example, Jesus Christ was 30 years old when He began His ministry. The number thirty integrates the concepts that He was spiritually perfect (3) and completely human (10).

Now, turning to the Biblical book of 2nd Peter, chapter 3, verse 8, Peter tells us:

But, beloved, do not forget this one thing, that with the Lord one day is as a thousand years, and a thousand years as one day.

And now consider Rev 20:2-6:

He laid hold of the dragon, that serpent of old, who is the Devil and Satan, and bound him for a thousand years; and he cast him into the bottomless pit, and shut him up, and set a seal on him, so that he should deceive the nations no more till the thousand years were finished. But after these things he must be released for a little while. And I saw thrones, and they sat on them, and judgment was committed to them. Then I saw the souls of those who had been beheaded for their witness to Jesus and for the word of God, who had not worshiped the beast or his image, and had not received his mark on their foreheads or on their hands. And they lived and reigned with Christ for a thousand years. But the rest of the dead did not live again until the thousand years were finished. This is the first resurrection. Blessed and holy is he who has part in the first resurrection. Over such the second death has no power, but they shall be priests of God and of Christ, and shall reign with Him a thousand years.

We must consider these two scriptures jointly to comprehend that the total time of history consists of a period of 6000 years during which Satan has authority and/or power on the earth, followed by a period of 1000 years during which Christ will be the sole regnal authority on the earth. You may recall that in the Gospels of Matthew and Luke, Satan tempts Jesus by offering to him all the kingdoms of the world if Jesus will only kneel before him. Satan had the authority to do this because he had been the ruler of the earth until the death of Christ, and still retains a power that will endure up until the return of Christ in the last days. As a final note, this view of the time of history is upheld in the Jewish Talmud. Some people refer to this theory as 'dispensationalism,' but that theory takes the construct further, grouping successive millennia into distinct 'days,' and assigning significance to each such era. To be clear, I am neither discounting nor subscribing to this broader aspect of dispensationalism since I have not yet invested sufficient time or effort into this area of my research, largely since it has not been pivotal in the scope of this work.

Because of my background, I take a sidebar to mention Sir Isaac Newton. We all associate Newton with his law of gravity, but he also essentially invented the field of physics as we know it today. His collective works in classical mechanics, optics, fluid dynamics, and mathematics remain foundational and relevant in science and technology today. In his *Principia Mathematica*, he effectively states that *his scientific works should underscore the existence of God*. Consider that without the orderly laws we have governing matter and energy, if there was indeed a big bang, what burst forth from it would have been nothing more than a mass of chaos, with matter and energy both disordered, if even distinct. (I examine this in greater detail in the section on dark matter.) As it is, we have a fixed set of elementary particles that all obey systematic laws that support an ordered universe, in which we have the culmination of this order manifest in the human form. It turns out that Newton also comprehended this septimillennial span for history. In fact, he deduced that history's end would be in the year 2060 AD, which is actually quite close to the figure of 2057 AD that I've deduced. So, as something of a fatalist in this regard, I believe that at the end of 6000 years, history will reach a terminus…not the final end, but the end of an era, marked by the return and reign of Christ as a real king over the physical world, for the final 1000 years.

Now, most Bible scholars believe that the year 1 AM (creation) occurred in the year 4004 BC. However, as it is presently 2021 AD, if that premise were true, we're already past the 6000 year mark by some 25 years. Being dedicated to this proposition, I concluded that there must be one or more errors in the work of James Ussher, who established creation at 4004 BC in his *Annals of the World* written back in the year 1658, and still widely accepted.

I believe that it was only a year or so after becoming a Christian that I started to put together my timeline from the Scriptures. What I did was use *Strong's Exhaustive Concordance of the Bible* on the words 'year' and 'years' and then strung together those verses that were connected to the timeline of AM years. The inferiority of my first effort yielded a date of about 4010 BC for 1 AM. There were significant Scriptural disconnects (e.g., the periods of the Judges and the divided kingdom) that prevented me from having confidence in this date. I also believe that I did this after I came to understand that the span of this era is 6000 years, but that was some 25 years ago, so at that time we had not yet reached what I thought might be 6000 AM, and had also sufficient worldly distractions to keep me from a comprehensive and proper reconciliation.

In starting the research for this book, I attempted to rebuild and correct my original timeline, this time drawing on the additional detail from the *Seder Olam*, the *Book of Jasher*, as well as the *Antiquities of the Jews*. This is presented in Appendix A, but I think it less tedious for both you and me, to simply cut to the chase. Most scholars connect the Biblical dates provided in Genesis to establish the year of Abram's birth at 1948 AM. While in the Biblical account (Gen 11:26), the births of all three of Terah's sons are conflated ("*After Terah had lived 70 years, he became the father of Abram, Nahor and Haran.*"), the Book of Jasher separates this apparently singular episode into two distinct events: the births of Haran and Nahor when Terah was 38 years old, and the birth of Abram when Terah was 70 years old. James Ussher, however, argues that Abram was born 60 years later. But Josephus agrees with the year 1948 AM, stating,

> *...Abraham, who accordingly was the tenth from Noah, and was born in the two hundred and ninety second year after the Deluge; for Terah begat Abram in his seventieth year.*
> [*Antiquities* I:VI:5].

Note that 1656 AM + 292 = 1948 AM (Josephus), and that 1878 AM + 70 = 1948 AM (Jasher). If we simply correct the year of Abram's birth, we regain 60 years. Thus, in the year 2021 AD, it should be 4004 BC + 2021 AD - 60 -1 = 5964 AM. (The -1 is necessary when accounting across BC and AD dates, as there is no year 0). Equivalently, we could say that 1 AM is 3944 BC. This, however, cannot be stated absolutely...there are still far too many variables and assumptions involved, and I believe this to be, at least in part, by divine intent: to have left these waters purposely muddied so that we cannot absolutely determine the day of His return, and thus must remain prepared for it at any time. Jesus Christ Himself said,

> *But of that day and hour no one knows, not even the angels of heaven, but My Father only.*
> [Mat 24:36]

Nonetheless, the prophet Daniel also tells us that in the end times "*knowledge will increase.*" Since knowledge would seem additive, generation over generation, and thus always to increase, this statement appears at first to be a simple truism. But I believe that Daniel is talking about specific knowledge: that which supports the veracity of Scripture, and/or the credence of prophecy. I've often speculated that possible discoveries supporting this postulate would be re-discovery of Noah's ark, finding the lost Ark of the Covenant, or perhaps even evidence of some of the theories presented herein. Trust me, I'm not claiming to be a prophet, but what if some of the conclusions I've reached herein might someday be substantiated archaeologically?

If we use the *Seder Olam*'s figures, as corrected by Ken Johnson, then the year as of this writing (2021) is 5944 AM. With due respect for Ken Johnson, I can't dispute his figure, as I haven't invested the time to determine if this date is better or worse than the 5964 AM figure I presented above. If I'm right, we are just 29 years away from the rapture and the start of the great tribulation in 2050 AD.

In either case, we are 50 years or less from the start of the Great Tribulation, which precedes the second coming of Christ (at the end of 6000 AM) by 7 years.

As a post-script, I find it interesting that Abram was born in 1948 AM and the modern nation of Israel was re-established in 1948 AD. I do not believe this is coincidental. The older I get, the less I believe in coincidence, and the more I believe in Providence. Frankly, I would've been more gratified had I calculated the year of the rapture to be 2048 (exactly 100 years after the nation of Israel was restored to the Jews), or even 2046 (49 + 49 years, or two jubilees after the restoration), and perhaps I will yet discover some obscure error that will yield one or the other of these 'more aesthetically preferable' dates.

CHAPTER 2: Creation, Supercontinent, and Talking Animals (Gen1)

Prelude: Evidence Supporting a Young Earth

Many criticize the idea of a young earth, preferring to believe in a Godless process taking billions of years. However, while I am ever eager to accept a well-founded theory, significant contrary evidence does exist that supports a different conclusion than a 4.6 billion-year old earth. There are many articles and books written about evidences of a young earth, and, to be fair, just as many that criticize these with alternate contrivances that claim to be scientific. The arguments on both sides lack the witness of verifiable events and conditions…that is, both have elements of speculation, insufficient facts, and confounding issues. And both creation and big bang advocates have biases that blind them to any concession to the other view. Here we are confronted with the disquieting issue that scientists almost never agree on the interpretation of data; and the facts aren't always unambiguous and don't always speak for themselves: data is inevitably interpreted, so while one scientist will view data with a bias favorable to his hypothesis, others will see it through their individual lenses that may not be rose colored, but colored nonetheless. I would caution anyone claiming to represent science against conflating the analytical terms of 'data,' 'theory,' 'evidence,' and 'fact,' the last being the most difficult to establish, as it infers absolute and unequivocal truth.

One of the most confounding issues I have with the figure of 4.6B years is that the earth's core is still so hot and the surface of the crust is so cool (i.e., a steep temperature gradient). According to an article in LiveScience (*Earth's Core 1,000 Degrees Hotter Than Expected,* April 25, 2013), the core temperature of the earth is about 6000°C, or about 10,800°F…comparable to the temperature at the surface of the sun. It seems to me that no matter how thermally resistive (i.e., slow to heat up) the earth's crust or mantle might be, after 4.6B years the surface should be hotter…a lot hotter. Without discounting the contribution from the greenhouse effect, could it possibly be that that our planet is indeed warming more significantly due to the conduction of heat from the core to the crust?

The Beginning

We'll now start at the beginning of the Biblical account…Creation. We'll keep track of the years from the first day of Creation in years designated AM. Thus, the first day of Creation is the first day of the year 1 AM. The *Book of Jubilees* often refers to a given year AM in terms of Jubilees, or periods of 49 years. Recall that the number 7, in Biblical expression, represents 'completion.' There were 6 days of Creation followed by a day of rest, the set of these comprising a period of completion. A week of years, being 7 years, is something of a completion, but a week of weeks in years (7 x 7 years) is 49 years, and is Biblically significant, referred to as a jubilee. In fact, the first day following a 49-year period is the beginning of the 50th, or 'Jubilee year,' in which the closure of the prior 49 years was celebrated. We'll run into this where I cite verses in the *Book of Jubilees*.

Now the Biblical Creation account is strictly pre-history…no human witnesses were present until the 6th day. So who wrote the Genesis account and when? Well, it's Jewish *tradition* that God instructed Moses to write things down that He <u>dictated</u> to him on Mount Sinai. Thus, it is apparent that Moses recorded the Torah *in God's exact words*. I stress this verbatim point because the exact words are critical to the centuries-old postulate by Isaac Newton and others, and more recently confirmed discovery, of concealed codes in the Hebrew text of these books which are statistically inexplicable without Divine conception, and thus deemed intentional. You can read more about these codes in Michael Drosnin's *"The Bible Code,"* Chuck Missler's *"Cosmic Codes,"* and other books on this subject matter. The more recent books will have more instances, as computers are now being used to ferret out more such occurrences. While I've read that some scholars challenge Moses' authorship, it is much more widely accepted that Moses was the scribe. Indeed, Josephus states in his *Antiquities* (I:I:1), regarding the first day of creation, that "…*Moses said it was one day*…." Thus, at least one scholarly, rabbinic view in the first century AD upholds this conviction that Moses wrote the Genesis account. As you'll see below, in the *Book of Jubilees*, God instructs the "angel of the presence" to dictate primeval history to Moses, who in turn instructs him to write it.

So, here we go with the prehistoric, Biblical account of creation, starting in the first chapter of Genesis:

In the beginning God created the heavens and the earth. The earth was without form, and void; and darkness was on the face of the deep. And the Spirit of God was hovering over the face of the waters.

Then God said, "Let there be light"; and there was light. And God saw the light, that it was good; and God divided the light from the darkness. God called the light Day, and the darkness He called Night. So the evening and the morning were the first day.

Then God said, "Let there be a firmament in the midst of the waters, and let it divide the waters from the waters." Thus God made the firmament, and divided the waters which were under the firmament from the waters which were above the firmament; and it was so. And God called the firmament Heaven. So the evening and the morning were the second day.

Then God said, "Let the waters under the heavens be gathered together into one place, and let the dry land appear"; and it was so. And God called the dry land Earth, and the gathering together of the waters He called Seas. And God saw that it was good.

Then God said, "Let the earth bring forth grass, the herb that yields seed, and the fruit tree that yields fruit according to its kind, whose seed is in itself, on the earth"; and it was so. And the earth brought forth grass, the herb that yields seed according to its kind, and the tree that yields fruit, whose seed is in itself according to its kind. And God saw that it was good. So the evening and the morning were the third day.

Then God said, "Let there be lights in the firmament of the heavens to divide the day from the night; and let them be for signs and seasons, and for days and years; and let them be for lights in the firmament of the heavens to give light on the earth"; and it was so. Then God made two great lights: the greater light to rule the day, and the lesser light to rule the night. He made the stars also. God set them in the firmament of the heavens to give light on the earth, and to rule over the day and over the night, and to divide the light from the darkness. And God saw that it was good. So the evening and the morning were the fourth day.

Then God said, "Let the waters abound with an abundance of living creatures, and let birds fly above the earth across the face of the firmament of the heavens." So God created great sea creatures and every living thing that moves, with which the waters abounded, according to their kind, and every winged bird according to its kind. And God saw that it was good.

And God blessed them, saying, "Be fruitful and multiply, and fill the waters in the seas, and let birds multiply on the earth." So the evening and the morning were the fifth day.

Then God said, "Let the earth bring forth the living creature according to its kind: cattle and creeping thing and beast of the earth, each according to its kind"; and it was so. And God made the beast of the earth according to its kind, cattle according to its kind, and everything that creeps on the earth according to its kind. And God saw that it was good.

Then God said, "Let Us make man in Our image, according to Our likeness; let them have dominion over the fish of the sea, over the birds of the air, and over the cattle, over all the earth and over every creeping thing that creeps on the earth." So God created man in His own image; in the image of God He created him; male and female He created them. Then God blessed them, and God said to them, "Be fruitful and multiply; fill the earth and subdue it; have dominion over the fish of the sea, over the birds of the air, and over every living thing that moves on the earth."

And God said, "See, I have given you every herb that yields seed which is on the face of all the earth, and every tree whose fruit yields seed; to you it shall be for food. Also, to every beast of the earth, to every bird of the air, and to everything that creeps on the earth, in which there is life, I have given every green herb for food"; and it was so. Then God saw everything that He had made, and indeed it was very good. So the evening and the morning were the sixth day. [Gen 1:1-31]

Josephus' account is very faithful to the Genesis record. Remember, he was employed by the Romans to write a complete history of the Jews, so his account is, in many places, taken word-for-word, or phrase-for-phrase, from the Law and the Prophets; but he was also attempting to provide a more complete history beyond the Biblical record. Thus, he adds elements of Jewish oral history, and perhaps even elements from other books such as *Jasher*, *Enoch*, and *Jubilees*, as all of these pre-dated his *Antiquities*, and were apparently widely read and even referenced in the Bible. As it turns out, he added almost no significant facets to the Biblical account of the first 7 days.

Now the phrase "*In the beginning*" makes no sense as a reference to God as He is eternal…more precisely, existing outside of the confines of time. When He created the heavens and the earth and all that is therein, He also created time itself. Time has no meaning without space and conversely; time is the medium of change. Thus, if all we have is *empty* space, time cannot be measured, since there is nothing to change. It is only after we introduce matter and energy within the space that that time has its purpose. I submit to you that this phrase in fact should be understood as "in the beginning of time, space, matter, and energy, as well as the laws that govern them."

On the fourth day (Gen 1:14) we have the creation of the lights in the firmament, of which it says "*…and let them be for signs and seasons….*" In Chapter V (*Babylonian Legend of the Creation*) of his book *The Chaldean Account of Genesis* (1876), George Smith presented a translation of the fifth tablet of the creation legend. It reads as follows:

It was delightful, all that was fixed by the great gods.
Stars, their appearance [in figures] of animals he arranged.
To fix the year through the observation of their constellations,
Twelve months (or signs) of stars in three rows he arranged,

From the day when the year commences unto the close.
[line number references omitted; public domain]

It goes on from there. But this is a clear reference to the Mazzaroth of Job 38:

Can you bind the cluster of the Pleiades,
Or loose the belt of Orion?
Can you bring out Mazzaroth in its season?
Or can you guide the Great Bear with its cubs?
Do you know the ordinances of the heavens?
Can you set their dominion over the earth?
[Job 38:31-33]

The "Mazzaroth" (Strong's 4216) is identified with the twelve signs of the zodiac. There are many books written about the signs and their original meanings, which provide the comprehensive story of God's plans for mankind, although these renderings have been lost and/or altered over the ages. While it is a fascinating subject, there are sufficient resources on this matter for it to be unnecessary for treatment herein, beyond this mention. Nevertheless, the stars, as contrasted with lunar cycles or even solar days, were intended to convey the length of a year.

Dark Matter?

I want to focus for a moment on the first sentence of Gen 1:2: *"The earth was without form, and void; and darkness was on the face of the deep."* I've recently looked into the hypothetical, so-called 'dark matter.' This type of matter has mass and the consequential gravitational properties, but does not have any properties in the quantum realm. Imagine for a moment that God creates time, space, matter, and energy, but that the laws of quantum mechanics (laws that govern subatomic particles) have not yet been imposed. Without this structural framework for electrons, protons, and neutrons, etc., the matter would be 'dark,' (actually transparent…invisible, which is what is implied in the word 'dark' as applied to such matter) and chaotic…not ordered. Without quantum properties there would be no compounds, no atoms, no distinct elementary particles…only mass. This Biblical description would seem a fitting description not only of dark matter, but also of the mass of the earth before quantum dimensionality. All collectives of matter in space would be simple, spherical lumps of mass. Only at the moment that God imbued the mass with the quantum dimensions would the matter become ordered, with some of these lumps then becoming stars, and others planets. When in Gen 1:3 God says *"Let there be light,"* could this be when the quantum and electromagnetic orderings were imparted to matter and energy? Is it then possible that God left some of the matter of the universe in this primordial form, without a full set of dimensional properties, and that the effects of this are what we now witness as the evidence for dark matter? If indeed the quantum dimensions are strictly a property of some matter (but not all), it then seems that a unified theory of gravitation and quantum mechanics would remain problematic. (I'm admittedly out of my depth here.)

Note that when the earth was created, it was completely covered with "waters." The word rendered "waters" in Gen 1:2 is the Hebrew word "mayim," (Strong's 4325) that is actually a more general term for 'fluids.' With only gravitational properties, all such matter could well be a truly continuous fluid. With the institution of quantum ordering, elementary particles and the elements are instantaneously formed, along with planets, as well as the ignition of sufficiently massive objects to become stars, and light would be the immediate by-product.

On the second day, there is a separation of waters above and below the firmament. Some of these waters above the firmament are re-introduced during the global deluge, and removed once again supernaturally. When, in the first verse of Genesis, He describes the earth as *"without form and void,"* you can imagine the surface of our globe being nothing but a fluidic mass, even without wind or moon to disturb the surface, it would indeed be void…a completely smooth, transparent ball in the blackness of space, without a single feature to distinguish it, nor even weather to disturb the surface thereof. There is no sun, no moon, no other planets or stars, and no electromagnetic radiation to impinge on the face of the earth. So darkness would indeed be on the face of the deep.

In verses 6-8, it is said that God created a firmament that divides the waters from the waters, and that God called this firmament "heaven." It seems that there is a place beyond the earth where the waters removed from the earth are stored, with the firmament separating them from us. Is there water stored somewhere within the three physical dimensions of our existence, but hidden somewhere beyond our atmosphere, in space…even perhaps on another planet, or is this firmament an interdimensional barrier with the extraterrestrial waters stored outside of even the possibility of our discovery? If we look at verse 14 of Gen 1, the lights (stars & planets) are created *"in the firmament;"* thus, with the waters on the other side of the firmament, it would seem that they are indeed kept outside of our three spatial dimensions, beyond our reach or detection.

For those without an understanding of hyper-dimensional space, imagine that we are two-dimensional creatures living within a plane…like an endless sheet of paper. Everything in our universe would have length and width, but no height. Constrained to two dimensions, even the concept of height would be difficult to grasp...such would have no meaning to us. Imagine now a pencil piercing through the paper into a third dimension of space, and the storage of two-dimensional objects in this third dimension, parallel to the plane of our existence. Since we are two dimensional creatures, our eyes would not work on things in such parallel spaces, and we could not leave our two-dimensional space to even discover what is 'above' us…the word itself would seem beyond our comprehension.

Chapter 1 of the *Book of Jubilees* begins at the first year of the exodus, but Chapter 2 recounts Creation, and provides some supplementary details.

And the angel of the presence spake to Moses according to the word of the Lord, saying: Write the complete history of the creation, how in six days the Lord God finished all His works and all that He created, and kept Sabbath on the seventh day and hallowed it for all ages, and appointed it as a sign for all His works.

For on the first day He created the heavens which are above and the earth and the waters and all the spirits which serve before him -the angels of the presence, and the angels of sanctification, and the angels [of the spirit of fire and the angels] of the spirit of the winds, and the angels of the spirit of the clouds, and of darkness, and of snow and of hail and of hoar frost, and the angels of the voices and of the thunder and of the lightning, and the angels of the spirits of cold and of heat, and of winter and of spring and of autumn and of summer and of all the spirits of his creatures which are in the heavens and on the earth, (He created) *the abysses and the darkness, eventide <and night>, and the light, dawn and day, which He hath prepared in the knowledge of his heart.* [Jub 2:1-2]

The author of *Jubilees* says that the heavens were created on the first day, which appears to be at odds with the Biblical account; however, if we assume that the reference to the heavens here actually refers to space and time, it is indeed a necessary prerequisite as the medium for the light. However, he adds the detail of the creation of the angels, delineating some of their domains. In the tenth chapter of the Book of Daniel, it is mentioned that there are also angels (referred to there as Princes) appointed with domain over nations and rulers, so this is apparently not a complete list of angelic domains. Note also that the author states that the "angel of the presence" told Moses to write the history of creation. Since we have distinct accounts of Creation, one dictated by God Himself, and the other dictated by the "angel of the presence," could it be that the angel of the presence is "The angel of the LORD" elsewhere cited in the Bible? That is, a so-called "Christophany" (i.e., appearance of the pre-incarnate second person of the Trinity in the OT)? I suspect this to be the very case here, as it reconciles the two accounts.

While the specific day of the creation of angels is not critical, angelic interactions with mankind are crucial to an understanding of many aspects of our history, and we'll deal with this in more detail when we get to Chapter 7 in this book, covering the sixth chapter of Genesis.

Is the Earth Flat?

This issue of the nature of the firmament touches on the theory of a flat earth. The other crucial text used to support the flat-earth view is Isa 40:22 which reads:

It is He who sits above the circle of the earth,
And its inhabitants are like grasshoppers,
Who stretches out the heavens like a curtain,
And spreads them out like a tent to dwell in.

When I started this journey, I was challenged by my very good friends, William and his wife, Robin. Like the Bereans in Acts 17:11, they searched the Scriptures daily to discover truth. As myself, he believes fully in the truth of all Scripture. I admit that I had a difficult time with the idea of a flat earth, as I felt that there was sufficient scientific evidence that the earth was a globe. I attempted to persuade them through arguments such as the Coriolis force that determines the circular direction of water flow down a drain that differs in northern and southern hemispheres, the seasonal differences by hemisphere, and the movement of the horizon around the globe. Believe it or not, I prayed to God that I was willing to accept the truth of a flat earth if indeed it were so; and I asked God to help me accept the truth, whatever that might be. Now I've already addressed my beliefs on the firmament, and where the waters are held. As I researched the contrary arguments (against a flat earth), some declared that the word for "*circle*" in Isa 40:22 (Strong's 2329) could actually mean "globe." This turns out <u>not</u> to be the case. The definition reads "*from 2328; a circle: -circle, circuit, compass.*" And the definition for 2328 says "*to describe a circle: -compass.*" The image is not that of a static circle such as a flat disk, but one of movement, as of a compass in the process of scribing out a circle. Thus, I believe the key to understanding this verse lies in the use of the secondary definition, "circuit." This means then that God sits above the 'circuit of the earth,' as it scribes out such circuit in its orbit around the sun. The circle of the earth, then, is not the earth itself, but the earth's orbit. I want to stress that I am willing to accept the truth, even if it flies in the face of what I think I know.

Paul Knauber

Chapter 3: The Garden of Eden (Gen 2)

Our ancient history continues in the second chapter of Genesis. Herein we have the events surrounding the Garden of Eden, eastward of where Adam and Eve were formed. I specifically avoid use of the word creation here, as the word creation implies formation out of nothing (Latin: *ex nihilo*... "from nothing"). Eve was formed from the rib of Adam, and Adam himself from the dust of the ground, so while creation was completed in 6 days, God appears also to have done what I'll call *formative engineering* to fashion them. Picking up the Genesis record in Chapter 2:

> *Thus the heavens and the earth, and all the host of them, were finished. And on the seventh day God ended His work which He had done, and He rested on the seventh day from all His work which He had done. Then God blessed the seventh day and sanctified it, because in it He rested from all His work which God had created and made.*
>
> *This is the history of the heavens and the earth when they were created, in the day that the Lord God made the earth and the heavens, before any plant of the field was in the earth and before any herb of the field had grown. For the Lord God had not caused it to rain on the earth, and there was no man to till the ground; but a mist went up from the earth and watered the whole face of the ground.*
>
> *And the Lord God formed man of the dust of the ground, and breathed into his nostrils the breath of life; and man became a living being.*
>
> *The Lord God planted a garden eastward in Eden, and there He put the man whom He had formed. And out of the ground the Lord God made every tree grow that is pleasant to the sight and good for food. The tree of life was also in the midst of the garden, and the tree of the knowledge of good and evil.*
>
> *Now a river went out of Eden to water the garden, and from there it parted and became four riverheads. The name of the first is Pishon; it is the one which skirts the whole land of Havilah, where there is gold. And the gold of that land is good. Bdellium and the onyx stone are there. The name of the second river is Gihon; it is the one which goes around the whole land of Cush. The name of the third river is Hiddekel; it is the one which goes toward the east of Assyria. The fourth river is the Euphrates.*
>
> *Then the Lord God took the man and put him in the garden of Eden to tend and keep it. And the Lord God commanded the man, saying, "Of every tree of the garden you may freely eat; but of the tree of the knowledge of good and evil you shall not eat, for in the day that you eat of it you shall surely die."*
>
> *And the Lord God said, "It is not good that man should be alone; I will make him a helper comparable to him." Out of the ground the Lord God formed every beast of the field and every bird of the air, and brought them to Adam to see what he would call them. And whatever Adam called each living creature, that was its name. So Adam gave names to all cattle, to the birds of the air, and to every beast of the field. But for Adam there was not found a helper comparable to him.*

And the Lord God caused a deep sleep to fall on Adam, and he slept; and He took one of his ribs, and closed up the flesh in its place. Then the rib which the Lord God had taken from man He made into a woman, and He brought her to the man.

And Adam said:

*"This is now bone of my bones
And flesh of my flesh;
She shall be called Woman,
Because she was taken out of Man."*

Therefore a man shall leave his father and mother and be joined to his wife, and they shall become one flesh.

And they were both naked, the man and his wife, and were not ashamed. [Gen 2: 1-25]

Before I address this excerpt, I want to present the accounts of this period from both *Jubilees* and Josephus' *Antiquities*, starting with *Jubilees*:

And on the six days of the second week we brought, according to the word of God, unto Adam all the beasts, and all the cattle, and all the birds, and everything that moves on the earth, and everything that moves in the water, according to their kinds, and according to their types: the beasts on the first day; the cattle on the second day; the birds on the third day; and all that which moves on the earth on the fourth day; and that which moves in the water on the fifth day. And Adam named them all by their respective names, and as he called them, so was their name. And on these five days Adam saw all these, male and female, according to every kind that was on the earth, but he was alone and found no helpmeet for him. And the Lord said unto us: 'It is not good that the man should be alone: let us make a helpmeet for him.' And the Lord our God caused a deep sleep to fall upon him, and he slept, and He took for the woman one rib from amongst his ribs, and this rib was the origin of the woman from amongst his ribs, and He built up the flesh in its stead, and built the woman. And He awaked Adam out of his sleep and on awaking he rose on the sixth day, and He brought her to him, and he knew her, and said unto her: 'This is now bone of my bones and flesh of my flesh; she shall be called [my] wife; because she was taken from her husband.' Therefore shall man and wife be one and therefore shall a man leave his father and his mother, and cleave unto his wife, and they shall be one flesh. In the first week was Adam created, and the rib -his wife: in the second week He showed her unto him: and for this reason the commandment was given to keep in their defilement, for a male seven days, and for a female twice seven days. And after Adam had completed forty days in the land where he had been created, we brought him into the garden of Eden to till and keep it, but his wife they brought in on the eightieth day, and after this she entered into the garden of Eden. And for this reason the commandment is written on the heavenly tablets in regard to her that gives birth: 'if she bears a male, she shall remain in her uncleanness seven days according to the first week of days, and thirty and three days shall she remain in the blood of her purifying, and she shall not touch any hallowed thing, nor enter into the sanctuary, until she accomplishes these days which (are enjoined) in the case of a male child. But in the case of a female child she shall remain in her uncleanness two weeks of days, according to the first two weeks, and sixty-six days in the blood of her purification, and they will be in all eighty days.' And when she had completed these eighty days we brought her into the garden of Eden, for it is holier than all the earth besides and every tree that is planted in it is holy. [Jub 3:1-12]

The Jubilees account immediately adds temporal details to this part of history. First, it tells us that it was in the second week of our history that the angels (one of which narrates the Book of Jubilees) brought the animals, birds, fish, and other living creatures to Adam, whereupon he named them. On the 6th day of this second week, Eve was formed. More interestingly, Adam and Eve were not yet in Eden; the angels brought Adam first into Eden 40 days after his creation, and it was another 40 days before Eve was brought in. Verses 10-11 constitute compliance with Leviticus 12:1-5, instituted much later, but observed and explained here in the foreknowledge of this element of the law. This passage of Leviticus addresses the times of purification following the birth of a male and female child. For a male child it is 7 + 33 days (= 40 days); for a female child it is 14 + 66 days (= 80 days). While the verses read as applicable to the mother, it seems clear from the Jubilees account that it applies equally to the children. According to the *Jewish Study Bible*, this purification is more ethereal than physical, and must be accomplished before the mother or child can enter a holy place, in this case, Eden, <u>where God meets man</u>, much as the Holy of Holies in the sanctuary of the Temple. Eden thus appears to be a picture of heaven just as is the Temple.

Let's now turn to Josephus' account in section 3 of Chapter I, Book I of his *Antiquities*:

Moses says further, that God planted a paradise in the east, flourishing with all sorts of trees; and that among them was the tree of life, and another of knowledge, whereby was to be known what was good and evil; and that when he brought Adam and his wife into this garden, he commanded them to take care of the plants. Now the garden was watered by one river, which ran round about the whole earth, and was parted into four parts. And Phison, which denotes a multitude, running into India, makes its exit into the sea, and is by the Greeks called Ganges. Euphrates also, as well as Tigris, goes down into the Red Sea. Now the name Euphrates, or Phrath, denotes either a dispersion, or a flower: by Tigris, or Diglath, is signified what is swift, with narrowness; and Geon runs through Egypt, and denotes what arises from the east, which the Greeks call Nile.

First, I want to address the creation of the angels. The Biblical account of creation in chapter 1 of Genesis seems to make no mention at all of their creation. Some suppose that this means that the angels were created beforehand. However, verse 1 of chapter 2 states *"Thus the heavens and the earth, and all the host of them, were finished."* The word translated "host" is the Hebrew word "tsaba" meaning "a mass of persons (or fig. things) espec. reg. organized for war (an army)." Given

Figure 1: Pangaea. By robin2/shutterstock.com

this insight, the inference that this refers to angels fits perfectly with later Scripture where the angels indeed function as an army, consistent in both the OT and NT. And, as within an army with ranks and branches, we have distinct ranks and functions of angels: messengers, combatants, guards, etc.

The Supercontinent

Gen 2:10 says that *"Now a river went out of Eden to water the garden, and from there it parted and became four riverheads,"* and goes on to tell us the names of each. Now, Josephus also describes that one river ran around the whole earth, and was divided into four parts. Josephus identifies them by name as the rivers Nile (in Africa), Ganges (in India), as well as Tigris & Euphrates (in the Middle East). How can this be and can we reconcile this with modern geography? Well, it is easily reconciled if one recognizes that the land mass of the earth prior to the time of Peleg was yet undivided into separate continents. You may be familiar with Alfred Wegener's theory proposed in 1912 that the earth's land masses were indeed conjoined as a single supercontinent that he named "Pangaea," (Greek for "all the earth;" see Figure 1) and he also coined the term "continental drift" to describe the process of its gradual division. However, Wegener's theory was actually founded on the earlier work of Antonio Snider who, in 1859, proposed a _rapid_ continental separation. This earlier concept has been recast in the modern age as "catastrophic plate tectonics." Similarly, the mechanics of Wegener's theory have been superseded by the more widely accepted theory of plate tectonics, but the underlying evidence that Wegener discovered tying the continents together at very specific adjoining areas remains sound. He was not just fitting the pieces together, but was looking at the types of rock, fossils, sediments, and other factors in order to justifiably match the shorelines as he did. (See Figure 2) As a youth, I did see such sketches showing how the continents fit together as in a jigsaw, but dismissed this as people seeing animal shapes in the clouds, or Abraham Lincoln's face in a corn flake. However, with a much better understanding now of a reconciled historical account, it makes perfect sense, and there's scientific evidence supporting the concept implicit in the Biblical account.

But if this is so, why does Josephus refer to the Tigris and Euphrates as emptying into the Red Sea? Recall that he is writing his account to the Romans in relatively modern times, and uses contemporary geographic references identifying these rivers as the then-surviving vestiges of the four parts of this one ancient river, even though they were even then to be found on separated continents. Note too that ancient Greek mythology also describes a single river that ran around the earth. Indeed, in Hesiod's *Theogony* the river Okeanos circles the earth.

So, when was the one land mass divided into the modern continents? Genesis 10:25 provides the answer: *"To Eber were born two sons: one was named Peleg, for in his days the earth was divided...."* The most prevalent interpretation of this verse is that in Peleg's time the lands were 'divided up' or 'allocated' to the various tribes of people. Although this indeed happened, there is more to it. It would be sensible to stop with this abbreviated explanation were it not for the reference to the name of Peleg. According to Strong's Concordance, Peleg in Hebrew means "earthquake!" Thus, it was

Figure 2: The Pillars of Evidence for Wegener's Continental Drift Theory.

in Peleg's life that the supercontinent was separated into the continents we know today, that process being accomplished by rapid tectonic shifts, accompanied by concomitant earthquakes, which is exactly what we witness today when tectonic plates shift. Can we reconcile this with other events during Peleg's life? Indeed we can, as Genesis Chapter 11 tells us:

> *Eber lived thirty-four years, and begot Peleg. After he begot Peleg, Eber lived four hundred and thirty years, and begot sons and daughters. Peleg lived thirty years, and begot Reu. After he begot Reu, Peleg lived two hundred and nine years, and begot sons and daughters.* [Gen 11:16-19]

Genesis provides a detailed chronology of these historical events, so we know from this that Peleg was born in 1757 AM and died in 1996 AM. The confusion of languages is the consequence of the construction of the Tower of Babel, which occurs in 1996 AM, making Peleg's death concurrent with the confusion and separation. If the land was indeed divided into the modern continents at the end of Peleg's life, it is thoroughly consistent with the distinct languages in the far flung countries on the separated continents and island nations we know today, without necessitating the relatively sophisticated design and construction of ships capable of long voyages over the high seas and the attendant navigational skills that would otherwise be indispensable for multiple transoceanic migrations. Noah's ark was capable in these regards, but was designed by God, and Noah was shown by Him how to build it. The engineering rules governing the stability and durability of such vessels did not otherwise yet exist. Peleg was not given his name as a consequence of the earthquakes, but rather prophetically, as is the case with many of the ancients' names.

I believe there may be one last Biblical clue to this event in the genealogy. Now 'hermeneutics' is the combination of art and science of interpretation, principally as applied to understanding Scripture. There is an established hermeneutic tool called by some the "Meaning-of-Names" code that been demonstrated as a valid method showing that prophecy is nested within the names of those in the direct lineage from Adam to Christ. The first case of this demonstrated to me was in the lineage from Adam to Noah which sequence encodes a Messianic prophecy. Once I became aware of this device, I decided to consider its application to the division of the supercontinent. Now Eber begets Peleg and Peleg begets Reu. The Hebrew word "eber" (Strong's 5676) means "a region across," or "on the opposite side." As previously noted, Peleg means "earthquake." And the Hebrew word Reu (Strong's 7466) means "friend." The implication here may be that "friends were separated to opposite sides with earthquakes." This is exactly what this rapid continental separation was intended to accomplish.

I'm already well ahead of myself, but I had to leap forward almost 2000 years to reconcile this incredibly significant, but obscured part of our ancient history.

The Piri Reis Map

We have another piece of evidence that supports the hypothesis of a supercontinent divided: the Piri Reis map. (See Figure 3) The map is apparently the only remaining fragment of a larger, global map, the fragment having been discovered in 1929 by German theologian Gustav Deissmann, while working in the Topkapi Palace Library in Istanbul. The subject map was created in 1513 by Turkish (Ottoman) Admiral and cartographer Hagii Ahmed Muhiddin Piri, aka Piri Reis ("Reis" meaning "Chief" or "Admiral," the latter clearly preferred by context, given his command of a naval fleet). Piri's own note numbered "VI" on the map provides information on the sources used to develop this map. (Note that the reference to "Colombo" in Reis' note is actually to Christopher Columbus.) The note reads:

> *This section shows in what way this map was drawn. In this century there is no map like this map in anyone's possession. The [--] hand of this poor man has drawn it and now it is constructed. From about twenty charts and Mappae Mundi--these are charts drawn in the days of Alexander, Lord of the Two Horns, which show the inhabited quarter of the world; the Arabs name these charts Jaferiye--from eight Jaferiyes of that kind and one Arabic map of Hind, and from the maps just drawn by four Portuguese which show the countries of Hind, Sind and China geometrically drawn, and also from a map drawn by Colombo in the western region I have extracted it. By reducing all these maps to one scale this final form was arrived at. So that the present map is as correct and reliable for the Seven Seas as the map of these our countries is considered correct and reliable by seamen.* [From *Life and Works of Piri Reis: The Oldest Map of America*, by Professor Dr. A. Afetinan, Ankara, 1954, pp. 28-34. Translated from the original Turkish. Public domain.]

Now the most compelling part of this map is the detailed coastline of Antarctica <u>without the icecap that presently encases the southern continent</u>! First, the continent of Antarctica is consistently convconveyedconveyed in history books as first speculated by Capt. James Cook in 1773, with this postulate not born out until 1820. What's more, in modern times, the underlying coastline of Antarctica was not determined 1949 during the Swedish-British Antarctic Expedition launched in 1949 and concluding in 1952. The purpose of the expedition was climatic investigation, but part of that investigation employed the use of seismic charges to determine the thickness of the ice cap across the continent. This part of the work, though, yielded a more accurate map of the actual coastline beneath the ice.

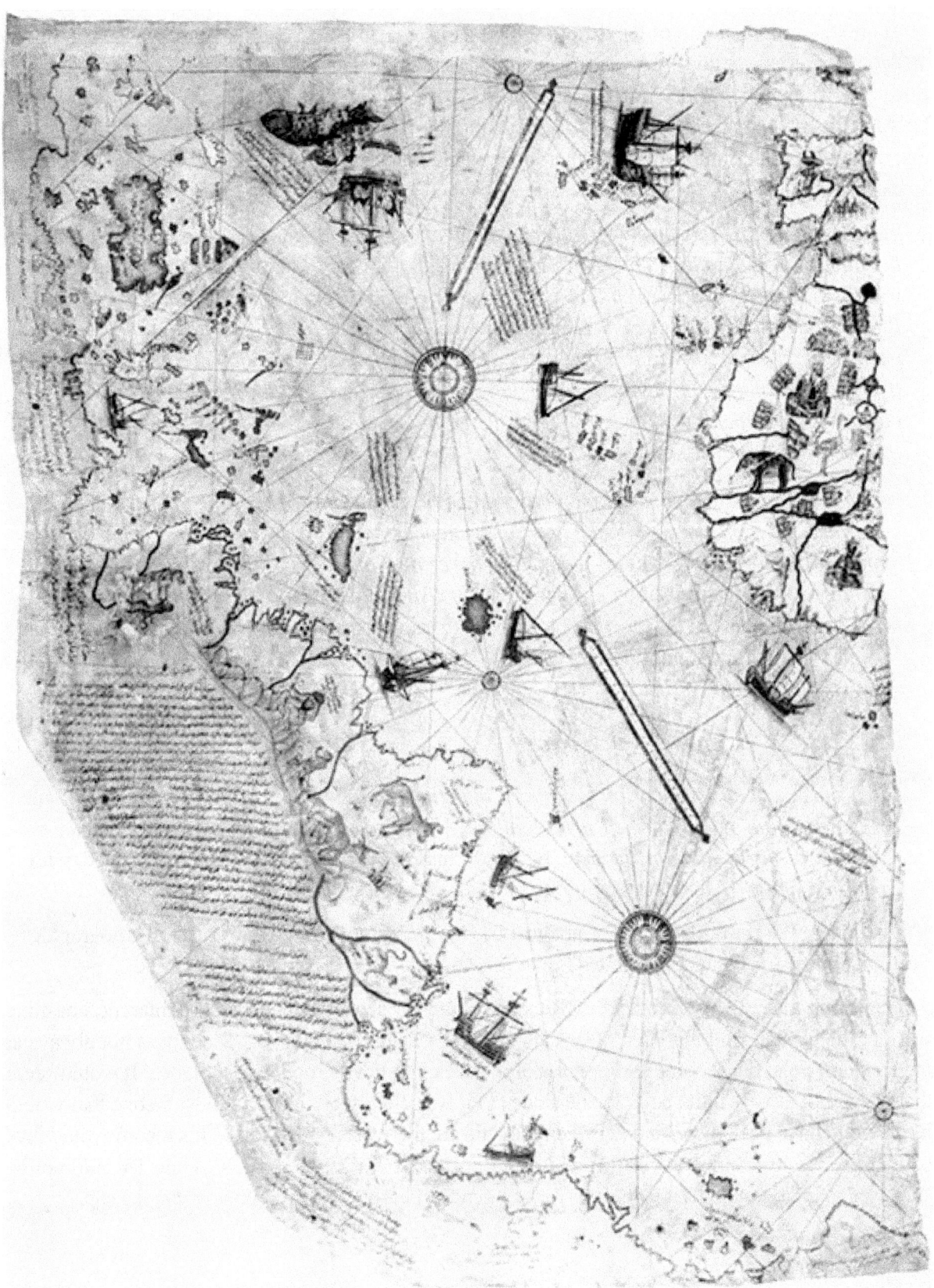

Figure 3: The Piri Reis Map. Wikipedia.com

While the interpretation of the detail on the Piri Reis map is not without some controversy, it is difficult to dismiss the confirmations by the USAF and notable endorsement of the renowned Albert Einstein. In his book *Maps of the Ancient Sea Kings*, Charles Hapgood reprints two letters from USAF officers that evaluated his work correlating the coastline in the lower portion of the map to that of the Antarctic continent. The later letter, dated August 1961 provides an excellent summary, an extract of which I've included herein:

The following is a brief summary of our findings. The solution of the portolano projection used by Admiral Reis, developed by your class in Anthropology, must be very nearly correct; for when known geographical locations are checked in relationship to the grid computed by Dr. Richard Strachan (MIT), there is remarkably close agreement. Piri Reis' use of the portolano projection (centered on Syene, Egypt) was an excellent choice, for it is a developable surface that would permit the relative size and shape of the earth (at that latitude) to be retained. It is our opinion that those who compiled the original map had an excellent knowledge of the continents covered by this map.

a. As stated by Colonel Harold Z. Ohlmeyer in his letter (July 6, 1960) to you, the Princess Martha Coast of Queen Maud Land Antarctica, appears to be truly represented on the southern sector of the Piri Reis map. The agreement of the Piri Reis map with the seismic profile of this area made by the Norwegian-British-Swedish Expedition of 1949, supported by your solution of the grid, places beyond a reasonable doubt the conclusion that the original source maps must have been made before the present Antarctic ice cap covered the Queen Maud Land coasts.

[...]

d. We are convinced that the findings made by you and your associates are valid, and that they raise extremely important questions affecting geology and ancient history, questions which certainly require further investigation. [Maps of the Ancient Sea Kings: Evidence of Advanced Civilization in the Ice Age, by Charles H. Hapgood, 1966; re-printed with permission from Adventures Unlimited Press]

The letter was issued by USAF Captain Lorenzo W. Burroughs, Chief of the Cartographic Section, 8th Reconnaissance Technical Squadron, at Westover AFB in Massachusetts.

Questions indeed! How could Piri Reis have had an accurate map of the Antarctic coastline without the ice cap, and that over 400 years earlier? Could it be that Antarctica was not always at the southern pole, but at some earlier point at a more climatically moderate latitude? It would seem that it was not always in its polar locale since (1) it was clearly mapped out by someone that would have had to have been there, and (2) when they did so, there was no ice cap. This record would thus be consistent with continental drift (rapid or not) of the Antarctic land mass. Thus, I would not be surprised at the possible future discovery of evidence of early civilization below the ice cap.

Dragons Were Real

The Genesis account of Creation provides a broad overview of the creation of the animals, but lacks detail regarding specific creatures. The Biblical Book of Job provides detailed descriptions, in God's own words, of various creatures, including the lion (38:39-41), mountain goats (39:1-4), the onager (or Asiatic wild ass) (39:5-8), the wild ox (39:9-12), the ostrich (39:13-18), the horse (39:19-

Figure 4: A wall with dragon in China.   By cowardlion/shutterstock.com

25), the hawk (39:26-30), the hippopotamus (called "behemoth") (40:15-24), and the dragon, called Leviathan (40:25-41:26). We can certainly identify the Leviathan with the dragon as this association is made in the Biblical book of Isaiah, chapter 27, verse 1, which reads, *"In that day the LORD with his sore and great and strong sword shall punish leviathan the piercing serpent, even leviathan that crooked serpent; and he shall slay the dragon that is in the sea."* [KJV] But the description in Job expounds with undeniable specifics:

> *"I will not conceal his limbs, His mighty power, or his graceful proportions. Who can remove his outer coat? Who can approach him with a double bridle? Who can open the doors of his face, with his terrible teeth all around? His rows of scales are his pride, Shut up tightly as with a seal; One is so near another That no air can come between them; They are joined one to another, They stick together and cannot be parted. His sneezings flash forth light, and his eyes are like the eyelids of the morning. Out of his mouth go burning lights; Sparks of fire shoot out. Smoke goes out of his nostrils, as from a boiling pot and burning rushes. His*

breath kindles coals, and a flame goes out of his mouth. Strength dwells in his neck, and sorrow dances before him.
The folds of his flesh are joined together; they are firm on him and cannot be moved. His heart is as hard as stone, even as hard as the lower millstone. When he raises himself up, the mighty are afraid; Because of his crashings they are beside themselves. Though the sword reaches him, it cannot avail; nor does spear, dart, or javelin. He regards iron as straw, And bronze as rotten wood. The arrow cannot make him flee; Slingstones become like stubble to him. Darts are regarded as straw; He laughs at the threat of javelins. His undersides are like sharp potsherds; He spreads pointed marks in the mire. He makes the deep boil like a pot; He makes the sea like a pot of ointment. He leaves a shining wake behind him; one would think the deep had white hair. On earth there is nothing like him, which is made without fear. He beholds every high thing; He is king over all the children of pride." [Job 41:12, 14-34; poetic lines concatenated for space]

I recall having a Bible study one evening with friends of ours at our home. As I was preparing for the study in the Book of Job, I remember reading about the Leviathan. The first 14 verses of chapter 41 do not reveal any characteristics that could be uniquely associated with any creature. But in v15, we see interlocking scales; in v16 sparks coming from its mouth; in v20, we have smoke coming from its nostrils; and v21 says that flame goes out of its mouth. As I pondered this, I glanced downward…I was seated at our dining room table beneath which was a Chinese rug with the image of a dragon in its center. I then realized that the Book of Job was describing a real creature. We have seen many depictions of dragons, in various cultures around the world, but probably none more abundant as in China. (See Figure 4) We have seen depictions of dragons also in the middle ages, being slain by knights. (See Figure 6) But dragons are depicted in art across many cultures and

Figure 5: Greek Mosaic of a Sea Dragon, 8th century BC (from Wikipedia.com)

continents: ancient Mesopotamian, ancient Egyptian, Arabian, Armenian, Babylonian, Korean,

Japanese, Chinese, eastern and western European, Norse, ancient Grecian (see Figure 5) and Roman, East Indian, Tibetan, Persian, Sumerian, Philippine, Mayan, Aztec, and Native American. With no apparent remaining species, it is clear that these terrible creatures were feared by all, and consequently hunted to extinction, probably by the end of the middle ages.

Figure 6: Illustration by Caspar Schott, from Physica Curiosa, 1697. Courtesy of UW-Madison's Ebling Library, Rare Books & Special Collections, Madison, Wisconsin. Special thanks to Micaela Sullivan-Fowler, M.S., M.A., Distinguished Academic Librarian, Head of Marketing & Special Communications, Curator & History of the Health Sciences Librarian, Ebling Library for the Health Sciences, for her provision of the digital image.

Chapter 4: The Fall of Man (Gen 3)

Now there is a bit of a gap in the Biblical record from Adam & Eve's entry into the Garden of Eden to their fall. We only know this from the Book of Jubilees which provides a specific period of their stay.

And in the first week of the first jubilee, Adam and his wife were in the garden of Eden for seven years tilling and keeping it, and we gave him work and we instructed him to do everything that is suitable for tillage. And he tilled (the garden), and was naked and knew it not, and was not ashamed, and he protected the garden from the birds and beasts and cattle, and gathered its fruit, and eat, and put aside the residue for himself and for his wife [and put aside that which was being kept]. And after the completion of the seven years, which he had completed there, seven years exactly, and in the second month, on the seventeenth day (of the month), the serpent came and approached the woman....
[Jub 3:15-17]

Note that they were in the Garden for *exactly* 7 years when the serpent approaches Eve…on the 17th day of the second month. Recall that Adam waited 40 days after his formation on the 6th day to enter the garden. Thus, the 17th day of the second month (30 + 17 = 47th day) referred to here is the day after the six plus forty days.

We now pick things up in Genesis chapter 3 (in the year 8 AM) wherein we have the account of the fall of Adam and Eve in the Garden of Eden.

Now the serpent was more cunning than any beast of the field which the Lord God had made. And he said to the woman, "Has God indeed said, 'You shall not eat of every tree of the garden'?" And the woman said to the serpent, "We may eat the fruit of the trees of the garden; but of the fruit of the tree which is in the midst of the garden, God has said, 'You shall not eat it, nor shall you touch it, lest you die.'"

Then the serpent said to the woman, "You will not surely die. For God knows that in the day you eat of it your eyes will be opened, and you will be like God, knowing good and evil."

So when the woman saw that the tree was good for food, that it was pleasant to the eyes, and a tree desirable to make one wise, she took of its fruit and ate. She also gave to her husband with her, and he ate. Then the eyes of both of them were opened, and they knew that they were naked; and they sewed fig leaves together and made themselves coverings.

And they heard the sound of the Lord God walking in the garden in the cool of the day, and Adam and his wife hid themselves from the presence of the Lord God among the trees of the garden.

Then the Lord God called to Adam and said to him, "Where are you?"

So he said, "I heard Your voice in the garden, and I was afraid because I was naked; and I hid myself."

And He said, "Who told you that you were naked? Have you eaten from the tree of which I commanded you that you should not eat?"

Then the man said, "The woman whom You gave to be with me, she gave me of the tree, and I ate."

And the Lord God said to the woman, "What is this you have done?" The woman said, "The serpent deceived me, and I ate."

So the Lord God said to the serpent:
  "Because you have done this,
  You are cursed more than all cattle,
  And more than every beast of the field;
  On your belly you shall go,
  And you shall eat dust
  All the days of your life.
  And I will put enmity between you and the woman,
  And between your seed and her Seed;
  He shall bruise your head,
  And you shall bruise His heel."

To the woman He said:
  "I will greatly multiply your sorrow and your conception;
  In pain you shall bring forth children;
  Your desire shall be for your husband,
  And he shall rule over you."

Then to Adam He said, "Because you have heeded the voice of your wife, and have eaten from the tree of which I commanded you, saying, 'You shall not eat of it':
  "Cursed is the ground for your sake;
  In toil you shall eat of it
  All the days of your life.
  Both thorns and thistles it shall bring forth for you,
  And you shall eat the herb of the field.
  In the sweat of your face you shall eat bread
  Till you return to the ground,
  For out of it you were taken;
  For dust you are,
  And to dust you shall return."

And Adam called his wife's name Eve, because she was the mother of all living.

Also for Adam and his wife the Lord God made tunics of skin, and clothed them.

Then the Lord God said, "Behold, the man has become like one of Us, to know good and evil. And now, lest he put out his hand and take also of the tree of life, and eat, and live forever"-- therefore the Lord God sent him out of the garden of Eden to till the ground from which he was taken. So He drove out the man; and He placed cherubim at the east of the garden of Eden, and a flaming sword which turned every way, to guard the way to the tree of life. [Gen 3:1-24]

I've always thought it odd that Eve seems not at all astonished that the serpent spoke. Clearly, she did not consider either his presence or his speech out of the ordinary, but why not? As we see here, Josephus provides the background:

God therefore commanded that Adam and his wife should eat of all the rest of the plants, but to abstain from the tree of knowledge; and foretold to them, that if they touched it, it would prove their destruction. **But while all the living creatures had one language**, *at that time the serpent, which then lived together with Adam and his wife, shewed an envious disposition, at his supposal of their living happily, and in obedience to the commands of God; and imagining, that when they disobeyed them, they would fall into calamities, he persuaded the woman, out of a malicious intention, to taste of the tree of knowledge, telling them, that in that tree was the knowledge of good and evil; which knowledge, when they should obtain, they would lead a happy life; nay, a life not inferior to that of a god: by which means he overcame the woman, and persuaded her to despise the command of God. Now when she had tasted of that tree, and was pleased with its fruit, she persuaded Adam to make use of it also. Upon this they perceived that they were become naked to one another; and being ashamed thus to appear abroad,* **they invented somewhat to cover them; for the tree sharpened their understanding; and they covered themselves with fig-leaves; and tying these before them**, *out of modesty, they thought they were happier than they were before, as they had discovered what they were in want of. But when God came into the garden, Adam, who was wont before to come and converse with him, being conscious of his wicked behavior, went out of the way. This behavior surprised God; and he asked what was the cause of this his procedure; and why he, that before delighted in that conversation, did now fly from it, and avoid it. When he made no reply, as conscious to himself that he had transgressed the command of God, God said, "I had before determined about you both, how you might lead a happy life, without any affliction, and care, and vexation of soul; and that all things which might contribute to your enjoyment and pleasure should grow up by my providence, of their own accord, without your own labor and pains-taking; which state of labor and pains-taking would soon bring on old age, and death would not be at any remote distance: but now thou hast abused this my good-will, and hast disobeyed my commands; for thy silence is not the sign of thy virtue, but of thy evil conscience." However, Adam excused his sin, and entreated God not to be angry at him, and laid the blame of what was done upon his wife; and said that he was deceived by her, and thence became an offender; while she again accused the serpent. But God allotted him punishment, because he weakly submitted to the counsel of his wife; and said the ground should not henceforth yield its fruits of its own accord, but that when it should be harassed by their labor, it should bring forth some of its fruits, and refuse to bring forth others. He also made Eve liable to the inconveniency of breeding, and the sharp pains of bringing forth children; and this because she persuaded Adam with the same arguments wherewith the serpent had persuaded her, and had thereby brought him into a calamitous condition.* **He also deprived the serpent of speech**, *out of indignation at his malicious disposition towards Adam. Besides this, he inserted poison under his tongue, and made him an enemy to men; and suggested to them, that they should direct their strokes against his head, that being the place wherein lay his mischievous designs towards men, and it being* *easiest to take vengeance on him, that way.* **And when he had deprived him of the use of his feet, he made him to go rolling all along, and dragging himself upon the ground.** *And when God had appointed these penalties for them, he removed Adam and Eve out of the garden into another place.* [Ant I:I:4, emphasis mine]

So, as it was, all the creatures in the Garden of Eden were from their creation able to speak the same language as Adam and Eve. This explains Eve's lack of amazement when the serpent spoke. Josephus' account also discloses that as a consequence of the serpent's temptation causing Adam and Eve to fall, God deprived the serpent of speech, inserted the poison under its tongue, and deprived him of the use of his feet. It is interesting to note that in some species of snakes, there are found vestigial femurs and pelves, suspended within the muscle tissue, completely disconnected from the spine. There can be no other explanation for these than that these creatures once had functional legs. You can examine this yourself by looking into "pelvic spurs," as they are termed.

Incidentally, the Book of Jubilees tells us that this single language was Hebrew. However, it also tells us that after the confusion of tongues following the flood of Noah's time, Hebrew ceased to be spoken, but was reintroduced to mankind when God first called Abraham.

And the LORD God said: "Open his mouth and his ears, that he may hear and speak with his mouth, with the language which hath been revealed;" for it had ceased from the mouths of all the children of men from the day of the overthrow (of Babel). And I opened his mouth, and his ears and his lips, and I began to speak with him in Hebrew in the tongue of creation. [Jub XII:25-26]

I also found it interesting that Adam and Eve knew how to sew. Since they had no prior need for this skill, how did they each manage to do this? I looked into the Hebrew word used in the Biblical text and found that it means only to sew, in the sense of what a seamstress would do...that is, real sewing. I thought that perhaps the word might have also been rendered "to weave," which would have been, to me, more sensible. But Josephus explains above that the tree "sharpened their understanding," allowing them to accomplish the task of sewing their leafy garments.

So, Adam and Eve were expelled from the Garden of Eden. According to the Book of Jubilees, Ch. 3, v32:

And on the new moon of the fourth month, Adam and his wife went forth from the Garden of Eden, and they dwelt in the land of 'Eldâ, in the land of their creation.

Going back to v28-29 of this same chapter, we read:

And on that day was closed the mouth of all beasts, and of cattle, and of birds, and whatever walketh, and whatever moveth, so that they could no longer speak: for they had all spoken with one another with one lip and with one tongue. And He sent out of the Garden of Eden all that was in the Garden of Eden, and all flesh was scattered according to its kinds, and according to its types unto the places which had been created for them.

This explains that not all creatures went to all places, which is why we do not find all types of creatures on every continent.

Chapter 5: The Second Generation (Gen 4)

Chapter 4 in Genesis articulates the stories of the first sons of Adam: Cain, Abel, and Seth. While Josephus provides supplementary details, they are mostly not pertinent to our expanded history. Similarly, The *Book of Jasher* also offers new detail to this story that is quite captivating. I encourage those interested in this story to read it for an expanded revelation of the purported conversations between Cain and Abel, and between God and Cain subsequent to Abel's murder. Nonetheless, I do provide the account from the *Book of Jubilees*, as herein we find some temporal detail:

And in the third week in the second jubilee she gave birth to Cain, and in the fourth she gave birth to Abel, and in the fifth she gave birth to her daughter Âwân. And in the first (year) of the third jubilee, Cain slew Abel because (God) accepted the sacrifice of Abel, and did not accept the offering of Cain. And he slew him in the field: and his blood cried from the ground to heaven, complaining because he had slain him. And the Lord reproved Cain because of Abel, because he had slain him, and he made him a fugitive on the earth because of the blood of his brother, and he cursed him upon the earth. ... And Adam and his wife mourned for Abel four weeks of years, and in the fourth year of the fifth week they became joyful, and Adam knew his wife again, and she bare him a son, and he called his name Seth; for he said 'GOD has raised up a second seed unto us on the earth instead of Abel; for Cain slew him.' And in the sixth week he begat his daughter Azûrâ. And Cain took Âwân his sister to be his wife and she bare him Enoch at the close of the fourth jubilee. And in the first year of the first week of the fifth jubilee, houses were built on the earth, and Cain built a city, and called its name after the name of his son Enoch. And Adam knew Eve his wife and she bare yet nine sons. And in the fifth week of the fifth jubilee Seth took Azûrâ his sister to be his wife, and in the fourth (year of the sixth week) she bare him Enos. He began to call on the name of the Lord on the earth.
[Jub 4:1-4, 7-12]

In verse 1, with reference to the birth of Cain, we see the wording "*...in the third week of the second jubilee....*" Here, the word "week" refers to weeks of years. Thus, we don't have a specific year for Cain's birth, only that he would have been born somewhere between 64 AM and 70 AM. Remember, the first jubilee is considered the first set of 49 years, so the first year of the second jubilee is 49 AM +1 = 50 AM. But, we also see here that Cain slew Abel in the first year of the third jubilee, or 49+49+1 = 99 AM. As discovered in v7, Seth was born in the fourth year of the fifth week (of the third jubilee), or 98 + 28 + 4 = 130 AM, which agrees completely with the Biblical account. I reiterate here that while the dates given here in the *Book of Jubilees* are spot-on with those in the Biblical account, most others do not so synchronize. Thus, one must always check these dates against the other sources. As previously noted, I accept them when they are in alignment with a given the chain of events, but must dismiss those which are not in agreement with the same event dated otherwise in the Biblical record.

A final note before moving on. Cain was cursed to wander the earth. It is said that he was banished from the land of his family to Nod, East of Eden. In his *Antiquities,* Josephus states that Cain built the city that he called Nod. Nod in Hebrew (Strong's 5113) means "*vagrancy, homeless, or nomadic.*" If one accepts that Eden is somewhere close to the confluence of the Tigris and Euphrates rivers, at the northern end of the Red Sea, then the land East of Eden would be the Arabian peninsula, a land of nomadic tribes even into modern times. While there is the crucial discontinuity of the peoples and cultures there with the occurrence of the global deluge in the 17th century AM, it is curious that this land seems to have retained some of its characteristic nomadism.

Chapter 6: The Coming Biblical Deluge (Gen 5)

Chapter 5 of Genesis provides a genealogy of Adam. This is not an exhaustive list of his offspring, but only those that are pertinent in the lineage to Noah. Rather than reprint the chapter and verses in their entirety here, I've elected to simply tabulate the dates with the supporting scripture so that we can firmly establish the year of the global flood. I jumped ahead to Genesis Chapter 7 on the last entry in Table 1, just to complete the record to the year of the flood.

Now the Bible does not always present events in chronological order; rather, the chapters are frequently topical. For example, in Genesis Chapter 4, verses 16-24 outline Cain's offspring to the

Year (AM)	Reference	Text
0	Gen 1:1	Creation
130	Gen 5:3	When Adam had lived 130 years, he had a son in his own likeness, in his own image; and he named him Seth.
235	Gen 5:6	When Seth had lived 105 years, he became the father of Enosh.
325	Gen 5:9	When Enosh had lived 90 years, he became the father of Kenan.
395	Gen 5:12	When Kenan had lived 70 years, he became the father of Mahalalel.
460	Gen 5:15	When Mahalalel had lived 65 years, he became the father of Jared.
622	Gen 5:18	When Jared had lived 162 years, he became the father of Enoch.
687	Gen 5:21	When Enoch had lived 65 years, he became the father of Methuselah.
874	Gen 5:25	When Methuselah had lived 187 years, he became the father of Lamech.
1056	Gen 5:28-29	When Lamech had lived 182 years, he had a son. And he called his name Noah....
1556	Gen 5:32	After Noah was 500 years old, he became the father of Shem, Ham and Japheth.
1656	Gen 7:6	Noah was six hundred years old when the floodwaters came on the earth.

Table 1: Biblical Chronology from Adam to the Flood

7th generation; then in verse 25 we jump back in time to the birth of Seth. So, when we get to Gen 6:3, there is a similar set back, this time just 20 years, from 1556 AM to 1536 AM. Herein, God pronounces His intent to destroy all mankind (save for Noah's family):

And the LORD said, "My spirit will not strive with man forever, for he is indeed flesh; yet his days shall be one hundred and twenty years." [Gen 6:3]

When I read the Bible the first couple of times, I took this to mean that God was declaring that mankind's lifespan would have an upper limit of 120 years, which is, with a very few possible exceptions, what we have witnessed for the last three millennia. Indeed, in the Biblical account over the period of roughly one thousand years following the flood, we see a gradual decline in the lifespans of men up to the life of Moses, whose life ends up being the prototypical maximum of 120 years in length. I later realized that in this verse God is intentionally declaring a second meaning. Correctly understood, He is also declaring when the flood will come, 120 years hence. The *Book of Jasher* states this very specifically:

> *And after the lapse of many years,* ***in the four hundred and eightieth year of the life of Noah (1536 AM),*** *when all those men, who followed the Lord had died away from amongst the sons of men, and only Methuselah was then left, God said unto Noah and Methuselah, saying, Speak ye, and proclaim to the sons of men, saying, Thus saith the Lord, return from your evil ways and forsake your works, and the Lord will repent of the evil that he declared to do to you, so that it shall not come to pass. For thus saith the Lord, Behold I give you a period of one hundred and twenty years; if you will turn to me and forsake your evil ways, then will I also turn away from the evil which I told you, and it shall not exist, saith the Lord. And Noah and Methuselah spoke all the words of the Lord to the sons of men, day after day, constantly speaking to them. But the sons of men would not hearken to them, nor incline their ears to their words, and they were stiffnecked. And* ***the Lord granted them a period of one hundred and twenty years****, saying, If they will return, then will God repent of the evil, so as not to destroy the earth.* [Jash 5:6-11; emphasis mine]

This dual fulfillment is not at all unique among the Biblical prophecies.

So, we see the lives of Lamech and Methuselah were cut short in order to spare them from demise by drowning in the coming flood. Let's take a quick look at what Scripture reveals about the years in which these men died.

The last two entries in Table 2 declare that God took these last two men just prior to the flood, notably shortening the lifespan of Lamech, to spare them from death by drowning. Jasher 5:1-5 provides a supporting testament for this view:

> *And it was in the eighty-fourth year of the life of Noah, that Enosh the son of Seth died, he was nine hundred and five years old at his death. And in the one hundred and seventy ninth year of the life of Noah, Cainan (Kenan) the son of Enosh died, and all the days of Cainan (Kenan) were nine hundred and ten years, and he died. And in the two hundred and thirty fourth year of the life of Noah, Mahlallel the son of Cainan (Kenan) died, and the days of Mahlallel were eight hundred and ninety-five years, and he died. And Jared the son of Mahlallel died in those days, in the three hundred and thirty-sixth year of the life of Noah; and all the days of Jared were nine hundred and sixty-two years, and he died.* ***And all who followed the Lord died in those days, before they saw the evil which God declared to do upon earth.*** [Jash 5:1-5; emphasis mine]

The case of Enoch is clearly an exceptional one in this sequence, in that he was taken from this earth in a special way. According to the Genesis account in chapter 5:

> *After he begot Methuselah, Enoch walked with God three hundred years, and had sons and daughters. So all the days of Enoch were three hundred and sixty-five years. And Enoch walked with God; and he was not, for God took him.* [Gen 5:22-24]

The generally accepted explanation is that Enoch did not die, but was 'translated' (taken directly) to heaven. The *Book of Jasher* confirms this interpretation in chapter 3:

And in some time after, when the kings and princes and sons of men were speaking to Enoch, and Enoch was teaching them the ways of God, behold an angel of the Lord then called unto Enoch from heaven, and wished to bring him up to heaven to make him reign there over the sons of God, as he had reigned over the sons of men upon the earth.

...

And at that time the sons of men were with Enoch, and Enoch was speaking to them, and they lifted up their eyes and the likeness of a great horse descended from heaven, and the horse paced in the air; and they told Enoch what they had seen, and Enoch said to them, On my account does this horse descend upon earth; the time is come when I must go from you and I shall no more be seen by you.

And the horse descended at that time and stood before Enoch, and all the sons of men that were with Enoch saw him.

...

And it was after this that he rose up and rode upon the horse....

And when the kings returned they caused a census to be taken, in order to know the number of remaining men that went with Enoch; and it was upon the seventh day that Enoch ascended into heaven in a whirlwind, with horses and chariots of fire. [Jash 3:23-26, with omissions]

Once again, I digress, here only to explain the relatively short span of Enoch's life. We'll complete our investigation of the global deluge in a later chapter, because we must now deal with a most significant *expose'* of antediluvian history.

Reference	Text	Lifespan	Year (AM)
Gen 5:5	*Altogether, Adam lived a total of 930 years, and then he died.*	930	930
Gen 5:8	*Altogether, Seth lived a total of 912 years, and then he died.*	912	1042
Gen 5:11	*Altogether, Enosh lived a total of 905 years, and then he died.*	905	1140
Gen 5:14	*Altogether, Kenan lived a total of 910 years, and then he died.*	910	1235
Gen 5:17	*Altogether, Mahalalel lived a total of 895 years, and then he died.*	895	1290
Gen 5:20	*Altogether, Jared lived a total of 962 years, and then he died.*	962	1422
Gen 5:21-23	*When Enoch had lived 65 years, he became the father of Methuselah. After he became the father of Methuselah, Enoch walked faithfully with God 300 years and had other sons and daughters. Altogether, Enoch lived a total of 365 years. And Enoch walked with God; and he was not, for God took him.*	365	987
Gen 5:27	*Altogether, Methuselah lived a total of 969 years, and then he died.*	969	1656
Gen 5:31	*Altogether, Lamech lived a total of 777 years, and then he died.*	777	1651

Table 2: Lifespans from Adam to Noah

Chapter 7: Ancient Aliens (Gen 6)

The sixth chapter of Genesis is perhaps one of the most pivotal in our expanded history. It reveals so much that explains things such as the building of ancient megalithic structures using stones too massive to quarry and move reasonably by human means, the pyramids in Egypt and elsewhere, various ancient mythologies, magic, the great flood, the origin and destruction of dinosaurs, as well as archaeological finds of the skeletal remains of giants and elongated skulls. Let's read what Scripture says at the opening of Chapter 6:

> *Now it came to pass, when men began to multiply on the face of the earth, and daughters were born to them, that the sons of God saw the daughters of men, that they were beautiful; and they took wives for themselves of all whom they chose. And the Lord said, "My Spirit shall not strive with man forever, for he is indeed flesh; yet his days shall be one hundred and twenty years." There were giants on the earth in those days, and also afterward, when the sons of God came in to the daughters of men and they bore children to them. Those were the mighty men who were of old, men of renown. Then the Lord saw that the wickedness of man was great in the earth, and that every intent of the thoughts of his heart was only evil continually. And the Lord was sorry that He had made man on the earth, and He was grieved in His heart. So the Lord said, "I will destroy man whom I have created from the face of the earth, both man and beast, creeping thing and birds of the air, for I am sorry that I have made them."* [Gen 6:1-7]

This chapter was the seed of my personal journey to discover the whole truth of the ancient history of the world. The first few times I read through the Bible, I glossed over these verses without much thought. But, as I started to realize what they really said, I was quite intrigued, and that's what led me to search other sources for more information. So, first, who are the "sons of God" here? We go to Jude 6-7 for the clear answer:

> *And the angels who did not keep their proper domain, but left their own abode, He has reserved in everlasting chains under darkness for the judgment of the great day; as Sodom and Gomorrah, and the cities around them in a similar manner to these, having given themselves over to sexual immorality and gone after strange flesh, are set forth as an example, suffering the vengeance of eternal fire.* [Jude v6-7]

We can also turn to the book of Jasher where specifics are provided.

> *And their judges and rulers went to the daughters of men and took their wives by force from their husbands according to their choice, and the sons of men in those days took from the cattle of the earth, the beasts of the field and the fowls of the air, and taught the mixture of animals of one species with the other, in order therewith to provoke the Lord; and God saw the whole earth and it was corrupt, for all flesh had corrupted its ways upon earth, all men and all animals.* [Jash 4:18]

Chuck Missler, in his *Expositional Commentary on Genesis*, tells us that the phrase "sons of God" (Gen 6:2, Hebrew transliteration "Bene HaElohim") is used only a handful of times in the Old Testament, and in every case it is used of a "direct creation of God," as contrasted with the offspring of men and women, as we perceive by the normal course of reproduction. Adam was also a direct creation of God, and this term could be used to describe him; all human males since Adam are the sons of men. In addition, in every instance in the OT, these sons of God are clearly identifiable as angels. There are some that have argued that these are in fact men, but upon personal examination, I find that these arguments are very weak at best, clearly invented to deal with the otherwise vexing issues and consequences. The most compelling argument that these are not ordinary men is that their offspring had the unique characteristic of being giants. The footnote on Gen 6:2 in the NKJV Study Bible also makes it clear that these are angels:

> *The **sons of God** refer to a different group from either the **men** or their **daughters**. The phrase occurs elsewhere in the Bible and clearly means "angels." Job 1:6 presents Satan and his angels coming into the presence of the Lord for an audience with His Majesty. Satan's angels are there called "the sons of God," with the suggestion that these angelic beings were once holy ones who served the Lord, but were now allied with the evil one. Genesis assumes the existence of the good angels of the Lord (see 3:24) and of Satan and his angels. It also assumes that the latter are already fallen and under God's judgment (see 1:2). In 3:1, the serpent (Satan) was already at work as the father of lies (John 8:44). Here it appears that some of Satan's angels, spirit beings, took on human form (see 3:24) and, out of a perverted lust, seduced women. In response, God reserved these angels for special judgment (2 Pet 2:4; Jude 6) and cleansed the earth itself (with the Flood).*
> [Taken from NKJV Study Bible. Copyright © 1997, 2007 by Thomas Nelson. Used by permission of Thomas Nelson. www.thomasnelson.com; emphasis mine]

(I must point out that the footnotes in the various study bibles are not themselves Scripture, and thus must be construed as commentary. As such, they may be illuminating, but can also be deficient, speculative, and/or flawed.) The fact that these angels were able to have sexual relations with the daughters of men clearly reveals that these angels had flesh and blood bodies. One of my well-respected and biblically literate friends argued with me about angels being strictly spirit beings. When confronted with Gen 6, he argues that the angels were spirit beings, able to 'take on' fleshly bodies at will (consistent with the NKJV footnote, which also evades the matter of 'how' this might work or the implications of this conjecture). When I inquired of him about how this might work, his response was "I don't know, but that's what I was taught." He argued first that perhaps the angels took possession of the bodies of (presumably unwitting) men, but that fails to explain the uniqueness of the bodies of their offspring, the Nephilim; if the men so possessed were *homo sapiens*, their offspring would be also, undifferentiated from the other men on the earth. And, if these angels were able to take on flesh of their own volition, it would seem to elevate them to God-like status with the ability to create something *ex nihilo*, or 'out of nothing.' Either way, it is problematic to posit either that they are, or that they are not, intrinsically flesh and blood beings. To his point, and in my friend's defense, in the Biblical book of Hebrews, we find two verses that confirm the spirit nature of angels:

> *And of the angels He says: "Who makes His angels spirits And His ministers a flame of fire."*
> [Heb 1:7]

> *Are they not all ministering spirits sent forth to minister for those who will inherit salvation?*
> [Heb 1:14]

If this be singularly true (that is, that the angels do not have a dual nature, i.e., body and spirit, as do humans), from whence do their bodies derive? The Book of Enoch may provide further insight:

And, when they wished, they appeared as men. [1 Enoch 17:2]

Now, whether or not this speaks of the angels' ability to create for themselves fleshly bodies, *or* to move interdimensionally, revealing only three dimensions of a hyper-dimensionality, remains unclear. Specifically, let's go to the book of Ezekiel to which I referred earlier regarding the description of angels with multiple faces:

And I looked, and, behold, a whirlwind came out of the north, a great cloud, and a fire infolding itself, and a brightness was about it, and out of the midst thereof as the color of amber, out of the midst of the fire. Also out of the midst thereof came the likeness of four living creatures. And this was their appearance; they had the likeness of a man. And every one had four faces, and every one had four wings. And their feet were straight feet; and the sole of their feet was like the sole of a calf's foot: and they sparkled like the color of burnished brass. And they had the hands of a man under their wings on their four sides; and they four had their faces and their wings. Their wings were joined one to another; they turned not when they went; they went every one straight forward. As for the likeness of their faces, they four had the face of a man, and the face of a lion, on the right side: and they four had the face of an ox on the left side; they four also had the face of an eagle. Thus were their faces: and their wings were stretched upward; two wings of every one were joined one to another, and two covered their bodies. And they went every one straight forward: whither the spirit was to go, they went; and they turned not when they went. As for the likeness of the living creatures, their appearance was like burning coals of fire, and like the appearance of lamps: it went up and down among the living creatures; and the fire was bright, and out of the fire went forth lightning.
[Eze 1:4-13].

I believe that Ezekiel is doing his best to describe hyperdimensional beings in three dimensional terms. If these beings are indeed hyperdimensional, when they do appear in our three dimensions, some of the features of the rest of their dimensionality would be unseen. It is for this reason that some of the ancient images (petroglyphs) of angels recorded by the Assyrians and Sumerians show only a single face (sometimes that of a man, and other times that of an eagle), with a humanoid body, albeit with wings. Some of these images are shown later in this chapter. Now, in contrast, I submit an excerpt from the Book of Revelation. The author, John the Apostle, is provided with a vision of heaven, in like circumstance to Ezekiel in the preceding passage:

And before the throne there was a sea of glass like unto crystal: and in the midst of the throne, and round about the throne, were four beasts full of eyes before and behind. And the first beast was like a lion, and the second beast like a calf, and the third beast had a face as a man, and the fourth beast was like a flying eagle. And the four beasts had each of them six wings about him; and they were full of eyes within: and they rest not day and night, saying, Holy, holy, holy, Lord God Almighty, which was, and is, and is to come. [Rev 4:6-8]

I submit to you that in this vision, John, in contrast to Ezekiel, saw heaven in only three dimensions. However, the angels that John sees are described as having six wings, as compared with the angels in Ezekiel's vision which have four wings. So, it is possible that the six-winged angels do not have the multi-facial dimensionality of those with four wings. (I provide some additional detail on the different ranks of angels and their unique features in the paragraphs ahead.)

Josephus provides us with a testimony consistent with the Biblical account in Gen 6. In chapter 3 of his *Antiquities*, Josephus writes:

> *Now this posterity of Seth continued to esteem God as the Lord of the universe, and to have an entire regard to virtue, for seven generations; but in process of time they were perverted, and forsook the practices of their forefathers, and did not pay those honors to God which were appointed them, nor had they any concern to do justice towards men. But for what degree of zeal they had formerly shewn for virtue, they now shewed for their actions a double degree of wickedness, whereby they made God to be their enemy; for many angels* of God accompanied with women, and begat sons that proved unjust, and despisers of all that was good, on account of the confidence they had in their own strength, for the tradition is that these men did what resembled the acts of what the Grecians call giants. But Noah was very uneasy at what they did; and, being displeased at their conduct, persuaded them to change their dispositions and their acts for the better; -but, seeing that they did not yield to him, but were slaves to their wicked pleasures, he was afraid they would kill him, together with his wife and children, and those they had married; so he departed out of that land.* [Ant. I:III:1]

The translator of this particular edition of the *Antiquities* (William Whiston) provides the following footnote on the angels: **This notion, that the fallen angels were, in some sense, the fathers of the old giants, was the constant opinion of antiquity.* This is an important point as many modern theologians now dismiss the idea that the "sons of God" were angels, simply to avert the controversy it creates. This speaks to the very heart of the rationale for writing this book: as science has advanced, modern theologians have allowed 'scientific' constraints to infringe upon what was previously accepted theological doctrine. For example, scientists biased against the teachings of Scripture want to dismiss the Biblical accounts in favor of 'Godless' theories such as evolution, the big bang, and even aliens from other planets. <u>We were indeed visited by ancient aliens, but they were the angels of heaven.</u> Science and religion do not exist at the exclusion of one other; God created an ordered universe with physical laws so that we could live with consistent expectations for outcomes, and to discover His universal laws and thereby harness the manifold utility of His creation.

Back to the matter at hand, Gen 6 and the fall of angels. Now, we have two citations from the Book of Jubilees account that may reconcile this all:

> *And in the second week of the tenth jubilee Mahalalel took unto him to wife Dinah, the daughter of Barakiel the daughter of his father's brother, and she bare him a son in the third week of the sixth year, and he called his name Jared; for in his days* **the angels of the LORD descended on the earth, those who are named the Watchers, that they should instruct the children of men**, *and that they should do judgment and uprightness on the earth.* [Jub IV:15; emphasis mine]

*And it came to pass when the children of men began to multiply on the face of the earth and daughters were born unto them, that the angels of God saw them on a certain year of this jubilee, that they were beautiful to look upon; and they took themselves wives of all whom they chose, and they bare unto them sons and they were giants. And lawlessness increased on the earth and all flesh corrupted its way, alike men and cattle and beasts and birds and everything that walks on the earth -all of them corrupted their ways and their orders, and they began to devour each other, and lawlessness increased on the earth and every imagination of the thoughts of all men (was) thus evil continually. And God looked upon the earth, and behold it was corrupt, and all flesh had corrupted its orders, and all that were upon the earth had wrought all manner of evil before His eyes. And He said that He would destroy man and all flesh upon the face of the earth which He had created. But Noah found grace before the eyes of the Lord. And against the angels **whom He had sent upon the earth**, He was exceedingly wroth, and He gave commandment to root them out of all their dominion, and He bade us to bind them in the depths of the earth, and behold they are bound in the midst of them, and are (kept) separate. And against their sons went forth a command from before His face that they should be smitten with the sword, and be removed from under heaven. And He said 'My spirit shall not always abide on man; for they also are flesh and their days shall be one hundred and twenty years'. And He sent His sword into their midst that each should slay his neighbor, and they began to slay each other till they all fell by the sword and were destroyed from the earth. And their fathers were witnesses (of their destruction), and after this they were bound in the depths of the earth forever, until the day of the great condemnation, when judgment is executed on all those who have corrupted their ways and their works before the Lord. And He destroyed all from their places, and there was not left one of them whom He judged not according to all their wickedness. **And he made for all his works a new and righteous nature**, so that they should not sin in their whole nature forever, but should be all righteous each in his kind alway.* [Jub V:1-12] (Emphasis mine)

Well, these verses cast a whole, new light on this episode. It appears that God may have *sent* His angels to instruct men in various disciplines, and that they had already bodies, or that God gave them bodies to facilitate this task. But in the last verse of the latter passage, it says that "...*he (God) made for all his works a new and righteous nature*...." Does this then imply that God took the fleshly bodies He had given the angels away to restore their ranks to being strictly spirit beings thereafter? This would fail to explain the appearances of angels in the form of men later in Genesis, but it would reconcile the aforementioned verses from Hebrews, since the position that the angels "are" (present tense) spirit beings would be true, in spite of what the angels "were" (past tense). It does make for some interesting controversy.

Many people in the Bible were visited by angels, and in every case the angels had the general form of a man, sometimes with wings and at other times without. If angels were strictly spiritual, they would have no physical form, much as the first and third persons of the Holy Trinity; only Jesus Christ, the second person of the Trinity, has a physical form, and this is real flesh and blood. As messengers to mankind, the angels' physical form enables execution of this objective. When the prophets were given visions of heaven, they saw angels in a physical form. Again, I accept the controversy on this subject, but, to be clear, I absolutely believe that the angels have now, and have had, physical bodies, varying in form by their designated rank and particular function, since their creation.

So, these angels came down from heaven, having been attracted by the beauty of the daughters of men, and took wives from among them. Gen 6:1 establishes the fall of these angels; Gen 6:3 talks about their offspring. Gen 6:2 is where God declares 120 years until the flood. So we can view all these events as roughly concurrent. Why is this important? While the Bible puts forth God's rationale for the earth's destruction solely as the wickedness of men, why did He then not continue to destroy the peoples of the earth after the flood? After all, the wickedness of man has since continued unabated. To this very point, the Old Testament tells a continuing tale of the wickedness of Israel and of its surrounding neighbors. The far more compelling element of God's decision to annihilate all mankind (save for Noah and his family) is the corruption of man's DNA with angelic DNA. When the angels had sexual relations with the daughters of men, it is said that their offspring were giants, and the heroes of old. Angels are not men…they are distinct beings with inconceivable power and knowledge, some with wings, and some with heads that are not human…see Rev 4:6-8 and Eze 1:5-19. They have *real* DNA that is uniquely different from that of humans, but is also obviously compatible with it. Their offspring were the Nephilim ('fallen ones').

Gen 6:9 states that *"Noah was a just man, perfect in his generations."* The first half of this sentence deals with Noah's spiritual righteousness, while the phrase *"perfect in his generations"* deals with his physical state: it is the implication that his DNA was uncorrupted as contrasted with that of the angel-human hybrid Nephilim and their offspring. From Strong's Concordance, the word translated *"perfect"* is the Hebrew word "tamiym" that means *"without blemish, complete, full, perfect, sincerely (-ity), sound, without spot, undefiled, upright (-ly), whole."* The words 'generations,' 'genealogy,' and 'genetics' all come from the common root 'gene-:' *"perfect in his generations"* connotes 'undefiled in his genetics.' Verse 9 of Gen 6 must be interpreted in the context of preceding verses in that chapter.

The Book of Jubilees supports this rationale for the deluge:

> *For owing to these three things came the flood upon the earth, namely, owing to the fornication wherein the Watchers against the law of their ordinances went a whoring after the daughters of men, and took themselves wives of all which they chose: and they made the beginning of uncleanness. And they begat sons the Naphidim, and they were all unlike, and they devoured one another: and the Giants slew the Naphil, and the Naphil slew the Eljo, and the Eljo mankind, and one man another. And everyone sold himself to work iniquity to shed much blood, and the earth was filled with iniquity. And after this they sinned against the beasts and the birds, and all that moveth and walketh on the earth: and much blood was shed on the earth, and every imagination and desire of men imagined vanity and evil continually. And the Lord destroyed everything from off the face of the earth; because of the wickedness of their deeds, and because of the blood which they had shed in the midst of the earth He destroyed everything.* [Jub 7:21-25]

The three-fold motivation for the flood was comprised of (1) fornication of the fallen angels, (2) the resultant hybrid Nephilim (here expressed as "Naphidim"), and (3) the sinfulness of mankind. Now when I first read this passage, I assumed that the Giants were the Nephilim and that the Naphil and Eljo were tribes or nations of men. However, upon further reflection, it became clear that the

Giants, Naphil, and Eljo are various types or subspecies of the Naphidim (or Nephilim). The revealing phrase is that "...*they were all unlike, and they devoured one another*...," meaning that there was diversity within this hybrid species, killing each other first, and then ultimately killing men. This would be the natural consequence of each rank of angels having unique DNA.

Further as to their appearance, Josephus makes the following comment in his *Antiquities*:

There were till then left the race of giants, who had bodies so large, and countenances so entirely different from other men, that they were surprising to the sight, and terrible to the hearing. The bones of these men are shewn to this very day, unlike to any credible relations of other men. [Ant V:II:3]

Josephus declares that these beings are essentially <u>incredible</u>, in the strict sense of the word: that is, beyond belief except by the physical evidence, then still extant. And what is happening in the world today, but to an even greater extreme, is denial of both the physical evidence and the testimonies of trustworthy men.

Angels in the Outfield

Let's now investigate the orders of angels more closely. In the OT, the word translated "angels" occurs about 100 times, and is the translation of the Hebrew word "malak" derived from a root word meaning "to dispatch," as a messenger. Thus, the word is also applied in some passages of Scripture to prophets, ambassadors, and kings. The Greek counterpart in the NT is "aggelos," also translated as "messenger." However, these are not the only words used to describe these special creations of God. We find throughout Scripture references to specific classes (or ranks) of angels, by name: cherubim, seraphim, thrones, archangels, powers, dominions, and principalities (princes). These classes are defined by their functions.

Archangels – This word only occurs twice, both times in the NT, from the Greek word "arxaggelos," meaning "chief angel." This implies a rank above that of other angels. It seems that Michael, the only archangel named in Scripture (Jude 9 & Rev 12:7), has a military function, which is brought out in Rev 12:7, where a battle is described between Satan and his angels and Michael and his angelic forces. In the court of the LORD, I think it would be appropriate to deem Michael as the 5-star general of the angelic forces. Indeed, in the First Book of Enoch, chapter 24, verse 6, it says, "*Then answered Michael, one of the holy and honored angels who was with me, and was their leader.*"

Also in the First Book of Enoch, chapter 9, verse 1, Michael is named along with three other angels, as though these are peers: "*And then Michael, Uriel, Raphael, and Gabriel looked down from heaven and saw much blood being shed upon the earth, and all lawlessness being wrought upon the earth.*" In the following chapter of 1Enoch, God sends each of these four on missions that set the stage for the events that precede the Deluge. In Chapter 20 of 1Enoch, three more names are added in a list there (for a total of seven), also defining each one's domain:

And these are the names of the holy angels who watch. Uriel, one of the holy angels, who is over the world and over Tartarus. Raphael, one of the holy angels, who is over the spirits of men. Raguel, one of the holy angels who takes vengeance on the world of the luminaries. Michael, one of the holy angels, to wit, he that is set over the best part of mankind and over chaos. Saraqael, one of the holy angels, who is set over the spirits, who sin in the spirit. Gabriel, one of the holy angels, who is over Paradise and the serpents and the Cherubim. Remiel, one of the holy angels, whom God set over those who rise. [1Eno 20:1-8]

Thus, we may conclude that these seven are of comparable rank, all being archangels. But Michael is still described as *"their leader,"* and hence the 5-star general; so, the others would probably be most appropriately esteemed to be 4-star generals.

Raphael is also mentioned in the apocryphal Book of Tobit, considered part of the canon in the Catholic and Orthodox churches. Specifically, in Tobit 12:15 [NAB, ©1970, Catholic Book Publishing Co.] it says: *"I am Raphael, one of the seven angels, who enter and serve before the glory of the Lord."* In this book, Raphael has the appearance of a man (no wings), and poses as an ordinary man, a close relative of the narrator, Tobit. However, the rank of archangel is not specifically ascribed to him in this book. Similarly, Uriel is mentioned in 2Esdras, another apocryphal book. So we find an apparent agreement between 1Enoch and Tobit in terms of the number of this rank.

Cherubim – Mentioned over 90 times in the OT, the transliterated Hebrew word in the singular form is '*keruwb*,' ('cherub') the plural form being '*keruwbim*.' This root word is of uncertain derivation, so no direct translation exists. The only occurrence of the word "cherubim" in the NT occurs in the book of Hebrews, and is simply a transliteration of the Hebrew word. The first appearance of cherubim is in Gen 3, where God placed them at the East of Eden to prevent man's return to the Garden. In this instance, their role appears to be that of (armed) guards. The next occurrence of cherubim is in Exo 25 when God instructs Moses in the construction of the Ark of the Covenant. Two cherubim were to be fashioned of gold, facing one another on the top of the ark (the so-called "mercy seat") with their wings covering the seat, ostensibly shielding human eyes from direct observation of God's glory. In Exo 26, God instructs Moses to have images of cherubim woven into the curtains of the tabernacle, as well as the veil that separated the outer tabernacle from the Holy of Holies where the ark was to be sheltered from all but the high priests…again, a picture of guardians.

To this point, the cherubim are depicted as having one pair of wings, with the span of the wings as wide as the cherubim were tall…the same as for the span of a man's arms. In the Book of Ezekiel, he describes one of his visions in heaven where he sees cherubim that have the likeness of a man, but four faces (one of a cherub, one of a lion, one of a man, and one of an eagle), as well as four wings. [Let's also be clear here that not all angels have wings. In the book of Genesis, Abram is approached by angels with the appearance of men (no wings). When these angels are sent to bring Lot out of Sodom before its destruction by fire and brimstone, the Sodomites regarded them as men.] Ezekiel also describes the cherubim as having eyes all around (which is what you would ideally want a guard to have). In Eze 41, the cherubim only have two faces, one of a man and the other of a lion. So it seems that cherubim have various forms and perhaps multiple functions. Other than the function specified in Genesis as guards against human intrusion into the garden, the cherubim are always found in the immediate presence of God, apparently serving Him as guardians. Since God is omnipotent, the cherubim are clearly not protecting Him, but rather it would seem that they are nearby as ready to be dispatched for particular security tasks.

Seraphim – This term appears only twice in the Bible, both in the sixth chapter of the Book of Isaiah. The term is derived from the Hebrew "saraph," meaning burning, apparently deriving from their appearance, as glowing metal when heated. It can also be translated figuratively as "poisonous," as a venomous serpent. Going to Isaiah chapter 6, we'll start in verse 1 so we gather the fuller context of their purpose:

"In the year that King Uzziah died, I saw the Lord sitting on a throne, high and lifted up, and the train of His robe filled the temple. Above it stood seraphim, each one had six wings: with two he covered his face, with two he covered his feet, and with two he flew. And one cried to another and said: 'Holy, holy, holy is the Lord of hosts; the whole earth is full of His glory!' And the posts of the door were shaken by the voice of him who cried out, and the house was filled with smoke. So I said: 'Woe is me, for I am undone! Because I am a man of unclean lips, and I dwell in the midst of a people of unclean lips; for my eyes have seen the King, the LORD of hosts.' Then one of the seraphim flew to me, having in his hand a live coal which he had taken with the tongs from the altar. And he touched my mouth with it, and said: 'Behold this has touched your lips; your iniquity is taken away, and your sin is purged.'" [Isa 6:1-7]

So, it seems that the seraphim have a primary role declaring the holiness of God and reside in closest proximity around His throne.

Thrones, Dominions, Principalities, Powers – All four of these angelic orders are delineated in Col 1:16, as follows: *"For by Him all things were created that are in heaven and that are on earth, visible and invisible, whether thrones or dominions or principalities or powers."* The word "thrones" is from the Greek 'thronos' which is derived from the root word for the verb "to sit." Specifically, it applies to a stately seat, or by implication, power or a potentate. The word "dominions" is the Greek word 'kuriotes,' deriving from the Greek word for "mastery," and refers to 'rulers.' The spiritual or angelic sense of the words "thrones" and "dominions" is not particularly clear in this verse. However, this sense for the word "principalities" is made clear in a couple of other Biblical verses, and then by association, this sense can be applied to the other words. Specifically, let's look at Eph 3: 8-12, Eph 6:12, and Col 2:15:

*To me, who am less than the least of all the saints, this grace was given, that I should preach among the Gentiles the unsearchable riches of Christ, and to make all see what is the fellowship of the mystery, which from the beginning of the ages has been hidden in God who created all things through Jesus Christ; to the intent that now the manifold wisdom of God might be made known by the church to **the principalities and powers in the heavenly places**, according to the eternal purpose which He accomplished in Christ Jesus our Lord, in whom we have boldness and access with confidence through faith in Him.* [Eph 3:8-12, emphasis mine]

> *For we do not wrestle against flesh and blood, but against **principalities, against powers, against the rulers of the darkness of this age, against spiritual hosts of wickedness in the heavenly places***. [Eph 6:12, emphasis mine]
>
> *And you, being dead in your trespasses and the uncircumcision of your flesh, He has made alive together with Him, having forgiven you all trespasses, having wiped out the handwriting of requirements that was against us, which was contrary to us. And He has taken it out of the way, having nailed it to the cross. Having disarmed **principalities and powers**, he made a public spectacle of them, triumphing over them in it.* [Col 2:13-15, emphasis mine]

Here now we see more clearly the context of these terms. In fact, one might deduce that all four of these angelic classes constitute some or all of the fallen angels. Indeed, with regard to the term "principalities," the related word "prince" is frequently used throughout the Bible to apply to high ranking angels, both good and fallen (e.g., see Dan 10, Mat 9, Mat 12, Mrk 3, Jhn 12, Jhn 14, Jhn 16, & Eph 2).

The Creatures in Heaven (Ezekiel) – As previously mentioned, in the first chapter of the book of Ezekiel, he is having a vision of God in heaven, with four "creatures" all around. He describes these creatures in great detail with four faces (a man, a lion, an ox, and an eagle), four wings (two stretching upward and two covering their bodies), straight legs with feet like the soles of calves' feet, with hands of a man under their wings on their four sides, and sparkling like the color of burnished bronze, bright like burning coals of fire, with lightning emanating from them. However, it is not until we get to the tenth chapter of Ezekiel, where he refers to these as cherubim instead. From these readings, one might conclude that the creatures and the cherubim are distinct. However, Ezekiel makes it clear in 10:15 that they are one and the same.

The Watchers – This is a term used only four times in the Bible, but used throughout the Books of Enoch. Three of the four Biblical uses are in the Book of Daniel, all in chapter 4; the fourth is in the Book of Jeremiah, chapter 4 v16. Now in the Book of Daniel, the word used is Strong's 5894 (transliterated from the original Chaldee as "'iyr") which is defined as "*a watcher, i.e. an angel (as guardian).*" In Jeremiah, the Hebrew word is different (Strong's 5341): "natsar." Strong defines this word as follows: *a prim. root; to guard, in a good sense (to protect, maintain, obey, etc.) or a bad one (to conceal, etc.) – besieged, hidden thing, keep (-er, -ing), monument, observe, preserve (-r), subtil, watcher (-man).* The context of 5341 in Jeremiah does not appear to connote angels. On the other hand, 5894 is clearly a reference to angels in all three citations. In fact, Daniel [Dan 4:13] provides the further phrase to clarify *"...a holy one, coming down from heaven."* As to 5894, Strong's indicates that it is from a root corresponding to 5782, with the primary reference to 5783 (to bare) *"...through the idea of opening the eyes."* So does this provide us with a sense of their mission? Specifically, were they to open the eyes of humanity to the various mysteries of God's creations?

Petroglyphs of Angels

Let's now go back and look again at the cherubim and seraphim. These are described as having four and six wings, respectively. These may not be the only classes with this wing arrangement, but we can make an association of ancient Sumerian and Assyrian petroglyphs with some angels on this basis. These images apparently date from the 8th and 9th centuries BC. See two of these images in Figures 7 & 8.

These creatures are clearly depicted with four wings, one with the head of a man and the other with the head of an eagle. There are many other such images of petroglyphs to be found on the internet by a simple web browser search using such words as 'Sumerian petroglyphs angels,' or similar. I would also recommend searching on 'Khorsabad wall reliefs' for more images of these winged creatures.

*Figure 7: Sumerian winged genie.
By Viacheslav Lopatin/shutterstock.com.*

The Sumerian empire is deemed to be the oldest civilization, its dawning concurrent with the earliest generations of mankind. Not surprisingly, it was located in the so-called "Fertile Crescent," between the Tigris and Euphrates rivers, shown on the map below. In Hebrew, it is rendered "Shinar," which is found seven times in the OT. According to some, this civilization began before 5000 BC, which would place it well before the Biblical dawn of history. Others say that the first kings of Sumeria reigned in the 3rd millennium BC. There is an ancient artifact commonly referred to as the "Sumerian King List" that was apparently created about 2100 BC (about 190 years after the Flood) that delineates the Sumerian rulers to the earliest antediluvian period. In his article *"Reinvestigating the Antediluvian Sumerian King List"* (Journal of the Evangelical Theological Society, March 1993), R. K. Harrison states:

> *The List commenced with an "antediluvian preamble": "When kingship was lowered from heaven, it was in the city of Eridu." After two kings had ruled over Eridu, kingship was transferred to Badtibira, where the reigns of three kings were duly recorded in succession. The antediluvian portion of the King List concluded with three rulers who reigned in*

Larak, Sippar, and Shuruppak, respectively. At this point the narrative broke off with the terse words: "the flood swept over (the earth)."

Thus, it seems likely that eight (allegedly Sumerian) kings reigned before the Flood. Many dismiss these kings as mythological because of the record of incredibly long reigns, the shortest being 18,600 years, and the longest 36,000 years, the sum of these totaling 241,200 years. Now, Berossus the Chaldean, an historian who lived in the 3rd century BC (whom Flavius Josephus often cites to corroborate specific episodes delineated in his *Antiquities*), provided a revised version of the Sumerian Kings List, but adds two more kings and extends the period of their collective reigns to 432,000 years. However, he also used Greek names for these kings, and the names in the two lists have not been directly correlated. In the aforementioned article, R. K. Harrison proposes that the actual length of the reigns of these eight kings were factored, and provides an <u>arbitrary</u> formula that reduces the sum of the reigns of the ten kings to 120 years, which has no correspondence to any other record. I'm dismissive of this theory because his factoring is arbitrary.

Figure 8: Assyrian winged god with eagles' head. By Kamira/shutterstock.com.

Now, there is a very compelling case to be made that the reigns were real, but that the earliest part of the Sumerian Kings list, recorded on a prism-shaped stone, was actually copied from an earlier text, and that the years recorded therein were recorded in base 10, as compared with the base 60 numerical system in use at the time that the prism was created. (Note that the base 60 system is the foundation for our temporal measurements of 60 seconds per minute and 60 minutes per hour; in addition it is the basis of the 360 degrees in a circle, as well as the sub-increments of 60 minutes per degree of angle and 60 seconds per minute of angle.) This case is laid out in an article by Raul Lopez, entitled *The Antediluvian Patriarchs and the Sumerian Kings List*, in the December 1998 issue of the *Journal of Creation*. Lopez postulates that eight kings identified in the antediluvian portion of the Sumerian Kings List actually correspond to eight of the ten Biblical patriarchs (leaving out Adam and Noah). In the end, he shows an extraordinary correspondence of the corrected numbers with the Biblically recorded <u>ages</u> of these patriarchs. This almost completely reconciles the Biblical record with the archaeological evidence, and further explains why Berossus would have added two more names to the list. The case concludes that the ages of the patriarchs were misinterpreted to be the duration of reigns, which were then errantly summed, compounding the error.

If Raul Lopez' postulate is correct, then this supports that the fallen angels appeared in the Sumerian and/or Assyrian cultures after the flood, which is what is represented in the petroglyphs which are also postdiluvian.

In my research for this book, I found claims that there are as many as 600 ancient stories of a massive flood, many of which have other correlations with the Biblical flood record, including corruptions of the name Noah such as Nu-u, Nu-Wah, Noh, Nos, and Nuh. And there seem to be as many other and more radical corruptions within this multitude of tales. However, given the sheer number of these, as well as the global span of the cultures, it would seem difficult to escape the conclusion that there must be a common heritage.

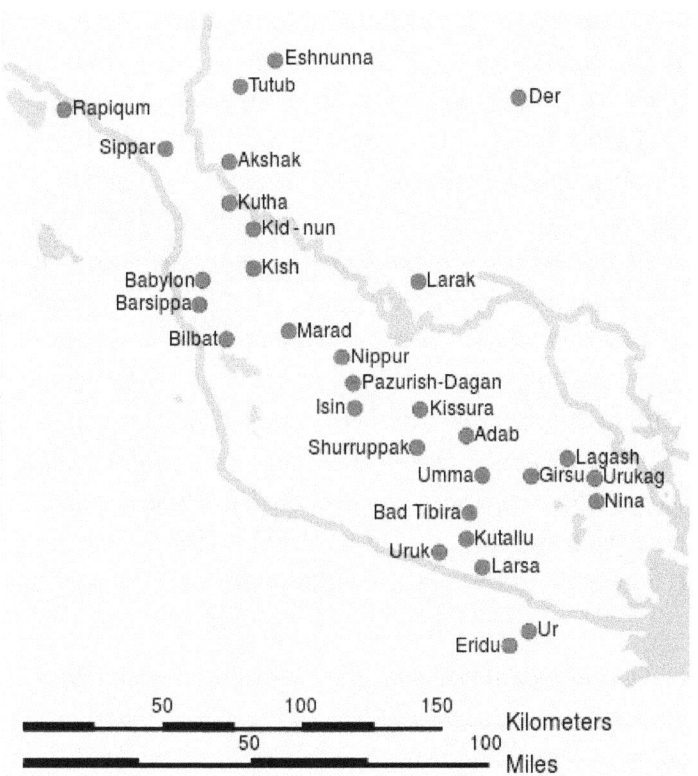

Figure 9: Map of Ancient Sumerian Empire. Wikipedia.com

Now, very interestingly, the Sumerians not only had this record of a global flood, but they also had an account of creation. I won't go into the detail of the account, other than to say that the god Enki made man, "Adamu," a woman, "Ti-Amat," in a garden called "Ed.in," and their children, "Ka-in," "Abael," and "Seth." This clearly demonstrates both the commonality with the Biblical account and the corruption of names.

Fallen Angels

Returning now to Gen 6:4 for a closer examination: *"There were giants on the earth in those days, and also afterward, when the sons of God came in to the daughters of men, and they bore children to them. Those were the mighty men who were of old, men of renown."* The Hebrew word here translated as "giants" is actually the Hebrew word "nephiyl," or Nephilim ("fallen ones"). How did this get to be translated as "giants?" In the Septuagint (the Greek translation of the Hebrew Tanakh), the Hebrew scholars of the day translated the Hebrew word "nephiyl" as the Greek word "gigantes." The definition of this Greek word is "earth-born," but is interestingly the same word used to describe the Greek Titans (also demigods) or the offspring of gods and women. Thus, in many English translations derived from the Septuagint, the word gigantes was rendered "giants." Now, in spite of this mistranslation, these angel-human hybrids were indeed giants, some three to six times the size of humans today. In his book *"Genesis 6 Giants: Master Builders of Prehistoric and Ancient Civilizations,"* Stephen Quayle documents many archaeological finds of the remains of giants.

After a short preamble comprising the first 5 chapters of the Book of Enoch (less than 3 pages), Enoch tells his version of the Gen 6 account, also starting with Chapter 6:

And it came to pass when the children of men had multiplied that in those days were born unto them beautiful and comely daughters. And the angels, the children of heaven, saw and lusted after them, and said to one another: 'Come, let us choose us wives from among the children of men and beget us children.' And Semjaza, who was their leader, said unto them: 'I fear ye will not indeed agree to do this deed, and I alone shall have to pay the penalty of a great sin.' And they all answered him and said: 'Let us all swear an oath, and all bind ourselves by mutual imprecations not to abandon this plan but to do this thing.' Then sware they all together and bound themselves by mutual imprecations upon it. And they were in all two hundred who descended in the days of Jared on the summit of Mount Hermon, because they had sworn and bound themselves by mutual imprecations upon it. [Author's note: Jared lived from 460 AM to 1422 AM.] *And these are the names of their leaders: Samiazaz, their leader, Arakiba, Rameel, Kokabiel, Tamiel, Ramiel, Danel, Ezeqeel, Baraqijal, Asael, Armoros, Batarel, Ananel, Zaqiel, Samsapeel, Satarel, Turel, Jomjael, Sariel. These are their chiefs of tens.* [1Eno 6:1-8; Author's note: 18 leaders of 10 = 18 x (10+1) = 198; adding the leader, Samlazaz (or Semjaza) = 199. If Samlazaz and Semjaza are indeed distinct co-leaders, then the total sums to 200.]

And all the others together with them went and took unto themselves wives, and each chose for himself one, and they began to go in unto them and to defile themselves with them, and they taught them charms and enchantments, and the cutting of roots, and made them acquainted with plants. And they became pregnant, and they bare great giants, whose height was three thousand ells: Who consumed all the acquisitions of men. And when men could no longer sustain them, the giants turned against them and devoured mankind. And they began to sin against birds, and beasts, and reptiles, and fish, and to devour one another's flesh, and drink the blood. Then the earth laid accusation against the lawless ones.

And Azazel taught men to make swords, and knives, and shields, and breastplates, and made known to them the metals of the earth and the art of working them, and bracelets, and ornaments, and the use of antimony, and the beautifying of the eyelids, and all kinds of costly stones, and all colouring tinctures. And there arose much godlessness, and they committed fornication, and they were led astray, and became corrupt in all their ways. Semjaza taught enchantments, and root cuttings, Amaros taught the resolving of enchantments, Baraqijal (taught) astrology, Kokabel the constellations, Ezeqeel the knowledge of the clouds, Araqiel the signs of the earth, Shamsiel the signs of the sun, and Sariel the course of the moon. And as men perished, they cried, and their cry went up to heaven. [1Eno 7: 1-6, 8:1-3]

Angel Name	Disciplines Taught to Men
Azazel	Metalwork: swords, knives, shields, breastplates, bracelets, ornaments, and make-up
Semjaza	Casting of spells, root cuttings
Amaros	Counter-spells
Baraqijal	Astrology
Kokabel	Constellations (portents)
Ezequeel	Clouds
Araqiel	The signs of the earth
Shamsiel	The signs of the sun
Sariel	The course of the moon

Table 3: The Disciplinary Domains of the Fallen Angels Named in 1Enoch.

So here we have specifics as to the numbers and some of the names of the fallen angels. There seem to be at least three ranks here: the highest leader(s), Samlazaz and/or Semjaza, the eighteen intermediate leaders, and the 180 lowest ranks. In military terms, one might say the general(s), the officers, and the enlisted ranks, respectively. We'll first look at the disciplines taught by each of these.

I could never fathom how early man could have developed skills in metalworking so quickly. First, you must be able to identify that there are metals. Then you must mine them, smelt them, separate them, and finally work them into tools and weapons. Working iron is no simple task, as very high temperatures are required to melt the ore: 2800°F...that's no simple matter even for most people in today's society without the advantage of modern, supporting technologies.

Ask anyone today if they have the least idea of how to construct a forge without the use of modern tools. Then ask them if they know where to get coal to fire it, and bellows to stoke it. Ancient man had none of these advantages. As far as they knew, the elements were air, fire, earth, and water. This theory of the makeup of substances was still held up to 3600 years after creation, to the time of Aristotle in the 4th century BC; and it would be another 2000 years until science had built a list of elements that started to resemble parts of the modern periodic table of the elements. How would they know of the real elements like iron, carbon, nickel, tin, aluminum, and so on? How could they know that each had melting points at all, and how long would it have taken them to develop the means to do this? The teaching by angels makes a lot of sense.

In the fourth chapter (*Babylonian Mythology*) of *The Chaldean Account of Genesis* (1876), author George Smith addresses the development of the pantheon of twelve gods, comprised of the gods of individual cities that were assimilated into the Babylonian kingdom. Following a delineation of these twelve as well as their domains and associated cities, he says:

Below these deities there was a large body of gods forming the bulk of the pantheon, and below these were arranged Igege, or angels of heaven, and the Annunaki, or angels of earth. Below these again came various classes of spirits or genii called Sedu, Vadukku, Ekimu, Gallu, and others; some of these were evil, some good.

Another captivating witness of good and evil angels on the earth.

Before moving on, I'd like to present a documented case of an angelic vision from the twenty first century. The case is documented in an article from 2017. Entitled "*A Strange Encounter with Angels. In Space*," the article was posted to the website mysteriousuniverse.org ("MU") in December 2017. The author, Brent Swancer, is an author and crypto expert living in Japan. Biology, nature, and cryptozoology are Brent Swancer's primary intellectual pursuits. He's written other articles for MU and dailygrail.com, and has been a guest on Coast to Coast AM and binnallofamerica.com. I reprint the article here in its entirety. [*Thanks to Brent Swancer and mysteriousuniverse.org for their permissions. The article can be found online at https://mysteriousuniverse.org/2017/12/a-strange-encounter-with-angels-in-space/.*]

Space is often touted as the last frontier, the final wilderness that we have yet to tame or understand, and in many ways this is very true. We have only within the last century really begun to comprehend some of its secrets to any appreciable degree, and there are certainly wonders beyond our imagination for us yet to behold. Yet some mysteries that have been encountered out there in the cold dark of space go well beyond conventional understanding, to propel out into the world of the paranormal and the universe of the truly bizarre. Certainly ranking among these mysteries is a curious close encounter between some of the first people in space and, well, something else.

In April of 1982, the Soviet Union launched its ambitious Salyut 7 space station as part of the Soviet Salyut Programme, which started in 1971 and had the aim of eventually sending up a total of four crewed scientific research space stations and two crewed military reconnaissance space stations. The last to be launched in the program and a precursor to the Mir space station, the Salyut 7 was the 10th space station ever put into orbit by mankind, and was designed to serve as a sort of test of a new system of modular space stations, which entailed the ability to attach new modules to expand the station or adapt it to whatever functions were required, as well as an outpost for various off-planet experiments. The Salyut 7 would end up staying in orbit for a total of 8 years and 10 months, which up until that time was the longest such a station had ever remained in continuous orbit. It is also known for a very bizarre series of bizarre, unexplained events witnessed by the crew.

In July of 1984, the Salyut 7 was on the 155th day of its mission and things were going in a routine fashion until there was a sudden transmission from cosmonauts Commander Oleg Atkov, Vladimir Solovyov, and Leonid Kizim in which they claimed that the space station had suddenly been surrounded by an oppressive, blinding orange light. The crew of three aboard the Salyut 7 all then allegedly looked out of the portals to try and see what was causing this inexplicable brilliant glow. At this point they would witness probably the last thing they had expected to see out there.

There hovering in space in front of the space station were what the crew would describe as seven enormous winged humanoid beings estimated as being around 90 feet in height and with calm, smiling faces, and it was from these bizarre entities that the ethereal light was apparently emanating. They were also claimed to exude a feeling of calm and peacefulness, and oddly the cosmonauts felt no fear during the encounter, merely wonderment. According to the witnesses, the colossal apparitions, which they described as "angels," matched the speed of the space station, remaining in the same position for around 10 minutes before fading away. Baffled by what they had all just seen, the three cosmonauts had a heated discussion on what the beings were and what rational explanation could account for it, but they could come up with nothing. In the end, although they had all seen exactly the same thing, they chalked it up to the stresses and rigors of being in space for so long, resigning themselves to the explanation that their minds had simply been playing tricks on them.

They may have gone on forever convinced that this was some sort of mass hallucination and a bout of temporary insanity, but it would not be their last encounter with these otherworldly beings. On Day 167 of the mission, the Salyut gained an additional three cosmonauts in the form of Svetlana Savitskaya, Igor Volk and Vladimir Dzhanibekov. Not long after these new crew members boarded, the station was once again bathed in that potent, bedazzling light, and this time all six of the crew looked out of the portholes to see several of the massive angelic beings swimming through the blackness of space outside, again with their benevolent smiling faces. Considering that this time they had again all seen the same thing, it appeared that there was perhaps something more going on beyond simple hallucinations.

When the Salyut mission was concluded and the cosmonauts returned to Earth, their strange experiences were allegedly covered up and swept under the carpet by the Soviet government, and the witnesses told in no uncertain terms that they were never to discuss what they had seen up there. Interestingly, intensive rounds of physical and psychological tests performed on the space station crew supposedly showed nothing out of the ordinary whatsoever. They were perfectly sound of body and mind.

Considering the thick secrecy surrounding the odd events, the story did not really get any wider coverage until after the Cold War, but when it did get out it immediately ignited a firestorm of debate and speculation as to what the cosmonauts had really seen. The most rational and scientific answer is that these cosmonauts experienced what they had suspected in the beginning, which is some sort of mass hallucination or madness brought on by the demanding stresses, fatigue, and the harsh conditions of space. After all, no one had ever really spent this much time continuously in space before, and so it should be only natural that they should have such visions.

Indeed, such surreal visual phenomena have been reported by other astronauts and cosmonauts who have been in space for long periods of time, and even earthbound pilots on long, demanding flights. The problem with this explanation is that six seasoned, experienced cosmonauts all saw the same thing at the same time, and all of them were given clean bills of mental and physical health afterward, making it seem rather unlikely that this could all be in their heads. It also seems rather implausible that a group of six highly trained, well-respected cosmonauts would get together and make up such a story as a hoax.

Another fairly rational explanation is that they witnessed some strange, unexplained natural phenomenon and simply misidentified what they were seeing, but even if this were true, why would they all give the exact same description of winged, angelic entities with smiling faces? Getting into more fringe ideas is that these were actual, literal angels, and that their appearance heralded some sort of prophetic information, or that it was even a portent of the

Biblical end of the world. There have also been all sorts of claims that everyone from NASA to world governments, to the Illuminati and even the Vatican itself know the truth about the existence of these "space angels," and that it is all being covered up and kept from the public, with conspiracy theorists routinely producing photographs from space stations and the Hubble Telescope that purportedly show photographic evidence of such entities.

So what in the world did the cosmonauts of the Salyut 7 see? Unbelievably, there have been other accounts of being visited by similar apparitions in space, with some cases coming even before the Salyut 7 sightings. Supposedly the very first human to go into space, cosmonaut Yuri Gagarin, had his own encounter with such a creature in April of 1961. At two points during his spaceflight aboard the Vostok-1, Gagarin inexplicably went silent and lost contact, and when he was asked about it later he was not sure what had happened, thinking he may have just briefly lost consciousness. During hypnotic regression, Gagarin claimed that he could remember seeing an enormous, mysterious figure floating in space in front of him, and that he had heard a voice in his head saying, "Do not worry, everything will be fine. You'll come back to Earth," before the apparition vanished into thin air right before his eyes. Hallucination or not?

More recently, in 2008 a former member of the Space Shuttle Fleet named Clark C. McClelland came forward to claim that he had years earlier observed a similar being while looking over some monitors of a space shuttle mission at the Kennedy Space Center while on duty at the Launch Control Center (LCC). He claims that over one of the 27-inch monitors he not only observed an enormous entity between 8 to 9 feet tall in the space shuttle's payload bay, but also that it was actually interacting with the astronauts. He would say of what he saw thus:

The ET was standing upright in the Space Shuttle Payload Bay having a discussion with TWO tethered US NASA Astronauts. I also observed on my monitors, the spacecraft of the ET as it was in a stabilized, safe orbit to the rear of the Space Shuttle main engine pods. I observed this incident for about one minute and seven seconds. Plenty of time to memorize all that I was observing.

McClelland claimed that others had seen the incident too, and that they had been told to keep quiet about what they had seen, meaning that he had sat on this hauntingly bizarre experience until after he retired. He also claims that the government has regular dealings with these creatures and that it is all kept top secret. In this case the entity mentioned is certainly described as an alien of some type, but its sheer size makes it interesting in relation to the space angel phenomenon, and makes one wonder just what it really was this man saw, if anything. Does this story have any credibility at all or is he just a loon?

So there you have it. Angels. In space. This last frontier has a lot of strange stuff in it, but perhaps not much that is as strange as this. Just what is going on here? Was this hallucinations seen by all of these crew members? Was it something else? Who knows? Considering the original news reports of the phenomenon have been quietly relegated to the background and are only really discussed on Internet forums by people who have noticed just how outlandish the story is, we may never know for sure. It remains just one more anomaly on perhaps a whole road of anomalies just waiting for us as we delve ever deeper into the reaches of our universe.

It is difficult to dismiss this and the other cited cases when men of the highest training, intellect, and composure are the witnesses. Who better could you conceive to be witness to any event in a court of law? Lawyers love to attack the credibility and character of witnesses; this is just a part of their tactics to win cases. But how do you attack credibility when multiple, educated, and composed witnesses all tell the same tale?

Magic is Real

Moving to the next discipline, we see that Semjaza, the leader, taught men about the casting of spells. Magic? Yes. Is magic real? Yes. Even the Bible tells us that this is so. While we're not yet anywhere close to completion of our study in Genesis, let's jump ahead by about 1100 years to 2448 AM when Moses comes before Pharaoh to deliver the message from God to let the Israelites leave Egypt. Let us examine the Biblical book of Exodus, starting in chapter 7:

So the LORD said to Moses: "See, I have made you as God to Pharaoh, and Aaron your brother shall be your prophet. You shall speak all that I command you. And Aaron your brother shall tell Pharaoh to send the children of Israel out of his land. And I will harden Pharaoh's heart, and multiply My signs and My wonders in the land of Egypt. But Pharaoh will not heed you, so that I may lay My hand on Egypt and bring My armies and My people, the children of Israel, out of the land of Egypt by great judgments. And the Egyptians shall know that I am the LORD, when I stretch out My hand on Egypt and bring out the children of Israel from among them.

"Then Moses and Aaron did so; just as the LORD commanded them, so they did. And Moses was eighty years old and Aaron eighty-three years old when they spoke to Pharaoh.

Then the LORD spoke to Moses and Aaron, saying, "When Pharaoh speaks to you, saying, 'Show a miracle for yourselves,' then you shall say to Aaron, 'Take your rod and cast it before Pharaoh, and let it become a serpent.' "So Moses and Aaron went in to Pharaoh, and they did so, just as the LORD commanded. And Aaron cast down his rod before Pharaoh and before his servants, and it became a serpent.

But Pharaoh also called the wise men and the sorcerers; so the magicians of Egypt, they also did in like manner with their enchantments. For every man threw down his rod, and they became serpents. *But Aaron's rod swallowed up their rods. And Pharaoh's heart grew hard, and he did not heed them, as the LORD had said.*

So the LORD said to Moses: "Pharaoh's heart is hard; he refuses to let the people go. Go to Pharaoh in the morning, when he goes out to the water, and you shall stand by the river's bank to meet him; and the rod which was turned to a serpent you shall take in your hand. And you shall say to him, 'The LORD God of the Hebrews has sent me to you, saying, "Let My people go, that they may serve Me in the wilderness"; but indeed, until now you would not hear! Thus says the LORD: "By this you shall know that I am the LORD. Behold, I will strike the waters which are in the river with the rod that is in my hand, and they shall be turned to blood. And the fish that are in the river shall die, the river shall stink, and the Egyptians will loathe to drink the water of the river.""" Then the LORD spoke to Moses, "Say to Aaron, 'Take your rod and stretch out your hand over the waters of Egypt, over their streams, over their rivers, over their ponds, and over all their pools of water, that they may become blood. And there shall be blood throughout all the land of Egypt, both in buckets of wood and pitchers of stone.'" And Moses and Aaron did so, just as the LORD commanded. So he lifted up the rod and struck the waters that were in the river, in the sight of Pharaoh and in the sight of his servants. And all the waters that were in the river were turned to blood. The fish that were in the river died, the river stank, and the Egyptians could not drink the water of the river. So there was blood throughout all the land of Egypt.

Then the magicians of Egypt did so with their enchantments; *and Pharaoh's heart grew hard, and he did not heed them, as the LORD had said. And Pharaoh turned and went into his house. Neither was his heart moved by this. So all the Egyptians dug all around the river for water to drink, because they could not drink the water of the river. And seven days passed after the LORD had struck the river.*

And the LORD spoke to Moses, "Go to Pharaoh and say to him, 'Thus says the LORD: "Let My people go, that they may serve Me. But if you refuse to let them go, behold, I will smite all your territory with frogs. So the river shall bring forth frogs abundantly, which shall go up and come into your house, into your bedroom, on your bed, into the houses of your servants, on your people, into your ovens, and into your kneading bowls. And the frogs shall come up on you, on your people, and on all your servants." ' "

Then the LORD spoke to Moses, "Say to Aaron, 'Stretch out your hand with your rod over the streams, over the rivers, and over the ponds, and cause frogs to come up on the land of Egypt.'" So Aaron stretched out his hand over the waters of Egypt, and the frogs came up and covered the land of Egypt. ***And the magicians did so with their enchantments, and brought up frogs on the land of Egypt****.*

Then Pharaoh called for Moses and Aaron, and said, "Entreat the LORD that He may take away the frogs from me and from my people; and I will let the people go, that they may sacrifice to the LORD."

And Moses said to Pharaoh, "Accept the honor of saying when I shall intercede for you, for your servants, and for your people, to destroy the frogs from you and your houses, that they may remain in the river only." So he said, "Tomorrow." And he said, "Let it be according to your word, that you may know that there is no one like the LORD our God. And the frogs shall depart from you, from your houses, from your servants, and from your people. They shall remain in the river only."

Then Moses and Aaron went out from Pharaoh. And Moses cried out to the LORD concerning the frogs which He had brought against Pharaoh. So the LORD did according to the word of Moses. And the frogs died out of the houses, out of the courtyards, and out of the fields. They gathered them together in heaps, and the land stank. But when Pharaoh saw that there was relief, he hardened his heart and did not heed them, as the LORD had said.

So the LORD said to Moses, "Say to Aaron, 'Stretch out your rod, and strike the dust of the land, so that it may become lice throughout all the land of Egypt.' "And they did so. For Aaron stretched out his hand with his rod and struck the dust of the earth, and it became lice on man and beast. All the dust of the land became lice throughout all the land of Egypt. Now the magicians so worked with their enchantments to bring forth lice, but they could not. So there were lice on man and beast. **Then the magicians said to Pharaoh, "This is the finger of God."** *But Pharaoh's heart grew hard, and he did not heed them, just as the LORD had said.* [Exo 7:1 - 8:19; emphasis mine]

God brought seven plagues on Egypt, and the Egyptian "wise men and sorcerers" ("magicians") duplicated the first three of these with their "enchantments." Other translations refer to these as "magic arts" (NLT), "secret arts" (NIV), "occult practices" (CSB), "secret powers" (CEV), "enchantments and certain secrets" (DRB), "magic spells" (GWT), and "secret lore" (OJB). The Bible does not say that these magicians created illusions or used trickery; it says that they "did so," in each case. Other translations say that the magicians "did the same things" (NIV et al.).

For another testament on magic, I present a passage from the year 2891 AM, as I calculate it. For this, we go to the Biblical book of 1st Samuel, chapter 28:

Now Samuel had died, and all Israel had lamented for him and buried him in Ramah, in his own city. And Saul had put the mediums and the spiritists out of the land.

Then the Philistines gathered together, and came and encamped at Shunem. So Saul gathered all Israel together, and they encamped at Gilboa. When Saul saw the army of the Philistines, he was afraid, and his heart trembled greatly. And when Saul inquired of the LORD, the LORD did not answer him, either by dreams or by Urim or by the prophets.

Then Saul said to his servants, "Find me a woman who is a medium, that I may go to her and inquire of her."

And his servants said to him, "In fact, there is a woman who is a medium at En Dor."

So Saul disguised himself and put on other clothes, and he went, and two men with him; and they came to the woman by night. And he said, "Please conduct a séance for me, and bring up for me the one I shall name to you."

Then the woman said to him, **"Look, you know what Saul has done, how he has cut off the mediums and the spiritists from the land.** *Why then do you lay a snare for my life, to cause me to die?"*

And Saul swore to her by the LORD, saying, "As the LORD lives, no punishment shall come upon you for this thing."

Then the woman said, "Whom shall I bring up for you?"

And he said, "Bring up Samuel for me."

When the woman saw Samuel, she cried out with a loud voice. And the woman spoke to Saul, saying, "Why have you deceived me? For you are Saul!"

And the king said to her, "Do not be afraid. What did you see?"

And the woman said to Saul, "I saw a spirit ascending out of the earth."

So he said to her, "What is his form?"

And she said, "An old man is coming up, and he is covered with a mantle." And Saul perceived that it was Samuel, and he stooped with his face to the ground and bowed down.

Now Samuel said to Saul, "Why have you disturbed me by bringing me up?"

And Saul answered, "I am deeply distressed; for the Philistines make war against me, and God has departed from me and does not answer me anymore, neither by prophets nor by dreams. Therefore I have called you, that you may reveal to me what I should do."

Then Samuel said: "Why then do you ask me, seeing the LORD has departed from you and has become your enemy? And the LORD has done for Himself as He spoke by me. For the LORD has torn the kingdom out of your hand and given it to your neighbor, David. Because you did not obey the voice of the Lord nor execute His fierce wrath upon Amalek, therefore the Lord has done this thing to you this day. Moreover the LORD will also deliver Israel with you into the hand of the Philistines. And tomorrow you and your sons will be with me. The LORD will also deliver the army of Israel into the hand of the Philistines."

Immediately Saul fell full length on the ground, and was dreadfully afraid because of the words of Samuel. And there was no strength in him, for he had eaten no food all day or all night.

And the woman came to Saul and saw that he was severely troubled, and said to him, "Look, your maidservant has obeyed your voice, and I have put my life in my hands and heeded the words which you spoke to me. Now therefore, please, heed also the voice of your maidservant, and let me set a piece of bread before you; and eat, that you may have strength when you go on your way."

But he refused and said, "I will not eat."

So his servants, together with the woman, urged him; and he heeded their voice. Then he arose from the ground and sat on the bed. Now the woman had a fatted calf in the house, and she hastened to kill it. And she took flour and kneaded it, and baked unleavened bread from it. So she brought it before Saul and his servants, and they ate. Then they rose and went away that night.

[1Sam 28:3-25; emphasis mine]

Saul was the first King of Israel and in this passage we find him in the last year of his reign. Saul had sinned multiple times and ways against God, so God would no longer respond to his inquiries. The Philistines, Israel's enduring enemy in the land of Canaan, were getting ready to attack Israel, and Saul was gripped with great trepidation for his own life. Since God would not respond to his inquiries, he sought out the services of a sorceress, and he is told there is one in En Dor. Other translations refer to this woman as "medium" (NIV et al.), "a woman who can talk to the spirits of the dead" (CEV), "a woman who has a spirit of Python" (DBT), "a woman that hath a divining spirit" (DRB), and "a woman who conjures up the dead" (GWT). This woman has a specific type of magic knowledge: to call upon the dead, see them, and converse with them. She very clearly accomplishes the task that Saul requests and immediately upon seeing Samuel, Saul's identity is revealed to her. This is neither accident nor coincidence, but a direct consequence of her conjuring. She had reservations about revealing her abilities to Saul, as he had previously "cut off" (i.e., killed) those with familiar spirits and wizards. For this reason, Saul disguised himself, but his ruse is exposed when she conjures up Samuel's spirit. She shrieks because she perceives that Saul, having now exposed her, will presently slay her.

Regarding magic and sorcery, *The Zondervan Encyclopedia of the Bible* states:

The reality of occult powers is acknowledged, *but magic and sorcery are consistently forbidden. A notable passage is Deuteronomy 18:10-14:*

"There shall not be found among you...anyone who practices divination, a soothsayer, or an augur, or a sorcerer, or a charmer, or a medium, or a wizard, or a necromancer. For

whoever does these things is an abomination to the Lord: ...these nations, which you are about to dispossess, give heed to soothsayers and to diviners: but as for you, the Lord your God has not allowed you so to do" (cf. Lev 19:26)

This verse incorporates practically all the OT types of magic, except those practiced by Egyptians and Babylonians. Two other words ḥrsm and kspm of Ugaritic and Akkadian provenance, are used to cover magic and sorcery in general (e.g. Exo 22:18; 2 Kings 9:22). [*The Zondervan Encyclopedia of the Bible,* by Merrill C. Tenney, Moisés Silva, ©2010, Zondervan. Used by permission of Zondervan. www.zondervan.com; emphasis mine]

There is at least one other Biblical account where the services of a sorcerer are used: the account of Balaam son of Beor. I won't provide the full account from Scripture, as it spans three chapters in the book of Numbers (22-24). The account is also described in Josephus' *Antiquities*, Book IV, chapter VI. As a quick summary, the Israelites had just annihilated the Amorites near Heshbon and then conquered the land of Bashan just to the north of there. These were both countries to the east of the Jordan, so Israel had not yet entered the Promised Land. The Moabites, just to the south of the Amorites, had been witnesses of these campaigns and were justifiably fearful that they might be next. Balak son of Peor, king of Moab, recognizing that they were no match for the Israelites, was quite distressed over the prospect of destruction. He realized that he needed supernatural support to defeat this enemy. Thus, he sent messengers to Balaam, a so-called "soothsayer," (one that employs divination to see the future) to call down curses from the gods upon Israel. Balak acknowledges that Balaam apparently has a successful track record from past episodes. Cutting to the chase, God intervenes and confounds Balaam's efforts.

After Balaam's failures, Balak dismisses him without compensation. But on his way out, Balaam offers Balak advice. He suggests that while nobody can defeat the Hebrews while God supports them, if the Moabites send some of their attractive women to consort with the Hebrew men, and draw them to worship the gods of the Moabites, they would thereby fall into sin and that God Himself would deal with them. But, Balaam also advised that this would only delay their inevitable defeat, and that only for a short while.

Now, interestingly, the Book of Jasher provides a tale of intersections of the lives of Moses and of Balaam. In the first instance, we find his name in a passage in chapter 67, just after the account of Miriam and Aaron (Moses' older sister and brother) being born. The account of Moses' birth is found in chapter 68. So, as Aaron was three years older than Moses, the year would have been about 2365 AM.

In those days died Zepho the son of Eliphaz, son of Esau, king of Chittim, and Janeas reigned in his stead. And the time that Zepho reigned over the children of Chittim was fifty years, and he died and was buried in the city of Nabna in the land of Chittim. And Janeas, one of the mighty men of the children of Chittim, reigned after him and he reigned fifty years. And it was after the death of the king of Chittim that **Balaam the son of Beor fled from the land of Chittim, and he went and came to Egypt to Pharaoh king of Egypt. And Pharaoh received him with great honor, for he had heard of his wisdom, and he gave him presents and made him for a counsellor, and aggrandized him. And Balaam dwelt in Egypt, in honor with all the nobles of the king, and the nobles exalted him, because they all coveted to learn his wisdom.** *And in the hundred and thirtieth year of Israel's going down to Egypt,*

Pharaoh dreamed that he was sitting upon his kingly throne, and lifted up his eyes and saw an old man standing before him, and there were scales in the hands of the old man, such scales as are used by merchants. And the old man took the scales and hung them before Pharaoh. And the old man took all the elders of Egypt and all its nobles and great men, and he tied them together and put them in one scale. And he took a milk kid and put it into the other scale, and the kid preponderated over all. And Pharaoh was astonished at this dreadful vision, why the kid should preponderate over all, and Pharaoh awoke and behold it was a dream. And Pharaoh rose up early in the morning and called all his servants and related to them the dream, and the men were greatly afraid. And the king said to all his wise men, Interpret I pray you the dream which I dreamed, that I may know it. And Balaam the son of Beor answered the king and said unto him, This means nothing else but a great evil that will spring up against Egypt in the latter days. For a son will be born to Israel who will destroy all Egypt and its inhabitants, and bring forth the Israelites from Egypt with a mighty hand. Now therefore, O king, take counsel upon this matter, that you may destroy the hope of the children of Israel and their expectation, before this evil arise against Egypt. And the king said unto Balaam, And what shall we do unto Israel? Surely after a certain manner did we at first counsel against them and could not prevail over them. Now therefore give you also advice against them by which we may prevail over them. And Balaam answered the king, saying, Send now and call thy two counsellors, and we will see what their advice is upon this matter and afterward thy servant will speak. And the king sent and called his two counsellors Reuel the Midianite and Job the Uzite, and they came and sat before the king. And the king said to them, Behold you have both heard the dream which I have dreamed, and the interpretation thereof; now therefore give counsel and know and see what is to be done to the children of Israel, whereby we may prevail over them, before their evil shall spring up against us. And Reuel the Midianite answered the king and said, May the king live, may the king live forever. If it seem good to the king, let him desist from the Hebrews and leave them, and let him not stretch forth his hand against them. For these are they whom the Lord chose in days of old, and took as the lot of his inheritance from amongst all the nations of the earth and the kings of the earth; and who is there that stretched his hand against them with impunity, of whom their God was not avenged? Surely thou knowest that when Abraham went down to Egypt, Pharaoh, the former king of Egypt, saw Sarah his wife, and took her for a wife, because Abraham said, She is my sister, for he was afraid, lest the men of Egypt should slay him on account of his wife. And when the king of Egypt had taken Sarah then God smote him and his household with heavy plagues, until he restored unto Abraham his wife Sarah, then was he healed. And Abimelech the Gerarite, king of the Philistines, God punished on account of Sarah wife of Abraham, in stopping up every womb from man to beast. When their God came to Abimelech in the dream of night and terrified him in order that he might restore to Abraham Sarah whom he had taken, and afterward all the people of Gerar were punished on account of Sarah, and Abraham prayed to his God for them, and he was entreated of him, and he healed them. And Abimelech feared all this evil that came upon him and his people, and he returned to Abraham his wife Sarah, and gave him with her many gifts. He did so also to Isaac when he had driven him from Gerar, and God had done wonderful things to him, that all the water courses of Gerar were dried up, and their productive trees did not bring forth. Until Abimelech of Gerar, and Ahuzzath one of his friends, and Pichol the captain of his host, went to him and they bent and bowed down before him to the ground. And they requested of him to supplicate for them, and he prayed to the Lord for them, and the Lord was entreated of him and he healed them. Jacob also, the plain man, was delivered through his integrity from the hand of his brother Esau, and the hand of Laban the Syrian his mother's brother, who had sought his life; likewise from the hand of all the kings of Canaan who had come together against him and his children to destroy them, and the Lord delivered them out of their hands, that they turned upon them and smote them, for who had ever stretched forth his hand against them with impunity? Surely Pharaoh the former, thy father's father, raised Joseph the son of Jacob above all the princes of the land of Egypt, when he saw his wisdom, for through his wisdom he rescued all the inhabitants of the land from the famine. After which he ordered Jacob and his children to come down to Egypt, in order that through their virtue, the land of Egypt and the land of Goshen might be delivered from the famine. Now therefore if it seem good in thine eyes, cease from destroying the children of Israel, but if it be not thy will that they shall dwell in Egypt, send them forth from here, that they may go to the land of Canaan, the land where their ancestors sojourned. And when Pharaoh heard the words of Jethro he was very angry with him, so that he rose with shame from the king's presence, and went to Midian, his land, and took Joseph's stick with him. And the king said to Job the Uzite, What sayest thou Job, and what is thy advice respecting the Hebrews? So Job said to the king, Behold all the inhabitants of the land are in thy power, let the king do as it seems good in his eyes. And the king said unto Balaam, What dost thou say, Balaam, speak thy word that we may hear it. And Balaam said to the king, Of all that the king has counselled against the Hebrews will they be delivered, and the king will not be able to prevail over them with any counsel. For if thou thinkest to lessen them by the flaming fire, thou canst not prevail over them, for surely their God delivered Abraham their father from Ur of the Chaldeans; and if thou thinkest to destroy them with a sword, surely Isaac their father was delivered from it, and a ram was placed in his stead. And if with hard and rigorous labor thou thinkest to lessen them, thou wilt not prevail even in this, for their father Jacob served Laban in all manner of hard work, and prospered. Now therefore, O King, hear my words, for this is the counsel which is counselled against them, by which thou wilt prevail over them, and from which thou shouldst not depart. If it please the king let him order all their children which shall be born from this day forward, to be thrown into the water, for by this canst thou wipe away their name, for none of them, nor of their fathers, were tried in this manner. And the king heard the words of Balaam, and the thing pleased the king and the princes, and the king did according to the word of Balaam. And the king ordered a proclamation to be issued and a law to be made throughout the land of Egypt, saying, Every male child born to the Hebrews from this day forward shall be thrown into the water. And Pharaoh called unto all his servants, saying, Go now and seek throughout the land of Goshen where the children of Israel are, and see that every son born to the Hebrews shall be cast into the river, but every daughter you shall let live. And when the children of Israel heard this thing which Pharaoh had commanded, to cast their male children into the river, some of the people separated from their wives and others adhered to them. And from that day forward, when the time of delivery arrived to those women of Israel who had remained with their husbands, they went to the field to bring forth there, and they brought forth in the field, and left their children upon the field and returned home. And the Lord who had sworn to their ancestors to multiply them, sent one of his ministering angels which are in heaven to wash each child in water, to anoint and swathe it and to put into its hands two smooth stones from one of which it sucked milk and from the other honey, and he caused its hair to grow to its knees, by which it might cover itself; to comfort it and to cleave to it, through his compassion for it. And when God had compassion over them and had desired to multiply them upon the face of the land, he ordered his earth to receive them to be preserved therein till the time of their growing up, after which the earth opened its mouth and vomited them forth and they sprouted forth from the city like the herb of the earth, and the grass of the forest, and they returned each to his family and to his father's house, and they remained with them. And the babes of the children of Israel were upon the earth like the herb of the field, through God's grace to them. And when all the Egyptians saw this thing, they went forth, each to his field with his yoke of oxen and his ploughshare, and they ploughed it up as one ploughs the earth at seed time. And when they ploughed they were unable to hurt the infants of the children of Israel, so the people increased and waxed exceedingly. And Pharaoh ordered his officers daily to go to Goshen to seek for the babes of the children of Israel. And when they had sought and found one, they took it from its mother's bosom by force, and threw it into the river, but the female child they left with its mother; thus did the Egyptians do to the Israelites all the days. [Jash 67:5-61; emphasis mine]

Chapter 79 of the Book of Jasher also provides an account of Moses' and Aaron's appearance before Pharaoh. In this account, though, Balaam is named as one of the magicians in Pharaoh's court:

And Moses and Aaron came to Egypt to the community of the children of Israel, and they spoke to them all the words of the Lord, and the people rejoiced an exceeding great rejoicing. And Moses and Aaron rose up early on the next day, and they went to the house of Pharaoh, and they took in their hands the stick of God. And when they came to the king's gate, two young lions were confined there with iron instruments, and no person went out or came in from before them, unless those whom the king ordered to come, when the conjurors came and withdrew the lions by their incantations, and this brought them to the king. And Moses hastened and lifted up the stick upon the lions, and he loosed them, and Moses and Aaron came into the king's house. The lions also came with them in joy, and they followed them and rejoiced as a dog rejoices over his master when he comes from the field. And when Pharaoh saw this thing he was astonished at it, and he was greatly terrified at the report, for their appearance was like the appearance of the children of God. And Pharaoh said to Moses, What do you require? And they answered him, saying, The Lord God of the Hebrews has sent us to thee, to say, Send forth my people that they may serve me. And when Pharaoh heard their words he was greatly terrified before them, and he said to them, Go today and come back to me tomorrow, and they did according to the word of the king. **And when they had gone Pharaoh sent for Balaam the magician and to Jannes and Jambres his sons, and to all the magicians and conjurors and counsellors which belonged to the king, and they all came and sat before the king.** *And the king told them all the words which Moses and his brother Aaron had spoken to him, and the magicians said to the king, But how came the men* *to thee, on account of the lions which were confined at the gate? And the king said, Because they lifted up their rod against the lions and loosed them, and came to me, and the lions also rejoiced at them as a dog rejoices to meet his master.* **And Balaam the son of Beor the magician answered the king, saying, These are none else than magicians like ourselves. Now therefore send for them, and let them come and we will try them, and the king did so.** *And in the morning Pharaoh sent for Moses and Aaron to come before the king, and they took the rod of God, and came to the king and spoke to him, saying, Thus said the Lord God of the Hebrews, Send my people that they may serve me. And the king said to them, But who will believe you that you are the messengers of God and that you come to me by his order? Now therefore give a wonder or sign in this matter, and then the words which you speak will be believed. And Aaron hastened and threw the rod out of his hand before Pharaoh and before his servants, and the rod turned into a serpent. And the sorcerers saw this and they cast each man his rod upon the ground and they became serpents. And the serpent of Aaron's rod lifted up its head and opened its mouth to swallow the rods of the magicians.* **And Balaam the magician answered and said, This thing has been from the days of old, that a serpent should swallow its fellow, and that living things devour each other. Now therefore restore it to a rod as it was at first, and we will also restore our rods as they were at first, and if thy rod shall swallow our rods, then shall we know that the spirit of God is in thee, and if not, thou art only an artificer like unto ourselves.** *And Aaron hastened and stretched forth his hand and caught hold of the serpent's tail and it became a rod in his hand, and the sorcerers did the like with their rods, and they got hold, each man of the tail of his serpent, and they became rods as at first. And when they were restored to rods, the rod of Aaron swallowed up their rods. And when the king saw this thing, he ordered the book of records that related to the kings of Egypt, to be brought, and they brought the book of records, the chronicles of the kings of Egypt, in which all the idols of Egypt were inscribed, for they thought of finding therein the name of Jehovah, but they found it not. And Pharaoh said to Moses and Aaron, Behold I have not found the name of your God written in this book, and his name I know not.* [Jash 79:19-44; emphasis mine]

According to other traditions, Noah's wayward and accursed son Ham brought the magic arts with him through the deluge. One such tale says that he had acquired books with spells and buried them in the earth before the flood and then afterward exhumed them. (As it turns out, this scheme proves unnecessary since there was a second fall of angels after the flood.)

Magic spells apparently appeal to the disembodied, demonic spirits to use their powers to accomplish specific ends, which include necromancy (calling upon the dead), divination (seeing the future and interpretation of signs and portents), enchantment (incantations and spells for various purposes including impartation of sickness or healing, confounding of plans and schemes, fertility and infertility, revealing of secrets, etc.), not having mentioned counter-spells to reverse or negate the effects of such spells.

In Smith's *The Chaldean Account of Genesis* (1876), he discusses the subject matter of tablets found in the Royal Assyrian Library in the mound of Kouyunjik, opposite the town of Mosul. The tablets, numbering more than 20,000, covered a variety of subjects, including mythology, grammar, mathematics, legends, history, geography, and law. About these, he said the following in Chapter 2 of his book:

> *Many of these texts take the form of charms to be used in sickness and for the expulsion of evil spirits; some of them are of great antiquity, being at least as old as the creation and Izdubar legends. One fine series concerns the cure of witchcraft, a superstition fully believed in in those days. Izdubar is mentioned in one of these tablets as lord of the oaths or pledges of the world.*

Note also that he identifies Izdubar with the Biblical Nimrod.

I wanted to be sure that magic is what I understood it to be. So, I looked up the word "magic" in Strong's Concordance, but found that it was nowhere listed therein. The word "magician" is there, and in all three cases referring to (1) the magicians in Pharaoh's court with Joseph, (2) those in Pharaoh's court with Moses, or (3) those in the Babylonian court with Daniel. Hmmm. I was pretty sure that magic was the work accomplished by demons, when called upon using specific incantations by which they are bound to respond. So maybe I should look up the word "demon." When I did this, I once again found that this word also was apparently missing from Scripture. So what's going on? I turned to the NT passages where demons were cast out, and found that the English word used in all cases was "devil," and not "demon." Now, the Greek word "δαίμων" (daemon, Strong's 1142) is always translated as "devil" in the NKJV, in spite of the fact that Strong's defines this word as "a demon, i.e., a fallen angel." Similarly for the variants, Strong's 1139, 1140, and 1141. Demons are disembodied fallen angels. This disembodiment was brought upon them as a punishment for their sin, and is apparently an uncomfortable state for them: they desire physical bodies and will take control when a person is weak or willing. We see this in the NT when demons are cast out of a man and they desire embodiment to such an extent that they possess the bodies of swine (see Mt 8:30-32, Mk 5:11-16, and Lk 8:32-33). Recall that earlier I delineated the disciplines taught by the fallen angels, which included casting of spells, root cuttings, and counter spells. What these angels conveyed was that they are, by certain methods, subject to the dictates of mankind.

Josephus, in Book VIII, Ch. II, Sec. 5 of his *Antiquities*, tells us that Solomon had learned "*...that skill which expels demons, which is a science useful and sanative to men.*" Josephus goes on to say that "*He composes such incantations also by which distempers are alleviated. And he left behind him the manner of using exorcisms, by which they drive away demons, so that they never return, and this method of cure is of great force unto this day....*" He says that he was witness to a case where a certain Jewish man by the name of Eleazar cast out a demon in the presence of Vespasian and members of his retinue.

Can these demons actually cure someone that is ill by their power? Maybe. Why is this a sin? Because these demons become intercessors to effect outcomes or access hidden knowledge, and we are to rely upon God alone for such. If we need healing, we are to ask God (in the name of Jesus Christ); similarly if we want an apparent outcome to be changed, or if we want to understand a dream. If we rely on other powers, other authorities, we are by such acts unfaithful. Nevertheless, magic is real, and I suspect that some of the incantations may have survived the generations. But further investigation of such is beyond the scope of this book.

The First, Second, and Third Falls of Angels

Let's go back for a moment to the Garden of Eden. Recall that the serpent is the source of temptation to Adam and Eve, and the cause of their fall into sin. Why was the evil one in the Garden of Eden? Again, if we suppose that God sent his angels to the earth with various educational objectives, it is not unreasonable to conclude that God put Satan into the garden with Adam and Eve to provide guidance or direction of some sort. It would also seem that he was then the only angel present on the earth. But then, it would seem that he fell victim to jealousy…that God treated man so lovingly, and he was envious of the relationship between God and man. Let's look again at what Josephus says in his Antiquities:

> *But while all the living creatures had one language*, **at that time the serpent, which then lived together with Adam and his wife**, *shewed an envious disposition, at his supposal of their living happily, and in obedience to the commands of God; and imagining that, when they disobeyed them, they would fall into calamities, he persuaded the woman, out of a malicious intention, to taste of the tree of knowledge, telling them that in that tree was the knowledge of good and evil; which knowledge when they should obtain, they would lead a happy life, nay, a life not inferior to that of a god: by which means he overcame the woman, and persuaded her to despise the command of God.* [Ant I:I:4; emphasis mine]

The Book of Revelation tells us that the serpent is the devil and Satan. Unlike the fallen angels in Gen 6, this angel was not drawn from his first estate by lustful drives for the daughters of men, but rather was driven by envy. He apparently wanted his special relationship with God to be unique, but his plan to restore such backfired, and that's another story. Thus, we can regard the fall of Satan in Gen 1 as the first fall of one angel. But the Gen 6 account is the first fall of a plurality of angels. The second fall of angels occurs later in Genesis, sometime between Noah's disembarkation from the ark and the Israelites crossing of the Jordan under Joshua. This has to be the case as there were Nephilim in the land of Canaan. Since the only survivors of the flood were Noah and his immediate family, there had to be a second fall that produced Nephilim. Genesis confirms that the Nephilim were there both before and after the deluge:

> *There were giants in the earth in those days;* **and also after that**, *when the sons of God came in unto the daughters of men, and they bare children to them, the same became mighty men which were of old, men of renown.* [Gen 6:4; emphasis mine]

This verse tells the tale that _**twice**_ the sons of God came unto the daughters of men and bore to them children…the Nephilim. There are alternate, corrupted flood stories that say that some of the Nephilim and/or angels survived the deluge, but the Biblical account clearly tells us that no one (human and/or hybrid) other than Noah and his family survived it. And there are others who claim that perhaps the hybrid DNA was carried through the flood by the wives of Noah's children. If that were true, though, at least one third of the postdiluvian population would have been hybrids, but this is clearly not the case. God is omniscient, and protected the unblemished DNA of the occupants of His ark. As well, the table of nations makes no reference to Nephilim, Raphidim, etc. So it must be the case that the Nephilim found in the land of Canaan were the result of a second fall of angels. And there will be a third fall of angels in the end times, but that is beyond the scope of this first volume.

Suffice it to say that three is a special number in the Bible: like the number seven in the Bible, the number three is also a symbol of completion.

One final digression. As I mentioned previously, the heavenly host refers to the angels of God. The word "stars" in the Bible is frequently, but not always, a reference to angels. I would say that in most cases, the word "star" simply means a stellar object like our sun. However, like so many words in the English language that have multiple meanings, and can also be used metaphorically, the word "stars" clearly has at least these two distinct meanings in the Biblical text. Let's examine several such passages wherein the former rendering will become clear.

> *...while the morning stars sang together and all the angels shouted for joy?* [Job 38:7, NIV]
>
> *After they had heard the king, they went on their way, and the star they had seen in the east went ahead of them until it stopped over the place where the child was.* [Mat 2:9, NIV]
>
> *How you have fallen from heaven, O morning star, son of the dawn! You have been cast down to the earth, you who once laid low the nations!* [Isa 14:12, NIV]
>
> *The fifth angel sounded his trumpet, and I saw a star that had fallen from the sky to the earth. The star was given the key to the shaft of the Abyss.* [Rev 9:1, NIV]
>
> *"I, Jesus, have sent my angel to give you this testimony for the churches. I am the Root and the Offspring of David, and the bright Morning Star."* [Rev 22:16, NIV]
>
> *From the heavens the stars fought, from their courses they fought against Sisera.* [Jdg 5:20, NIV]
>
> *...and the stars in the sky fell to earth, as figs drop from a fig tree when shaken by a strong wind.* [Rev 6:13, NIV]
>
> *His tail drew a third of the stars of heaven and threw them to the earth. And the dragon stood before the woman who was ready to give birth, to devour her Child as soon as it was born.* [Rev 12:4, NKJV]

In each of these cases, the stars are not stellar objects; this last one is the most pertinent to this point. If the stars in this verse are literal stars, the earth would be consumed. This verse clearly depicts the third fall of angels. In the last days, even more angels will be deluded by Satan and drawn into his ranks for the final battle at Armageddon.

The Fallen Ones

With the truly powerful angels now taking charge, chaos ensues. First, the offspring from their sexual relationships with women are giants with unbridled desires for fulfillment in their hybrid bodies. So we start with an examination of these hybrids. Gen 6:4 tells us that these Nephilim were the heroes ("mighty men" in the KJV) of old. The Hebrew word for "mighty" (Strong's 1368, transliterated "gibbowr") here means "powerful," or by implication, warrior or tyrant. What do the other histories tell us? The sixth chapter in the Book of 1Enoch provides the account of the fall of the angels. We pick things up in chapter 7, starting in verse 1:

> *And all the others together with them went and took unto themselves wives, and each chose for himself one, and they began to go in unto them and to defile themselves with them, and they taught them charms and enchantments, and the cutting of roots, and made them*

acquainted with plants. And they became pregnant, and they bare great giants, whose height was three thousand ells: Who consumed all the acquisitions of men. And when men could no longer sustain them, the giants turned against them and devoured mankind. And they began to sin against birds, and beasts, and reptiles, and fish, and to devour one another's flesh, and drink the blood. Then the earth laid accusation against the lawless ones. [1Eno 7:1-6]

The Book of Jasher provides further details, as follows:

And their judges and rulers went to the daughters of men and took their wives by force from their husbands according to their choice, and the sons of men in those days took from the cattle of the earth, the beasts of the field and the fowls of the air, and taught the mixture of animals of one species with the other, in order therewith to provoke the Lord; and God saw the whole earth that it was corrupt, for all flesh had corrupted its ways upon earth, all men and all animals. [Jash 4:18]

We've already provided an excerpt from Josephus' *Antiquities*, but I insert it again here for continuity.

But for what degree of zeal they had formerly shewn for virtue, they now showed by their actions a double degree of wickedness, whereby they made God to be their enemy; for many angels of God accompanied with women, and begat sons that proved unjust, and despisers of all that was good, on account of the confidence they had in their own strength, for the tradition is that these men did what resembled the acts of those whom the Graecians call giants. [Ant I:III:1]

Lastly, we look at the account in Jubilees:

And it came to pass when the children of men began to multiply on the face of the earth and daughters were born unto them, that the angels of God saw them on a certain year of this jubilee, that they were beautiful to look upon; and they took themselves wives of all whom they chose, and they bare unto them sons and they were giants. And the lawlessness increased on the earth and all flesh corrupted its way, alike men and cattle and beasts and birds and everything that walketh on the earth – all of them corrupted their ways and their orders, and they began to devour each other, and lawlessness increased on the earth and every imagination of the thoughts of all men (was) thus evil continually. And God looked upon the earth, and behold it was corrupt, and all flesh had corrupted its orders, and all that were upon the earth had wrought all manner of evil before His eyes. And He said, "I shall destroy man and all flesh upon the face of the earth which I have created." [Jub 5:1-4]

What can we summarize from these accounts? First, the Nephilim were powerful giants...according to one account, 3,000 ells. What's an ell? As I've been able to discover, it's nominally the same as a cubit. The word "ell" apparently means "arm," and a cubit is the distance from the elbow to the tips of the extended fingers of the hand. There are some slight variations in this, but all such variations are close enough to simply use the 1:1 correspondence to the cubit. This does, however, pose a real problem: 3,000 ells (cubits) is about 4500 feet. I think we must conclude that the figure is not 3,000, or the unit is not an ell, or that the ell referenced here is not the same unit of measure. But can we determine how tall they were? I propose that we look to the Biblical account of the flood.

> *Now the flood was on the earth forty days. The waters increased and lifted up the ark, and it rose high above the earth. The waters prevailed and greatly increased on the earth, and the ark moved about on the surface of the waters. And the waters prevailed exceedingly on the earth, and all the high hills under the whole heaven were covered. The waters prevailed fifteen cubits upward, and the mountains were covered.* [Gen 7:17-20]

This passage says that the depth of the waters was 15 cubits above the highest mountain peak, or about 22.5 feet using the standard 1.5 ft./cubit conversion. I suggest that this depth was not arbitrary, but that this probably places an upper limit on the height of the Nephilim at about 20 feet.

I looked into the subject of how body mass scales with height. Consider, for instance, that a typical 7 foot human is only about 16% taller than the average 6-foot man. But his weight will be about 36% greater. That is, body mass scales roughly with the square of height. Thus, a 12-foot tall hybrid, of otherwise typical human build, would probably weigh 800 pounds (i.e., height is 2x typical, and weight is therefore 2x2 = 4x typical). Similarly, an 18-foot hybrid would likely weigh about 1800 pounds (i.e., 3x typical height scales to 3x3 = 9x typical weight). If we can conceive a 25-foot hybrid, we're looking at almost 3500 pounds. Let's also consider how much weight a man can lift. Generally, trained power lifters can lift about 4 times their body weight. So, a power lifting athlete of 90kg (about 200 lbs.) can lift about 360kg (over 800 pounds). More typically, a non-athlete is going to be able to lift about his own body weight, but can carry no more than about a quarter of that while walking. However, the Nephilim were regarded for their great strength, so we can probably identify their abilities more closely with, and probably well exceeding, those of trained athletes. Why am I interested in this? Well, let's have a look at one account of giants in North America. The following is an excerpt from *The Life of Hon. William F. Cody, Known as Buffalo Bill, The Famous Hunter, Scout and Guide. An Autobiography*:

> *While we were in the sand-hills, scouting the Niobrara country, the Pawnee Indians brought into camp, one night, some very large bones, one of which a surgeon of the expedition pronounced to be the thigh-bone of a human being. The Indians claimed that the bones they had found were those of a person belonging to a race of people who a long time ago lived in this country. That there was once a race of men on the earth whose size was about three times that of an ordinary man, and they were so swift and powerful that they could run alongside of a buffalo, and taking the animal in one arm could tear off a leg and eat the meat as they walked. These giants denied the existence of a Great Spirit, and when they heard the thunder or saw the lightning they laughed at it and said that they were greater than either. This so displeased the Great Spirit that he caused a great rain-storm to come, and the water kept rising higher and higher so that it drove those proud and conceited giants from the low grounds to the hills, and thence to the mountains, but at last even the mountain tops were submerged, and then those mammoth men were all drowned. After the flood had subsided, the Great Spirit came to the conclusion that he had made man too large and powerful, and that he would therefore correct the mistake by creating a race of men of smaller size and less strength. This is the reason, say the Indians, that modern men are small and not like the*

giants of old, and they claim that this story is a matter of Indian history, which has been handed down among them from time immemorial.

As we had no wagons with us at the time this large and heavy bone was found, we were obliged to leave it. [Public domain]

This is an astounding account. This giant was about three times the height of an ordinary man. Adult American bison range in weight from about 800-2200 pounds. Given the height estimate already and using a 6-ft standard for comparison, we're looking at a humanoid weighing about 1800 pounds, and carrying a creature of roughly the same weight, while walking and eating it. This means that we are dealing with creatures of exceptional strength, their size notwithstanding, well above the normal laws of scaling. And this agrees with the general regard for their strength.

I'd like to go back for a moment to the ancient Assyrian petroglyphs depicting the angels, just as described in the Bible, particularly those pictured with the head of an eagle, wings, and the body of a man. Given that we have the story of the bones of giants, would not then angels have had to be there also? Figure 10 provides an artist's rendition of what is commonly referred to as the Native American "Eagle Dancer." What we see is an image that resembles the Assyrian petroglyphs in all respects other than the clothing. As to the purpose of this ritual dance, the following is an extract from kachinahouse.com's blog:

Eagles are the focus of many Native American legends and play a large role in many spiritually-based ceremonies among different tribes.
Native American tribes started preforming the "eagle dance" as they believed that the eagle could soar between heaven and earth because of how high it can fly. Native American tribes believed that eagles had supernatural powers; the ability to carry messages to the gods, and the ability to control weather such as rain. The eagle was considered powerful among tribes and was often admired and worshiped as a "god" would be. The eagle dance is performed when tribes seek help of a higher power or are in need of divine intervention. The tribes perform the dance in the hope of curing illness, asking for rain, winning a battle, and much more. [Reprinted with permission from kachinahouse.com]

Given that we have witness of both the bones of a giant and the history of the eagle dance with the associated supernatural aspirations, I believe that these evidences firmly support the theory of angels among the ancients in North America, and thus across the globe. These two examples independently support the postulate, but when considered together, the weight of the evidence is indeed greater than the sum of the parts.

*Figure 10: Sculpture of Native American "Eagle Dancer."
Image used by permission of the artist, Steve Streadbeck.*

Skeletal Remains of Giants and Elongated Skulls

Stephen Quayle's book, *Genesis 6 Giants*, documents myriad cases of not only ancient giants, but large men in modern times. Now, at some point we have to draw a distinction between abnormally large humans and genetically distinct giants. The line is not clear. There are many diagnosed cases of gigantism, an endocrine disorder of the pituitary gland wherein an overproduction of somatotropin (aka Human Growth Hormone, or simply GH or HGH) stimulates growth through an intermediary hormone called Insulin-like Growth Factor 1 ('IGF-1') produced by the liver. Overproduction of either of these can result in gigantism. This is so exceedingly rare that only about 100 cases have ever been documented. Acromegaly is a similar condition but its onset occurs at middle-age (mean age of diagnosed cases is mid-twenties), as contrasted with gigantism that occurs prior to fusion of the epiphyseal growth plates in the long bones of the body.

So, how large can humans with such endocrine disorders be? The largest ten cases on record are men with heights between 8' 1" and 8' 11". Thus, I think we'll refrain from the use of the term 'giant' in the context of angel-human hybrids as referring to anyone under 9' tall. Quayle's book documents many cases of people in the 7' and taller range, so I think we must reasonably disqualify virtually all cases under 9' in height as candidates for being first-generation Biblical (hybrid) giants. With this condition, the larger population of cases in Quayle's book are discounted...perhaps

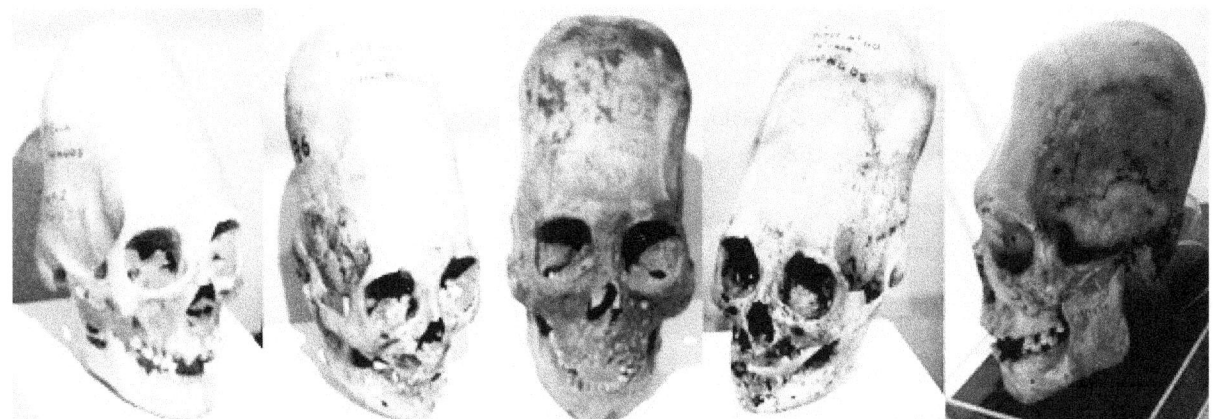

Figure 12: Elongated Skulls from Paracas Peru (Photo reprinted with permission from Brien Foerster.)

arbitrarily, but we needed to set a boundary somewhere. One other possibility to distinguish subspecies is to use the dentition; many of the giants' remains documented have "double rows of teeth." If we rule out those with the single row, normal to *Homo sapiens*, it provides a two-criteria qualification that would more certainly separate simple endocrine disorders from a more fundamental genetic distinction. There is a third criterion that might be applied, and this is that there are multiple accounts of giants as having six fingers. It remains unclear how we can apply all of these criteria, since the hybrids were described as being differentiated subspecies. So, we may not find evidence of hybrids with all three characteristics, and perhaps even pairs of these might provide a very limited number of documented cases.

In Figure 11 on page 91, we have a summary of some of the largest and well documented finds of humanoid remains. Again, the details of each of these cases can be found in Stephen Quayle's *Genesis 6 Giants*.

In Figure 12 you can see five "elongated skulls." Binding of the head in some cultures produces an elongation of the skull, but it does not increase the cranial volume. The skulls from Paracas have volumes about 20% larger than those of typical humans. In addition, the eye sockets are larger than those in humans, and the skulls lack the sagittal suture. One of these skulls was subjected to mitochondrial DNA (mtDNA) testing, and the results were definitely not human. Note that the full human genome is more than 3 billion base pairs, while mtDNA consists of less than 17,000 base pairs (approximately 0.0006%), so it provides a small but consistent subset of identifying genetic makeup.

Consider the shape of these skulls, and compare them with the sculpture (Figure 13a) of a "Daughter of Akhenaten" with a notably elongated head. The bust is dated to the 18th Dynasty, or about 1345 BC. Was this daughter of Akhenaten truly a demi-god…one of the Nephilim? Or was her head bound to produce the likeness of a demi-god? This would be just 100 years after the death of Joshua, and was neither the earliest nor the latest episode in the Biblical narrative involving the Nephilim. Thus, the period is consistent with the time that these hybrids were among us. And compare the images in Figures 12 and 13a with the Pharaonic headdress shown in Figure 13b. This piece is dated to "before 1862 BC" which would be just about 100 years after the dispersion of nations. There are certainly many images of Egyptian Pharaohs in which members of the general population are markedly smaller than the royals. Did the Pharaohs adopt such headwear to project the image of a god (Nephilim) once the true hybrids had been eliminated, thus to maintain the reverence and fear of the masses? Certainly the style lacks any practical design elements. And why did ancient cultures even begin the practice of head binding? What were they imitating…the awe and prominence of a god?

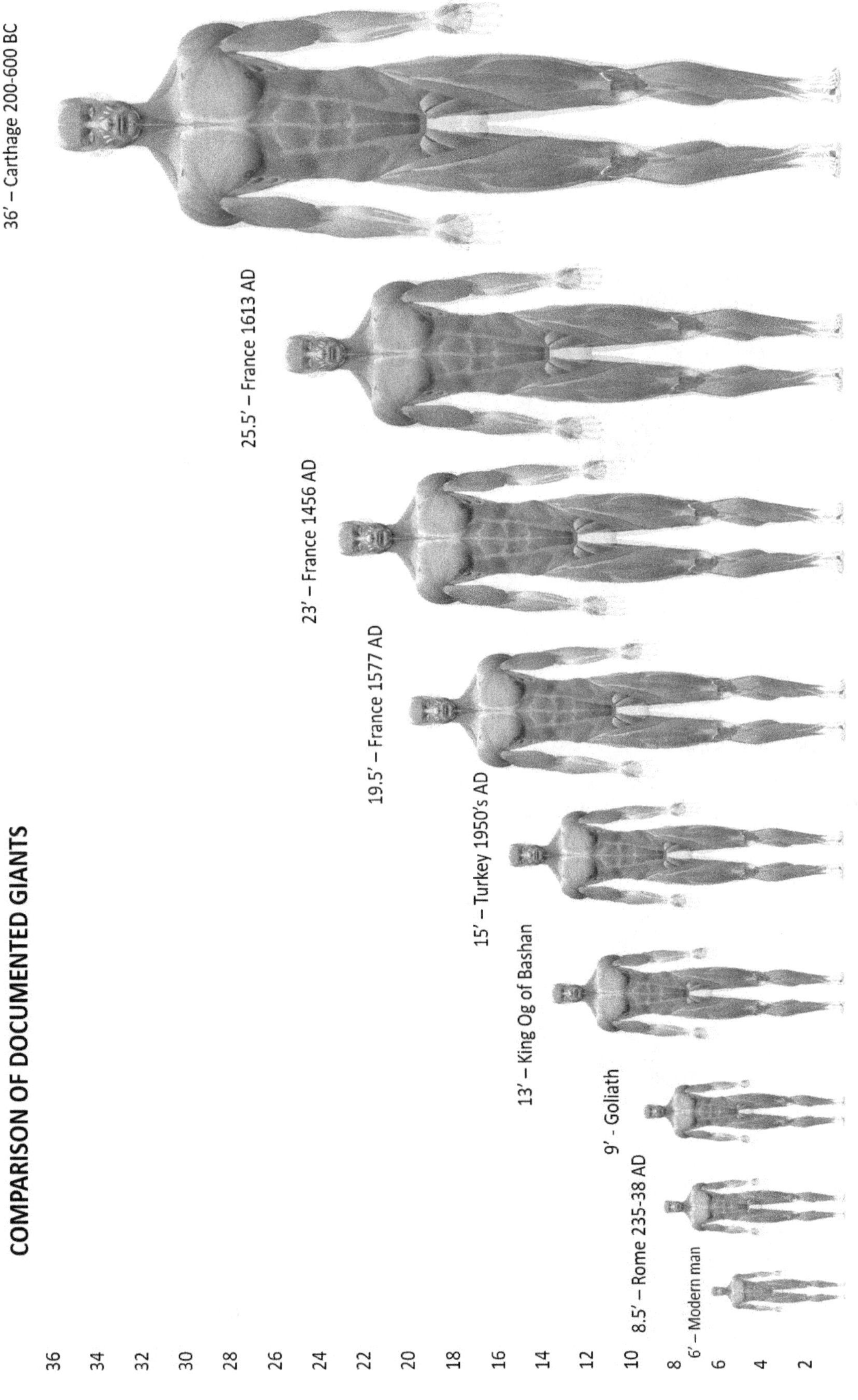
COMPARISON OF DOCUMENTED GIANTS
36' – Carthage 200-600 BC
25.5' – France 1613 AD
23' – France 1456 AD
19.5' – France 1577 AD
15' – Turkey 1950's AD
13' – King Og of Bashan
9' - Goliath
8.5' – Rome 235-38 AD
6' – Modern man
36
34
32
30
28
26
24
22
20
18
16
14
12
10
8
6
4
2

Figure 11: Comparison of Documented Giants

Figure 13a: Head of a Daughter of Akhenaten. Osama Shukir Muhammed Amin FRCP (Glasg), CC BY-SA 4.0 <https://creativecommons.org/licenses/by-sa/4.0>, via Wikimedia Commons

Figure 13b: Sculpture of Egyptian Pharaoh's head at The Louvre. By Celli07/shutterstock.com

Dinosaurs

Now, the giants were apparently eating the human inhabitants literally out of house and home. Given their size, they would have to consume many more calories than humans, in accordance with both their body mass and power. So while an average adult male human requires 1500-2000 Calories per day in sedentary occupations to maintain weight, an active, athletic counterpart could easily consume double that. Earlier, we estimated that an 18-foot hybrid would weigh about 1800 pounds. Typical bodybuilders consume about 45-50 Cal/kg or, 20-25 Cal/lb. Accounting for the increased body mass and strength of a hybrid giant, you're looking at perhaps 40-80,000 Calories per day to maintain fitness and health. Each of these creatures were probably consuming the equivalent intake of 25-30 men. So, a hundred hybrids would eat as much or more than 2500 ordinary men. It is easy to see how they could quickly consume crops and herds, ultimately turning to feeding on men...and each other.

The hybrids apparently learned from their fathers who "...*taught the mixture of animals of one species with the other....*" What on earth does this mean? Well, one theory is that this corruption of the natural order was done for a purpose. Consider the creatures we call dinosaurs (from Ancient Greek meaning 'fearsome reptile'). These creatures did not survive the great flood; apparently, none were on Noah's ark. Why? Because they were *not* God's creations; like the hybrid giants themselves, these were abominations. And consider that they were created for a purpose: giant men need giant creatures to sustain their dietary needs. So, I submit that they created these hybrid creatures, cross-breeding reptiles with birds and mammals. While we may have regarded this as beyond conception when I was young (Watson and Crick had their work on the structure of DNA published just a year before I was born, notwithstanding the fact that they stole the data for their work from Rosalind Franklin, but that's another story). And today, only 60-some years later, we are splicing genes and creating new "genetically modified organisms" ("GMOs" on your grocery labels), hybrid vegetables and plants, and God only knows what else they're working on that we don't know about. We know that they are cloning animals, but what about creating hybrids? Who knows what we'll be able to accomplish in the next 20 or 30 years, but it is not beyond comprehension that we may once again have dinosaurs or even giants among us. So, we can thus account not only for the extinction of dinosaurs, but also their origin.

As an addendum on the subject of genetic engineering, let's turn to the Biblical Book of Revelation. In chapter 9, John writes about the so-called "fifth trumpet judgment," which is a plague of locusts from the bottomless pit (Tartarus). These creatures torture all of mankind for a period of five months. In vv7-10, we are given a description of these hybrid entities:

The shape of the locusts was like horses prepared for battle. On their heads were crowns of something like gold, and their faces were like the faces of men. They had hair like women's hair, and their teeth were like lions' teeth. And they had breastplates like breastplates of iron, and the sound of their wings was like the sound of chariots with many horses running into battle. They had tails like scorpions, and there were stings in their tails. Their power was to hurt men five months.

Many are dismissive of the reality of John's depiction of the end times because of passages such as this, which bear no resemblance to anything we recognize today. Whether these creatures are a creation of God or of the fallen angels is not clear. However, the fallen angels performed genetic engineering once before, so there is no reason to doubt that they could and would undertake such again in the last days. While to many this passage is taken as strictly symbolic, I believe we have evidence and precedence that would lead us to conclude that this is more likely a factual account. While it is unquestionably conceivable that mankind could produce an abomination of nature such as this in another 20-30 years, I find this an unlikely origin because they emerge from the bottomless pit.

Figure 14: Kitakyushu Museum of Natural History and Human History. By kitwam/shutterstock.com.

CHAPTER 8: Egypt and the Pyramids

Could the angels or their offspring have been responsible for construction of the pyramids in Egypt…and those on other continents? The angels themselves are beings of indescribable power and abilities, beyond our conceptions of anything familiar. We know not the limits of their power, but we also know that the Nephilim were of great strength. While their hybridization rendered them lesser in power, abilities, or intellect than their angelic fathers, they were nonetheless beings physically far superior to *Homo sapiens*.

Though the most typical stones used in the construction of the great pyramid at Giza weigh about 2-3 tons, the largest are about 80 tons. Some are granite and others are limestone. All granite stones

Figure 15: Mass of Stones Comprising the Great Pyramid at Giza.
By Victor Jiang/shutterstock.com

were transported to Giza from Aswan (that's over 500 miles south, for the kids at home). And estimates put the number of these stones between 2.5 and 3 million. Just for perspective, consider the following quote from the book *Unwrapping the Pharaohs* (by Down & Ashton, ©2009, reprinted with permission from Master Books Publishing):

> *If this mass of stone was cut into cubes about a foot square (30 cm x 30 cm x 30 cm) in size and placed side by side around the coast of Australia, only half the stones would be used. There would be enough left over to circle the borders of the United States of America.*

Try to get your head around that. That task is neither small nor simple even with our modern technologies: to quarry, cut to precise size, transport, and set such massive limestone and granite blocks.

To give you some conception of the size for the largest stones, the density of granite is about 170 pounds per cubic foot. 80 tons (x2000 lbs. per ton) = 160,000 pounds. Dividing this by the density gives us nearly 1000 cubic feet. If in the form of a cube, this would be 10' H x 10' W x 10' L. That's about the size of a typical bedroom, or three or more typical, full sized automobiles. If you were to position men around the perimeter of such a stone, shoulder to shoulder, you might be able to accommodate twenty men. And if each man could lift twice his weight (not uncommon even among amateur athletes), at a nominal 400 pounds per man times twenty yields 8,000 pounds. *Each such stone weighed twenty times this amount.*

Even using logs on which to roll it, you still have to push (or float) each one 500 miles. Well, at least it is a slight downhill grade from Aswan to Giza. And this could work for the first tier of stones, but what about the higher tiers? For the second tier, you'd have to lift each stone 8-10'; for the third tier, 16-20', and so on.

So, what if, instead of men, we place Nephilim of, say, 18' in height around the block. Owing to their larger size, we may only be able to fit ten such giants around the block. And let's further assume that each one can lift four times his weight (still only a direct scaling based on human performance of typical weightlifters). So with each hybrid able to lift perhaps 8,000 pounds, ten such beings could lift 80,000 pounds. While the stone is still twice the weight they might lift, they would certainly be able to manipulate it much more easily. If we turn their bodies sideways to the stone, and place beams across the width, we might fit the twenty hybrids we need to actually lift and carry an eighty ton stone.

Now Josephus provides an interesting passage. Speaking of Seth's descendants, he says:

> *They were also the inventors of that peculiar sort of wisdom which is concerned with the heavenly bodies, and their order. And that their inventions might not be lost before they were sufficiently known, upon Adam's prediction that the world was to be destroyed at one time by the force of fire, and another time by the violence and quantity of water, they made two pillars; the one of brick, the other of stone: they inscribed their discoveries on them both, that in case the pillar of brick should be destroyed by the flood, the pillar of stone might remain, and exhibit those discoveries to mankind; and also inform them that there was another pillar of brick erected by them. Now this remains in the land of Siriad to this day.* [Ant. I:II:3]

In the following paragraph, Josephus goes on to tell how the posterity of Seth became perverted by the angels' accompaniment with women and begat sons that proved unjust.

At http://www.squirespublishing.co.uk/files/syriad.htm you can find a short article by Alexander Winslow entitled *"The Pillar in the land of Siriad."* In the article, Winslow starts by identifying the land of Siriad as Egypt. He goes on to state that Whiston's English translation (which I also used for this book) was based on a Latin translation from the original Greek. With Latin a far less precise language than Greek, the word used for the pillars was *columna*, although Winslow proposes that the original Greek word could have likely been *pyramos*. He then provides evidence not only that it was the descendants of Seth in Egypt that built the pyramids *before the deluge*, but that astronomical information was indeed inscribed on the casing stones that were stripped away long ago for use in the construction of mosques.

So, incorporating this account with what we have already proposed, we have a group of angels descending to the earth with specific knowledge that they imparted to mankind, and that their offspring built the pyramids to carry the information through the flood. It is intriguing to consider that perhaps magic spells may have also been inscribed here, and the secrets thereon removed and carried off after the deluge.

So, just the bulk movement of the stone blocks is a feat that is still veiled in mystery. But what of the quarrying and fitting of the stones? Yet another unanswered mystery, unless we acknowledge that ancient aliens from heaven and their offspring were the architects and builders.

Figure 16: Pyramids at Giza. By WitR/shutterstock.com.

Now we find the remains of massive pyramidal structures on several (arguably every) inhabited continent. In Egypt, we see the most famous grouping of these megalithic structures at Giza. It is generally assumed that the smaller, stepped pyramids were built first, perhaps as models or early attempts. Considering that if angels were directing the construction or actually building the pyramids themselves, they would not need to practice. With their unique and complete knowledge of all the sciences and thus engineering, they could go directly from concept to completed project without error. Their geometry would be perfect; their cuts would be precise; their placement would be faultless. And the structures would last for millennia because they are constructed of stone, an exceedingly durable material…even durable enough to survive a global flood. In modern times, we might use concrete and steel, but even concrete has a life expectancy of less than 100 years. Over the millennia, such would crack and crumble…but not so with stone. And the granite and limestone blocks were cased with a beautiful, _engineered_ limestone aggregate (yes, man-made; not natural by any means). In a 2007 article provided to LiveScience in partnership with the National Science Foundation entitled *The Surprising Truth About How the Great Pyramids Were Built*, the authors (Sheila Berninger & Dorilona Rose) discuss the foundational work done by Joseph Davidovits, Director of the Geopolymer Institute in St. Quentin, France. He discovered that the casing stones were cast using a composite of limestone, clay, lime, and water. The article goes on to describe another investigation undertaken two decades after the work of Davidovits, led by Michel Barsoum from Drexel University's Department of Materials Science and Engineering. The second investigation took some five years and ended up supporting Davdovits' findings with the aid of modern electron microscopy. Barsoum also looked into the adhesive used between the limestone casing stones and discovered another engineered material that is still holding up after nearly 4,500 years. The article states that the cement consists of either silica (quartz) or another silicate mineral.

In his book *The Great Pyramid Decoded: God's Stone Witness* (©1971), author E. Raymond Capt provides the following observations about the casing stones at Giza made by Colonel Howard Vyse, during an 1837 expedition to the site:

The few casing stones found "in situ" by Colonel Howard Vyse, Egyptologist, in 1837, made it possible to determine the original baseline of the structure and also the exact angle of its sloping sides.

The casing stones consist of dense, white, marble-like limestone and exhibit an amount of accuracy in fitting that equals the most modern optician's work. The joints, with an area of some 35 square feet each, are not thicker than aluminum foil; yet they include between the polished surfaces, an extraordinarily thin film of white cement.

Colonel H. Vyse, speaking of the cement says, "...such is the tenacity of this cement...that a fragment of a stone that has been destroyed remains firmly fixed in its original alignment, notwithstanding the lapse of time and the violence to which it has been exposed." Modern chemists have analyzed this cement but have been unable to compound one of such fineness and tenacity as that exhibited in the Great Pyramid.

Petrie in his account of these stones records, "The mean thickness of the joints is one-fiftieth part of an inch; and the mean variation of the cutting of the stone from a straight line, and from the true square, is but one-hundredth part of an inch in the length of 75 inches up the face." That they were able to maintain these tolerances despite the area and the weight of the stones moved – some 16 to 20 tons each – is seemingly almost impossible. This feat was duplicated in all the casing stones, which were numbered approximately 144,000. [p18, reprinted with permission from Artisan Publishers]

What the chemists of the 19th century could not do, Barsoum resolved in the 21st century. As for the precision of the squareness, the calculation yields a precision of less than 30 seconds of arc (i.e., one half of one minute of one degree…that is, <1 part in 10,000). It remains truly incredulous that the ancients could have achieved this with simple hand tools and crude instruments.

If you can imagine each side of this monument at about 5 acres in size, of a highly polished white stone, reflecting the impinging sunlight so brightly that it could be seen not only from the furthest horizon, but undoubtedly from the moon. I would venture to say that such precision would prove exceedingly difficult even today.

So, if the Great Pyramid and its two sisters were architected and built by the angels and Nephilim, what are the smaller, stepped pyramids? I postulate that these were actually built later than the larger, ideal pyramids, and that these are nothing more than crude attempts by the Mesraites (later, Egyptians), then unaided by hybrid giants or angels, to copy what was already there, with lesser, imperfect understanding, and lesser means to accomplish the tasks. Once the angels were accursed and disembodied, and the Nephilim defeated and (nearly) annihilated by the Israelites, the Egyptians were left only with the monuments and the absence of memory as to what happened. Although, it is possible that an oral history of the origins of the pyramids was passed down through Noah.

So why were the pyramids and other megalithic structures built by or through the guidance of the angels? One possibility is that it was a matter of self-aggrandizement: they wanted to give the men a place to worship the angels themselves and their demigod offspring. They regarded themselves as veritable gods among the mortals. Power corrupts, and absolute power corrupts absolutely. The pyramids would have been a beacon stretching hundreds of miles to draw men close to worship them. Another viable possibility, however, is that it was an educational tool provided for men, encoding the various mathematical, chronological, geographical, and astronomical information in a form not readily lost, and durable enough to last the entire span of world history. I'll provide further details about the information encoded a little ahead.

In the meantime, ponder for a moment: 18 leaders of ten, dividing six continents among themselves…that's three (archangels) per continent. How many ideal pyramids do we have at Giza…yes, three: one greater, and two lesser. Now, this is not to say that these angels had any evil intent, beyond pride. I abide by my opinion that these angels were sent to edify men and fell victim to their own desires. But that does not mean that they were above sinning. Clearly they sinned, and they were just as clearly punished for their sin, being now disembodied angels…that is, demons.

An interesting consideration about the great pyramid at Giza is the proposed date of construction. The dates vary somewhat, of course, as at the time of construction years were not consistently recorded outside of the Biblical record. However, that said, the accepted dates are around 2560 BC. Subtracting this from 3944, this would be 1384 AM…about 270 years *before* the global deluge of 1656 AM. Now God announced His intent to flood the globe 120 years before it occurred, and the Nephilim were already creating havoc by that time. So the fall of angels would have been sometime earlier. Certainly, with the assessed capabilities of the Nephilim and the angels themselves, it is not unreasonable that 150 years would be more than adequate for them to construct these megalithic monuments. As to the secular histories documenting the construction of the pyramids in the postdiluvian era around the time of the Hyksos kings, I suspect that the pyramids to which such refer are the inferior, stepped pyramids.

In his book *The Great Pyramid Decoded* (©1971), E. Raymond Capt presents an historical record regarding the orientation of the monument. He says, *"That the Architect knew where to find the poles of the earth is evidenced by the high degree of accuracy in orienting the building true north. Modern man's best effort, the Paris Observatory, is six minutes of a degree off true north. The Great Pyramid today is only off three minutes and that after 4200 years, due mainly to subsidence."*

If you are not already aware, the great pyramid at Giza is not of arbitrary dimensions. Myriad articles, websites, and books are devoted to this very subject, and it is thus a challenge to try to condense all that the great pyramid represents into a single chapter. Nevertheless, I attempt to provide the briefest overview herein.

The Great Pyramid at Giza, also designated Khafre, incorporates mathematical ratios such as Phi and Pi. Phi is the so-called "Golden Ratio," which is a unique number calculated from an equation

$$\frac{a+b}{a} = \frac{a}{b} \stackrel{def}{=} \varphi$$

Solving: $(a+b)b = a^2$

$a^2 - ab - b^2 = 0$

Dividing by b^2: $a^2/b^2 - ab/b^2 - b^2/b^2 = 0$

$(a/b)^2 - a/b - 1 = 0$

Since $\varphi = a/b$: $\varphi^2 - \varphi - 1 = 0$

By the quadratic formula, $\varphi = \frac{1+\sqrt{1+4}}{2}$ = 1.6180339... (irrational)

Figure 17: The Golden Ratio

that relates the lengths of two segments, as shown in Figure 17. And Pi, of course, is the more commonly recognized constant that is the ratio of the circumference of any circle to its diameter (c = πd) with and approximate value of 3.1415928....

We can create a rectangle of golden ratio dimension by adding sides of height 'a' to the lines shown in Figure 17, as in Figure 18. Now, simply adding a diagonal line through the golden rectangle, we divide it into two golden triangles.

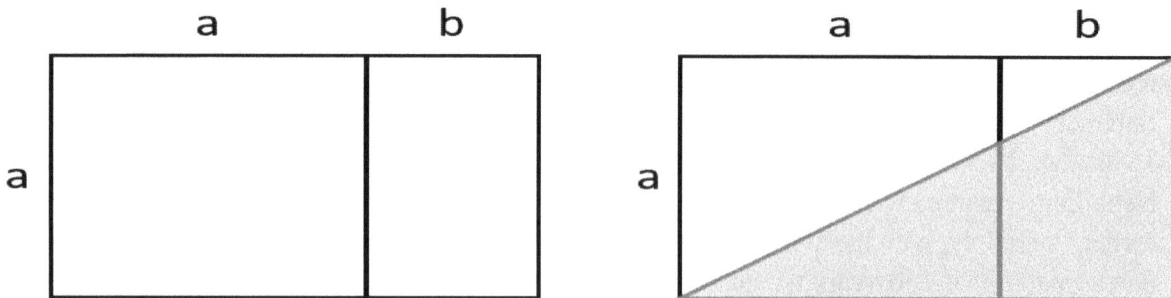

Figure 18: Golden Rectangle and Golden Triangle

So, the casing stones on the faces of the great pyramid have been mostly removed by later Egyptian monarchs and vandals over the ages. But, using the original height of the Great Pyramid with the casing (481 ft.), and divide this by half the width of the pyramid's base (756 ft.), we have 481/378 = 1.2724868…. If we square this number, it is 1.619… compared with the 1.618… or accurate to less than 0.1%. See Figure 19.

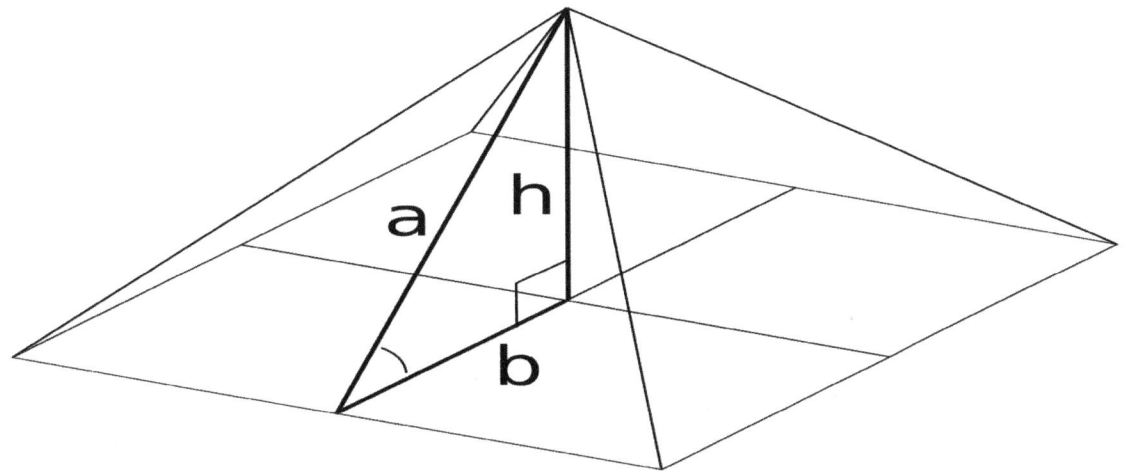

Figure 19: The Great Pyramid and the Golden Ratio (Wikipedia.com)
If b = 1, a = φ, and h = √φ.

Now if we take the finished (i.e., with the facing stones) base dimension of the pyramid to be 756 ft. and the original finished height (presently destroyed) to be 481 ft., then the circumference of the base would be 4x756 = 3024 ft. Dividing this by the height of 481 ft. we get approximately 6.2869023. Dividing this by 2 we get 3.14345…. This value is within the true value of Pi with accuracy again less than 0.1%.

The mathematical constant e, also called Euler's number (after the 18th century Swiss mathematician Leonhard Euler), is also encoded within the geometry of the great pyramid. The number e can be expressed as the sum of an infinite series, as follows:

$$e = \sum_{n=0}^{\infty} \frac{1}{n!} = 1/1 + 1/1 + 1/2 + 1/6 + 1/24 + \ldots$$

It is an irrational number, but has an approximate value of 2.71828. This number e is important in differential and integral calculus as the base for a logarithm. Specifically, you are probably familiar with base 10 powers: $10^0 = 1$, $10^1 = 10$, $10^2 = 10 \times 10 = 100$, $10^3 = 10 \times 10 \times 10 = 1000$, etc. The inverse function of this exponential function $f(x) = 10^x$, is the logarithm, expressed mathematically as $f(x) = \log_{10}(x)$, where the number 10 denotes the base. Thus, $\log_{10}(1) = 0$, $\log_{10}(10) = 1$, $\log_{10}(100) = 2$, $\log_{10}(1000) = 3$, etc. The interesting thing about the number e is that when it is the base for an exponential function (i.e., $f(x) = e^x$), the function is its own derivative. This means that the slope of the line mathematically tangent to the graph of the function at any given point on the graph is given by the value of function itself. See the graphic illustration in Figure 20.

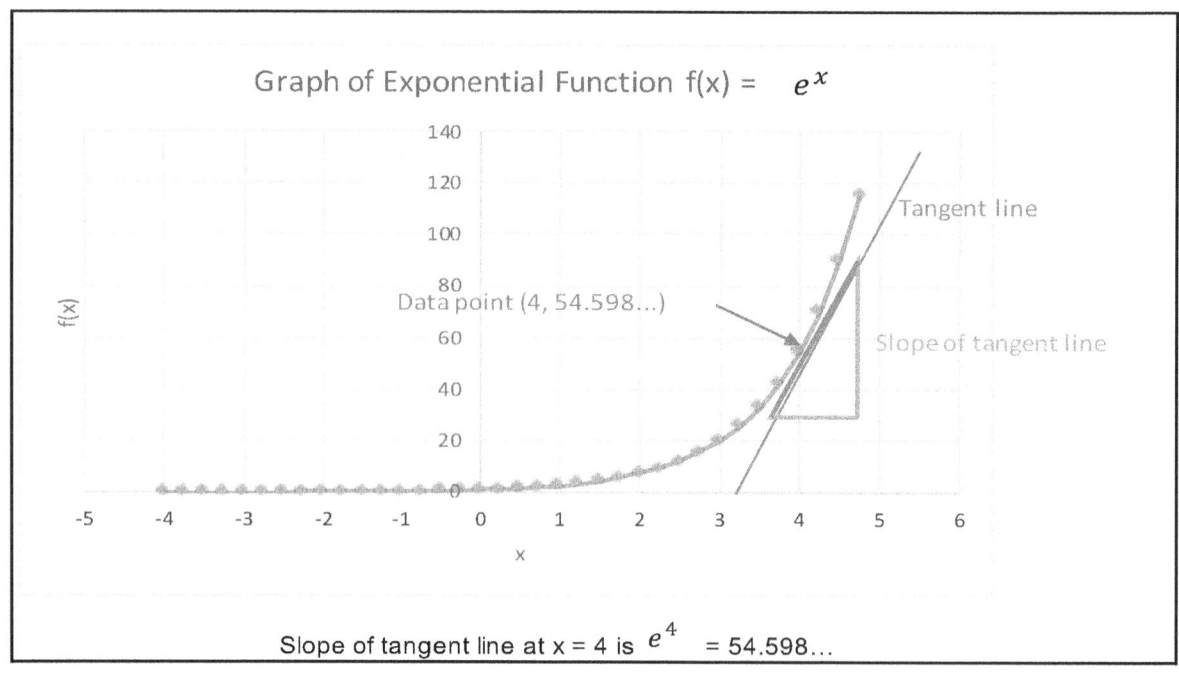

Figure 20: Exponential Function and Tangent Line at x=4

The number e is also encoded in the dimensions of the great pyramid. The angle that the faces of the pyramid make with respect to the horizontal plane is 51° 51' 00". Converting this expression from degrees-minutes-seconds to decimal it is 51.85°. Using the right-triangle geometry of the faces and base presented earlier, the complementary angle of this golden triangle is 38.15°, found at the apex of the pyramid. If we take the ratio of these two angles we have 51.85/38.15 = 1.359109…. Twice this is 2.71821… or Euler's number e precise to within less than 0.0025%, or less than 1 part in 40,000. Coincidence? I consider it highly unlikely.

While it is amazing that three mathematical constants could be so accurately encoded in a single geometric figure, we have not even addressed the geographical or astronomical alignments, nor even the architecture of the hidden passages. As previously stated, there are ample books and articles you can find on the internet that delve more completely into this enigma. I would challenge any twenty-first century architect to develop such a monument that would convey so much and survive so long.

The First Rabbit Hole

Whether or not the Khufu pyramid is antediluvian, if Egypt was indeed founded by Ham's son Mizraim, then the nation itself must be postdiluvian and cannot be older than 1948 BC; and we thus have a conundrum: the succession of Egyptian dynasties, as widely accepted today, appear to provide a (presumably) continuous chain of reigns from about 3150 BC to the Ptolemaic dynasty, following the death of Alexander the Great, right up to the first century BC. After Alexander, the Egyptian dynasties ceased and we have fairly reliable, modern histories from his death in the fourth century BC forward. If the accepted sequence of the 31 pre-Alexandrian dynasties is correct, we have no account therein of a global flood, much less the colossal consequences of this annihilation to any population and Pharaonic continuity. The entire culture would have been destroyed, with the identities of the pre-flood peoples completely distinct from the identity and culture of the post-flood inhabitants. While most modern historians resolve this dilemma by simply discarding the long accepted truth of a global flood, this is neither a just method nor a fully defensible conclusion. It is, however, convenient, and suits the further denial of the truth of Scripture by many modern teachers.

The process of writing a book is much more involved than I had originally imagined. While anyone can simply offer opinions unsupported, and they may find agreement among the like-minded, the critics will use the lack of evidence to impugn the hypothesis (and its author), even if such opinions are valid. I realize that if I'm going to disrupt accepted opinion with contrary and controversial ideas, I must find the evidence, examine it openly, present it, and even expose any deficiencies. If I fail in this, then my work is without merit, and I'm nothing short of another practitioner in pseudoscience, whom I despise. Thus, as I continue to discover the shortcomings in my education, I must address each through research and study. It seems lately that I find myself buying a book a week so that I can research such subjects as the history of Egypt now at hand. This is one of many such rabbit holes into which I've had to descend to determine if my hypotheses are defensible. Such is the case here: can I find a reasoned, rational sequence of the Egyptian dynasties that results in a strictly postdiluvian history?

Having examined the various accounts of the sequence of pharaohs and dynasties, the initial reaction was that I must discover grounds to compress the accepted, dynastic timeline. Though it sounds like an arbitrary strategy, it is a valid means that others have used to accomplish such compressions. How do we tactically proceed? Elimination of Pharaohs whose very existence is in question is one. Secondly, we have dynasties that may not be sequential, but rather concurrent. Having looked at the various regnal seats, I thought it most probable that some of the dynasties were concurrent. This idea is not as far-fetched as it might sound, nor is it even a novel conception. Having been confronted with the same discrepancy between the Biblical account and profane histories, I had to choose; and for me the selection was simple. However, that does not mean that I simply cast aside the more broadly accepted history and ignore the factual elements thereof. Ultimately, the discrepancies need to be resolved such that the two are coherent. Thus, my investigation begins.

First, I discovered that, like some of the Biblical chronology, the ancient history of Egypt is not at all fully documented, nor well understood. Newton well appreciated this issue; in Chapter II of his *Chronology* (the chapter entitled *Of the Empire of Egypt*), he says the following:

> *The Egyptians anciently boasted of a very great and lasting empire under their Kings Ammon, Osiris, Bacchus, Sesostris, Hercules, Memnon, &c. reaching eastward to the Indies, and westward to the Atlantic Ocean; and out of vanity have made this monarchy some thousands of years older than the world: let us now try to rectify the Chronology of Egypt; by comparing the affairs of Egypt with the synchronizing affairs of the Greeks and Hebrews.* [Sir Isaac Newton, *The Chronology of Ancient Kings Amended, A Short Chronicle from the first Memory of Things in Europe,* 1728; public domain]

What remains largely true even since Newton's time is that what we have for Egyptian history is still a patchwork of archaeological evidence, along with often conflicting second or third-hand accounts that have been pieced together, and for lack of ingenuity or need to find a better construct, arranged in a more or less straight timeline.

Gerard Gertoux is a French engineer, professor, and modern-day chronologist who has published multiple papers and books on chronologies of various, ancient historical eras. In his paper entitled "*Basic Astronomy for Historians to Get a Chronology*," Gertoux wrote the following:

> *Anyone interested in history has been able to see that every Egyptologist has their own chronology (and consequently their own truth about history) and all the history books just mention in their introduction that some dates are controversial and in order to solve this crucial problem they argue that most academic historians have used the "Middle Chronology" as reference (it's magic), because the truth always belongs to the majority in a democracy. How can one explain this anomaly? Academic historians claim that chronology is a complex science and historical documents are difficult to interpret. These two lame excuses are false. In fact the primary purpose of academic historians is to validate and to spread an official history aimed at magnify (sic) the national novel of their country (it's a part of the process called "manufacturing consent"). The official history is that of the winner (for every country) and the vanquished are always pictured as barbarians, unworthy of owning their own country such as the American Indians, the Palestinians in the West Bank, the Armenians in Turkey, etc. The only history that most academic historians are really seeking to promote is their own history (their* cursus honorum*), not the truth. The criticizing of ones colleagues is not very polite and it gets you immediately blacklisted, as was already the case for Herodotus (until today among Egyptologists!), but that's life (Luke 6:26).*

One facet about the commonly-accepted, linear construction that struck me particularly is that the seats of reign for the various dynasties were not all the same; we find that Pharaohs ruled from Thinnes (dynasties I & II), Memphis (dynasties II- VIII, XIX, & XXV), Heracleopolis Magna (dynasties IX, X, & XXIII), Thebes (dynasties XI, XVI, XVII, XVIII, XIX, & XXIII), Itjtawy (dynasties XII & XIII), Avaris (dynasty XV), Amarna (dynasty XVIII), Pi-Ramesses (dynasties XIX & XX), Tanis (dynasties XXI & XXII), Bubastis (dynasty XXII), Hermopolis (dynasty XXIII), Sais (dynasties XXIV, XXVI, & XXVIII), Babylon (dynasties XXVII & XXXI), Mendes (dynasty XXIX), and Sebennytos (dynasty XXX).

One scenario might be that the rulers moved the seat of power with episodic cause. However, it is an established fact that Egypt was not always a unified entity. In fact, Isaac Newton addresses this directly in his *Chronology*. Speaking of the period of the Shepherd Kings (i.e., the Hyksos Dynasty), he says:

> *The upper parts of Egypt were in those days under many Kings, Reigning at Coptos, Thebes, This, Elephantis, and other Places, which by conquering one another grew by degrees into one Kingdom, over which Misphragmuthosis Reigned in the days of Eli.* [Sir Isaac Newton, *The Chronology of Ancient Kings Amended, A Short Chronicle from the first Memory of Things in Europe*, 1728; public domain]

Misphragmuthosis (aka, Thutmose I and Aliphragmuthosis) was a Pharaoh of the 18th dynasty. The consequential implication is that the first 17 dynasties (not to mention any pre-dynastic kings) were rulers of smaller regions later comprising the nation we now know as Egypt. Fourth century historian Eusebius of Caesarea apparently had a similar observation regarding Manetho's account of the Pharonic dynasties when he wrote the following in his work *Chronicon*:

And now it is right and fitting for us to add to this Manetho's account of the Egyptians, which seems to be a reliable history.

From the Egyptian records of Manetho, who composed in three books commentaries about the gods, demi-gods, spirits, and the mortal kings who ruled over the Egyptians, up until the time of Dareius the king of the Persians.

The first man amongst the Egyptians was Hephaestus, who discovered fire for them; he was the father of Sol [the Sun]. After him came [(?)Agathodaemon; then] Cronus; then Osiris; then Typhon the brother of Osiris; and then Horus the son of Osiris and Isis. These were the first rulers of the Egyptians. After them, one king succeeded another until the time of Bidis, for a total of 13,900 years - calculated by lunar years, which lasted for 30 days. That is the period which we now call a month, but the men of that time called it a year.

After the gods, a race of demi-gods ruled for 1,255 years. After them, other kings ruled [the country] for 1,817 years. After them, 30 kings from Memphis [ruled] for 1,790 years; and then another ten kings from Thinis ruled for 350 years. And then the shades and demi-gods were kings, for 5,813 years. The total for all of these is 11,000 years - which are lunar years, or months.

The total time, which the Egyptians assign to the gods and demi-gods and spirits is 24,900 lunar years - which is the equivalent of 2,206 solar years. If you compare this figure with the chronology of the Hebrews, you will find almost the same number of years. For Aegyptus is called Mizraim by the Hebrews; and he was born many years after the time of the flood. **It was after the time of the flood that Ham the son of Noah became the father of Mizraim, who was also called Aegyptus; and when the nations were scattered around the earth, Mizraim set off for Egypt to live there.** *According to the Hebrews, there were 2,242 years in all from Adam until the flood.*

So let the Egyptians boast of their antiquity, in the ancient times which preceded the flood. They say that they had some gods, demi-gods and shades. If the years which are recorded by the Hebrews are converted to months, the total is over 20,000 lunar years, so that there are about the same number of months as are contained in the years recorded by the Hebrews, when we count the years from the first-born man up until Mizraim. Mizraim was the patriarch of the Egyptians, and the first dynasty of the Egyptians was descended from him.

But if, even so, the number of years is found to be too large, then we must investigate the reason for this. **Perhaps it happened that there were many kings in Egypt at the same time. They say that some of them were kings of Thinis, some of Memphis, some of Sais, and some of Ethiopia; and there were yet others in other places. And as it seems that these dynasties ruled each in its own (?) nome, it is very unlikely that they ruled in succession to each other. Rather, some of them ruled in one place, and others in another place. Therefore the increase in the number of years can be explained in that way.** *But we will leave this matter, and proceed to the details of the chronology of the Egyptians.* [Eusebius, *Chronicon*, Vol I, c325 AD, English translation of the Latin translation of the Armenian translation from the original Greek; public domain; emphasis mine]

While the concluding paragraph of this extract is the pertinent one to the subject matter at hand, it is interesting to see that gods and demi-gods were believed to have ruled in Egypt before men. I suspect that the most ancient Egyptian records blend and corrupt the antediluvian history regarding the angels (gods), the Nephilim (demi-gods), and disembodied angels (shades) with the account starting with Mizraim after the confusion of languages at Babel.

Given that Misphragmuthosis is a known alias for Thutmose I, and that Thutmose I was part of the 18th dynasty, we can deduce directly that several of the first 17 dynasties were concurrent with one or more of the others, in the various regions of Egypt. Unfortunately, I think Newton misses the mark in his comment regarding "the days of Eli," as Thutmose I is reasonably identifiable as the Pharaoh of the Exodus. His reign is commonly accepted as c1504 -1492 BC. Since the Exodus of the Hebrews from Egypt occurred in 1496 BC, this coincides nearly perfectly with Thutmose I's reign. Eli died about 400 years later in the year 1105 BC. Josephus confirms Thutmose as the Pharaoh of the Exodus, stating:

> *When this people or shepherds were gone out of Egypt to Jerusalem, Tethmosis the king of Egypt, who drove them out, reigned afterward twenty five years and four months, and then died; after him his son Chebron took the kingdom for thirteen years;....* [Flavius Josephus, *Against Apion*, Book I, Ch. 15]

I included the latter clause from Josephus to be clear so as not to confuse this Tethmosis (i.e., Thutmose I, the third Pharaoh of the 18th dynasty) with any of the other Pharaohs also taking the name Thutmose. Thus, we have a synchronizing data point in the timeline that aligns the Biblical record with the secular. Again, the Exodus occurs at the end of the 15th dynasty (Hyksos), which would thus be concurrent with the 18th (Thutmosid) dynasty.

It was at the same time both a surprise and a consolation to me that Josephus' account turns out to be in agreement with the most widely accepted chronology of Egyptian rule from the Ptolemaic dynasty all the way back to the early 18th dynasty. Perhaps I should not have been so surprised, as the more recent dynasties are probably better documented and understood.

What we seek here is a realignment within the first 17 dynasties such that they do not extend earlier than the global deluge of Genesis. The balance of dynasties might also be scrutinized for the various seats of power to determine if they also are candidates for such realignment. I do not pretend to know enough about Egyptian history to undertake this without great reservation. But I will attempt to lay out evidence from the various accounts I've reviewed to see if I can indeed find viable, alternate timelines.

Now, as a rabbit hole within a rabbit hole, some have hypothesized that a vizier of Sestrosis I of the twelfth dynasty is identifiable as Joseph, though the implication is associative, by description of his eminence, rather than nominative. Sestrosis I reigned c1971-1926 BC, and the accepted reign for Thutmose I is c1503-1493 BC. If the hypothesis is correct, Joseph becomes vizier sometime during the reign of Sestrosis I…let's say 1930 BC. If we add 430 years to this (the Biblical span of the subjection of the Israelites "in a country not their own"), we find ourselves right in the reign of Thutmose I (1500 BC)! While this would seem a very gratifying and substantiating calculation, it is not in alignment with the true Biblical account, for the Biblical account only has the Israelites in Egypt for 210 years. The other 220 years were spent in Canaan. This is only clearly stated in the Septuagint translation (LXX) and the Samaritan Pentateuch, and missing from other manuscripts, where in Exo 12:40 (LXX) it says, *"And the sojourning of the children of Israel, while they sojourned in the land of Egypt and the land of Chanaan, four hundred and thirty years."* Thus, I must dismiss this hypothesis which, while compelling, is so speciously.

If we work the math the other way, let's see where that leads. We'll start with Thutmose I in the year of the Exodus at 1496 BC, and subtract 210 years. That takes us to 1706 BC. This would be the year that Jacob and family come to Egypt from Canaan, which is the ninth year of Joseph's service as vizier. Amazingly, the accepted years of Salatis' reign are c1715 - c1702 BC, first Pharaoh of the Hyksos dynasty in Avaris, in Goshen. This is the land that Pharaoh gave to Jacob and his family. So, which Pharaoh reigned in Egypt, and from what city, when Salatis reigned in Avaris? The conventional chronology of Egypt would put us somewhere in the 12th or 13th dynasties. However, given that compression in this range is necessary, there are other candidates. As an example, Donovan Courville, a twentieth century college professor with his PhD in chemistry and emeritus professor of biochemistry at the Loma Linda University School of Medicine, maintained an interest in Egyptology and Biblical chronology. In 1971 he published a book entitled *The Exodus Problem and Its Ramifications: A Critical Examination of the Chronological Relationships between Israel and the Contemporary Peoples of Antiquity*. In his book he proposes an alternative arrangement of the Egyptian dynasties wherein several of the dynasties are concurrent (see chart in Figure 21). While I

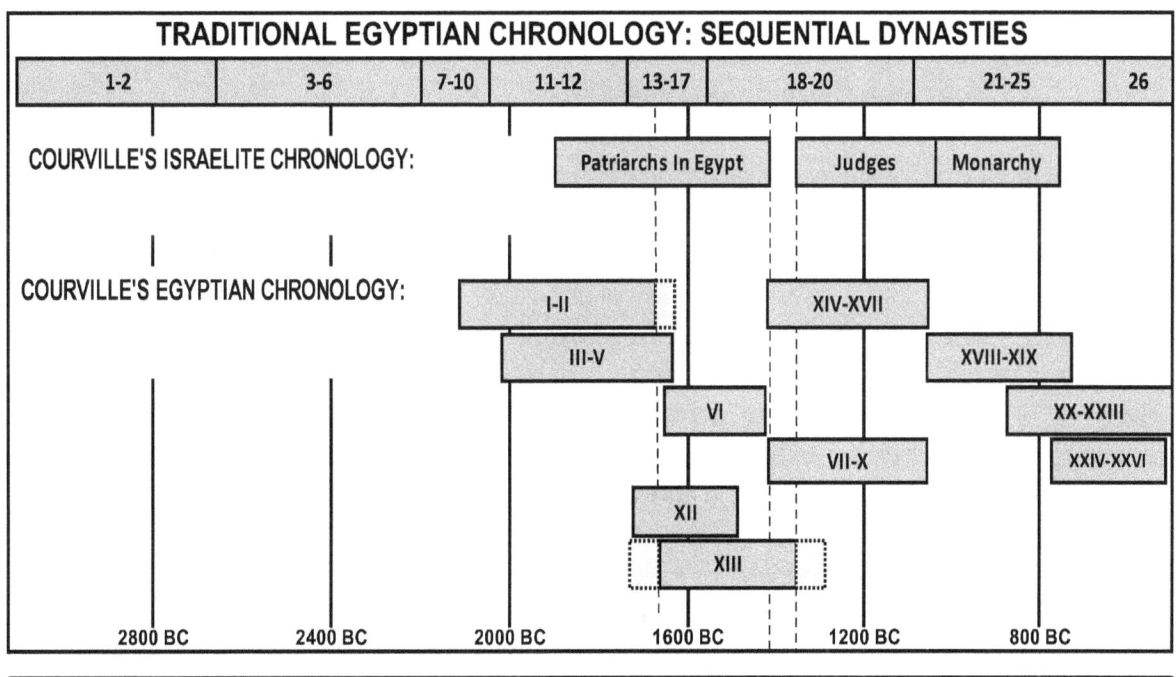

Figure 21: Courville's Revised Chronology

do not generally agree with Courville's proposed realignment of the Biblical Exodus and other events (as I've already shown the Exodus to align nicely with the conventional Egyptian chronology), I use this example simply to illustrate that other researchers have proposed compression of the timeline with rationalized concurrency of multiple dynasties. I am not prepared at this time to delve any more deeply into my own dynastic realignment; perhaps a future revision of this book will incorporate such, once I've had more time (not to mention the inclination) to undertake the requisite research.

A Brief Departure on the Hyksos Dynasty

Before I move from the alignment of the dynasties, I want to take a moment to address the Hyksos Dynasty. For those unfamiliar with the Biblical story of Jacob's eleventh son, Joseph, I suggest you read the account in the book of Genesis, chapters 37-50 and Exodus, chapters 1-14. Here's the briefest summary: Joseph, sold by his brothers to Midianite merchants as a slave at the age of 17, finds himself in Egypt, servant to Potiphar, a priest of On. Based on false claims of affront by Potiphar's wife, Joseph is committed to prison, but because of a reputation he gains in prison for the interpretation of dreams, he is brought before Pharaoh who had been disturbed by two foreboding dreams, the interpretation of which eluded his court wise men. The dreams were given to Pharaoh by God to forewarn him of a coming famine, and God reveals this to Joseph, who then provides the interpretation of these to Pharaoh. As a result, Joseph, now 30 years of age (the year is 2229 AM, or 1715 BC), is elevated by God's Providence to become governor of the land, second only to Pharaoh himself in authority over all Egypt. Several years later, with the famine now at its height, Joseph is highly regarded for his successful management of Egypt's affairs to this point, and has consequently found great favor with Pharaoh. When Pharaoh is made aware that Joseph has found his family, their having travelled to Egypt for food, Pharaoh invites them all (the entire clan of Jacob, his children and grandchildren, 70 in all) to remove from Canaan, offering them a land grant in Goshen, a significant and fertile region of Lower Egypt.

Now fast forward just over 200 years, well after Joseph's death at age 110, and we find that the Hebrews have grown into a significant population of well over a million (600 thousand men, not including women and children) and the Egyptians grew fearful of their numbers. Thus, the then-current Pharaoh, who, of a new dynasty and having no memory of Joseph's auspicious deeds for the benefit of Egypt, not only subjects the Hebrews to slavery and forced labor, but gives orders to the Egyptian mid-wives that newborn males of the Hebrews are to be killed to prevent further increase of the Hebrew population. Moses, born in Egypt almost 60 years after Joseph's death, is saved from such demise by Pharaoh's daughter, and is raised by the royal family. Once grown to adulthood, he is called by God to deliver the Hebrews from their oppressions, and through a series of divine plagues, the Hebrews are finally allowed to depart Egypt for Canaan (the "Exodus"). Pharaoh shortly thereafter regrets his decision and sends his army after them, but this military force meets its demise when God, having parted the Red Sea to allow the Hebrews to escape, now collapses the waters over the Egyptians, drowning them.

Flavius Josephus, in his work *Against Apion*, presents a compelling parallel account from the works of the 3rd century BC Egyptian historian Manetho. Josephus adds commentary between quotes from Manetho (whose original manuscripts are no longer extant). I insert here Josephus' entire treatment of this episode, Book I, chapters 14-16:

> *I shall begin with the writings of the Egyptians; not indeed of those that have written in the Egyptian language, which it is impossible for me to do. But Manetho was a man who was by birth an Egyptian, yet had he made himself master of the Greek learning, as is very evident; for he wrote the history of his own country in the Greek tongue, by translating it, as he saith himself, out of their sacred records; he also finds great fault with Herodotus for his ignorance and false relations of Egyptian affairs. Now, this Manetho, in the second book of his Egyptian history, writes concerning us in the following manner. I will set down his very words, as if I*

were to bring the very man himself into a court for a witness: - "There was king of ours, whose name was Timaus. Under him it came to pass, I know not how, that God was averse to us, and there came, after a surprising manner, men of ignoble birth out of the eastern parts, and had boldness enough to make an expedition into our country, and with ease subdued it by force, yet without our hazarding a battle with them. So when they had gotten those that governed us under their power, they afterwards burnt down our cities, and demolished the temples of the gods, and used all the inhabitants after a most barbarous manner: nay, some they slew, and led their children and their wives into slavery. At length they made one of themselves king, whose name was Salatis; he also lived at Memphis, and made both the upper and lower regions pay tribute, and left garrisons in places that were the most proper for them. He chiefly aimed to secure the eastern parts, and foreseeing that the Assyrians, who had then the greatest power, would be desirous of that kingdom and invade them; and as he found in the Saite Nomos [Seth-roite] a city very proper for his purpose, and which lay upon the Bubastic channel, but with regard to a certain theologic notion was called Avaris, this he rebuilt, and made very strong by the walls he built around it, and by a numerous garrison of two hundred and forty thousand armed men whom he put into it to keep it. Thither Salatis came in summer-time, partly to gather his corn, and pay his soldiers their wages, and partly to exercise his armed men, and thereby to terrify foreigners. When this man had reigned thirteen years, after him reigned another, whose name was Beon, for forty-four years; after him reigned another, called Apachnas, thirty-six years and seven months: after him Apophis reigned sixty-one years, and then Jonias fifty years and one month; after all these reigned Assis forty-nine years and two months. And these six were the first rulers among them, who were all along making war with the Egyptians, and were very desirous gradually to destroy them to the very roots. This whole nation was styled HYCSOS, that is, Shepherd-kings; for the first syllable HYC, according to the sacred dialect denotes a king, as is SOS a shepherd – but this according to the ordinary dialect; and of these is compounded HYCSOS: but some say that these people were Arabians." Now, in another copy it is said, that this word does not denote Kings, but on the contrary denotes Captive Shepherds, and this on account of the particle HYC; for that HYC, with the aspiration, in the Egyptian tongue denotes Shepherds, and that expressly also; and this to me seems the more probable opinion, and more agreeable to ancient history. [But Manetho goes on]: -"These people, whom we have before named kings, and called shepherds also, and their descendants," as he says, "kept possession of Egypt five hundred and eleven years." After these, he says, "That the Kings of Thebais and of the other parts of Egypt made an insurrection against the shepherds, and that a terrible and long war was made between them." He says further, "After a king whose name was Alisphragmuthosis, the shepherds were subdued by him, and were indeed driven out of other parts of Egypt, but were shut up in a place that contained ten thousand acres: this place was named Avaris." Manetho says, "That the shepherds built a wall round all this place, which was a large and strong wall, and this in order to keep all their possessions and their prey without a place of strength, but that Thummosis the son of Alisphragmuthosis made an attempt to take them by force and by siege with four hundred and eighty thousand men to lie round about them; but that, upon his despair of taking the place by that siege, they came to a composition with them, that they should leave Egypt, and go without any harm to be done them, whithersoever they would; and that, after this composition was made, they went away with their whole families and effects, not fewer in number than two hundred and forty thousand, and took their journey from Egypt, through the wilderness for Syria: but that, as they were in fear of the Assyrians, who had then the dominion over Asia, they built a city in that country which is now called Judea, and that large enough to contain this great number of men, and called it Jerusalem." Now Manetho, in another one of his books says, "That this nation, thus called Shepherds, was also called Captives in their sacred books." And this account of his is the truth; for the feeding of sheep was the employment of our forefathers in the most ancient ages; and as they led such a wandering life in feeding sheep, they were called Shepherds. Nor was it without reason that they were called Captives by the Egyptians, since one of our ancestors, Joseph, told the king of Egypt that he was a captive, and afterwards sent for his brethren into Egypt by the king's permission.

But now I shall produce the Egyptians as witnesses to the antiquity of our nation. I shall therefore here bring in Manetho again, and what he writes as to the order of the times in this case, and thus he speaks: -"When this people or shepherds were gone out of Egypt to Jerusalem, Tethmosis the king of Egypt, who drove them out, reigned twenty-five years and four months, and then died; after him his son Chebron took the kingdom for thirteen years; after whom came Amenophis, for twenty years and seven months: then came his sister Amesses, for twenty-one years and nine months; after her came Mephres, for twelve years and nine months; after him was Mephramuthosis, for twenty-five years and ten months; after him was Tethmosis, for nine years and eight months; after him came Amenophis, for thirty years and ten months; after him came Orus, for thirty-six years and five months; then came his daughter Acenchres, for twelve years and one month; then was her brother Rathotis, for nine years; then was Asencheres, for twelve years and five months; then came another Acencheres, for twelve years and three months; after him Armais, for four years and one month; after him was Rameeses, for one year and four months; after him came Armesses Miammoun, for sixty years and two months; after him Amenophis, for nineteen years and six months; after him came Sethosis, and Ramesses, who had an army of horse, and naval force. This king appointed his brother Armais, to be his deputy over Egypt." [In another copy it stood thus: -"After him came Sethosis, and Ramesses, two brethren, the former of whom had a naval force, and in a hostile manner destroyed those that met him upon the sea: but he slew Ramesses in no long time afterward, so he appointed another of his brethren to be his deputy over Egypt.] "He also gave him all the other authority of a king, but with these only injunctions, that he should not wear the diadem, nor be injurious to the queen, the mother of his children, and that he should not meddle with the other concubines of the king; while he made an expedition against Cyprus, and Phoenicia, and besides against the Assyrians and the Medes. He then subdued them all, some by his arms, some without fighting, and some by the terror of his great army; and being puffed up by the great successes he had had, he went on still the more boldly, and overthrew the cities and countries that lay in the eastern parts; but after some considerable time, Armais, who was left in Egypt, did all those very things, by way of opposition, which his older brother had forbidden him to do, without fear; for he used violence to the queen, and continued to make use of the rest of the concubines, without sparing any of them; nay, at the persuasion of his friends he put on the diadem, and set up to oppose his brother; but then, he who was set over the priests of Egypt, wrote letters to Sethosis, and informed him of all that had happened, and how his brother had set up to oppose him: he therefore returned back to Pelusium Immediately, and recovered his kingdom again. The country also was called from his name Egypt: for Manetho says that Sethosis himself was called Egyptus, as was his brother also called Danaus."

This is Manetho's account; and evident it is from the number of years by him set down belonging to this interval, if they be summed up together, that these shepherds, as they are here called, who were no others than our forefathers, were delivered out of Egypt, and came thence, and inhabited this country three hundred and ninety three years before Danaus came to Argos; although the Argives look upon his as their most ancient king. Manetho, therefore, bears this testimony to two points of the greatest consequence to our purpose, and those from the Egyptian records themselves. In the first place, that we came out of another country into Egypt; and that withal our deliverance out of it was so ancient in time, as to have preceded the siege of Troy almost a thousand years; but then, as to those things which Manetho adds, not from the Egyptian records, but, as he confesses himself, from some stories of an uncertain original, I will disprove them hereafter particularly, and shall demonstrate that they are no better than incredible fables. [Against Apion, I.14-16]

One can hardly deny the harmony of Manetho's account of the Shepherd-Kings and the Biblical account of Joseph through the Exodus. There is clearly an anti-Semitic spin in Manetho's account, which may have simply been the best record he had, previously distorted for the sake of Egyptian dignity, or that he himself may have altered the account to favor the Egyptian perspective. That, unfortunately, is the quandary of all history written by men with biases, and the modern equivalent with which I concern myself herein.

From this, we conclude two things: first, that the Biblical account from Joseph through Moses is corroborated by Manetho, albeit with readily rationalized corruptions; and secondly, that the Hyksos Dynasty was at its end concurrent with the reign of Tethmosis, aka Thutmose I.

I shall now return to the matter of a proper reconciliation of the Egyptian dynasties. David Down worked as an archaeologist and tour guide in the Middle East for some 50 years. He was the author of the monthly archaeology journal "*Diggings*," as well as the bimonthly magazine "*Archaeological Diggings*," and authored two books on this subject. He is one of several experts that has proposed an alternate chronology for the Egyptian dynasties, shown in Figure 22. Notice first that the timeline is shifted forward by nearly a millennium. This is still not quite in harmony with my proposed timeline, wherein Mizraim (Menes) cannot start his rule until after 1948 BC, but it is close. Notice the multiple overlaps of dynasties. And with that, we'll move on to the next subject.

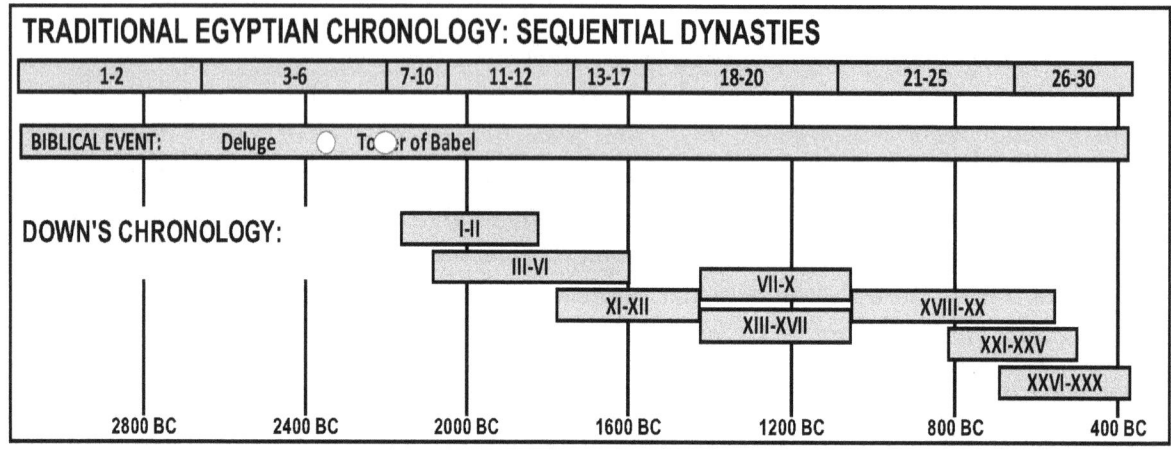

Figure 22: Down's Revised Dynastic Chronology

CHAPTER 9: The Deluge (Gen 7)

I'll admit that I've gotten quite a bit off track here, but Gen 6 is so packed with clues about our secreted ancient history, that the overarching objective got pushed aside. So, I now pull us back to Genesis chapter 7 in which the global deluge is detailed. The year is 1656 AM, or as I calculate it, 2288 BC. For starters, let me make one thing clear: the earth was flooded supernaturally, and the waters were similarly removed supernaturally. Anyone arguing against the actuality of the deluge on the basis of failure to explain it by natural events here is squandering their time and energy. Gen 7:18 states that *"The waters prevailed and greatly increased on the earth...."* The Book of Jasher uses virtually identical language here. The water on our earth *increased*. In addition, Gen 8:2 tells us that *"The fountains of the deep and the windows of heaven were also stopped, and the rain from heaven was restrained."* The flood waters were not all natural. And the animals were brought to Noah supernaturally, as well. The Bible tells us that as the waters receded, the ark came to rest on Ararat.

I want also to address a different flood myth: that the Biblical account of the flood drew on the Sumerian Epic of Gilgamesh. It is widely accepted that this Sumerian tale was passed down via oral tradition from about 2100 BC, but was not committed to writing until somewhere between 1800-1200 BC. Since the actual flood occurred in about 2288 BC, the Biblical account would also have been passed down orally before the story of Gilgamesh by about 200 years. The issue at hand is that none of the history of the Hebrews was committed to writing until God so instructed Moses to do so in about 2448 AM or about 1496 BC. Given the wide range of dates for the Gilgamesh tablet, one can as easily conclude that it was based on the Biblical account, and/or that both had a common origin. Profane historians have collectively determined that the Gilgamesh Epic predates the Biblical flood account so as to undermine the authenticity of Bible itself, framing it as just another mythical tale, hijacked by the Hebrews.

Now, as to the reality of the deluge, I call Josephus as a witness, who in turn cites Berosus the Chaldean. In his *Antiquities*, he writes:

> *Now all the writers of barbarian histories make mention of this flood and of this ark; among whom is Berosus the Chaldean; for when he is describing the circumstances of the flood, he goes on thus: -"It is said there is still part of this ship in Armenia, at the mountain of the Cordyaeans; and that some people carry off pieces of the bitumen, which they take away and use chiefly as amulets for the averting of mischiefs." Hieronymus the Egyptian, also, who wrote the Phoenician Antiquities, and Mnaseas, and a great many more, make mention of the same. Nay, Nicolaus of Damascus, in his ninety-sixth book, hath a particular relation about them, where he speaks thus: -"There is a great mountain in Armenia, over Minyas, called Baris, upon which it is reported that many who fled at the time of the Deluge were saved; and that one who was carried in an ark came on shore upon the top of it; and that the remains of the timber were a great while preserved. This might be the man about whom Moses, the legislator of the Jews wrote.* [Ant I:III:6]

Josephus continues in Ant I:III:9 telling how Noah lived 350 years after the flood, at which point he dies at the age of 950 years. Josephus goes on to delineate 11 historians, *"...both among the Greeks and barbarians..."* that attest to the extraordinarily long lives of the ancients.

One early twentieth century cartographer by the name of William R. Shepherd at Columbia University, created *Shepherd's Historical Atlas,* published in 1923, that included a map that shows Mt. Baris at the location of Mt. Ararat. See page 20 from the atlas in Figure 23 below (The low resolution of the image makes it a little difficult to read here, but you may view it online at www.lib.utexas.edu/maps/historical/shepherd/asia_minor_p20.jpg.).

Compare this map to a modern map (Figure 24) of the same region, this one showing Mount Ararat instead. Using the city of Van as the common reference, you can see that Mount Ararat is indeed the same as Mount Baris.

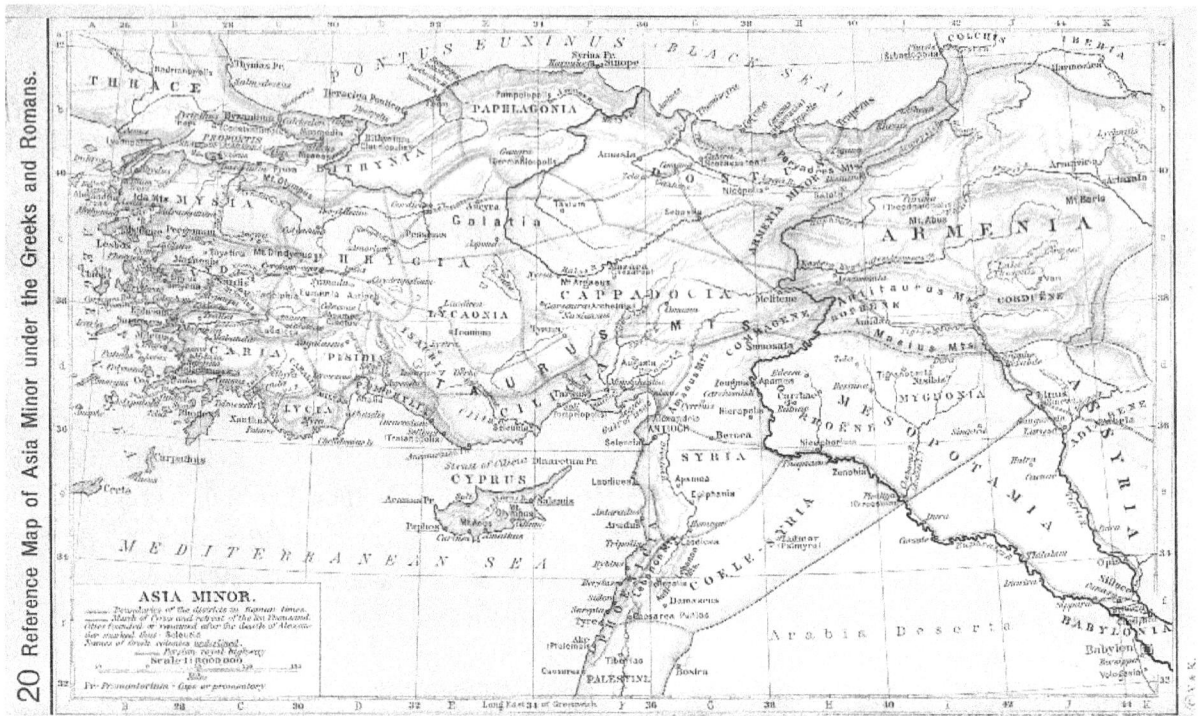

Figure 23: Modern Map of Turkey. By Peter Hermes Furian/shutterstock.com

Josephus also tell us in his Antiquities [Ant I:III:5] that "*After this the ark rested on top of a certain mountain in Armenia.*" Indeed, Mount Ararrat is in Armenia, as shown on both maps. He goes on further to say that "*...the Armenians call this place (Αποβατήριον) The place of Descent; for the ark being saved in that place, its remains are shown there by the inhabitants to this day.*" William Whiston adds the following footnote on this passage:

> *This Αποβατήριον, or Place of Descent, is the proper rendering of the Armenian name of this very city. It is called in Ptolemy Naxuana, and by Moses Chorenensis, the Armenian historian, Idsheuan; but at the place itself, Nachidsehduan, which signifies The First Place of Descent, and is a lasting monument of the preservation of Noah in the ark, upon the top of that mountain, at whose foot it was built, as the first city or town after the Flood.*

Figure 24: Sheet 20 from Shepherd's Historical Atlas. (Courtesy of the University of Texas Libraries, The University of Texas at Austin.)

Chapter 10: Origin of Nations and Languages (Gen 10-11)

Genesis chapters 8 & 9 tell of the receding flood waters, Noah's sacrifices to God, and God's covenant with Noah. None of the extra-Biblical sources I used add anything of significance to the Genesis account in these chapters. This brings us then to Gen 10: the table of nations.

Since Noah and his family were the only survivors of the deluge, then all mankind is descended from Noah. In his genes were all races…another sense in which he was perfect (i.e., complete) in his generations. Chapter 10 of Genesis delineates all of the families of the sons of Noah, in their nations, up until the incident of the Tower of Babel. The last verse in this chapter says "…*and from these nations were divided on earth after the flood*." Chapter 11 then begins thus:

> *Now the whole earth had one language and one speech. And it came to pass as they journeyed from the east, that they found a plain in the land of Shinar, and they dwelt there. Then they said to one another, "Let us make bricks and bake them thoroughly." They had brick for stone, and they had asphalt for mortar. And they said, "Come, let us build ourselves a city, and a tower whose top is in the heavens; let us make a name for ourselves, lest we be scattered abroad over the face of the whole earth."* [Gen 11:1-4]

As previously mentioned, Shinar is extensively acknowledged to be Sumer. If this be so, then Noah's descendants would have to migrate mostly south from their original settlements in the foothills of Ararat. Sumer was at the southern end of what would later be the Babylonian empire. It is interesting that just as many translations render the text of 11:2 as "from the east" as alternately render it "eastward," both of which are problematic. I did refer to Strong's Concordance as a first attempt for resolution, but unfortunately, the expression has many connotations, including "in front," and "before" (temporally). I think perhaps the best translation that averts the controversy here is the Good News Translation (GNT) which renders Gen 11:2 as follows: "*As they wandered about in the East, they came to a plain in Babylonia and settled there.*" This, however, is still a little disquieting; I mean, what is it about things being *east*? The land of Nod was *east* of Eden, a land inferior to it. When this verse says that they "…*journeyed from the east*…," what is the reference? That is, east of what? Could it mean east of the Promised Land? Notably, the plain of Shinar (Sumer) is indeed <u>directly</u> east of the Promised Land.

The Tower of Babel

So, we have the descendants of Noah gathered together in the plain of Shinar. They conceived to build there a city with a tower *"…whose top is in the heavens; let us make a name for ourselves, lest we be scattered abroad over the face of the whole earth."* [Gen 11:4] Pride in their own abilities to construct something that could, to their thinking, confound God in His plans was both their motivation and their undoing. The Book of Jasher tells us that Nimrod was the sole regent over the land at that time:

> *And king Nimrod reigned securely, and all the earth was under his control, and all the earth was of one tongue and words of union.* [Jash 9:20]

The author of Jasher goes on to tell that Nimrod and his father and uncles (collectively, all the sons of Ham) conspired to maintain this unity in order to continue to reign "*mightily*" over the whole world. It was all about power and control. Josephus underscores this in his Antiquities as follows:

Now the plain in which they first dwelt as called Shinar. God also commanded them to send colonies abroad, for the thorough peopling of the earth, -that they might not raise seditions among themselves, but might cultivate a great part of the earth, and enjoy its fruits after a plentiful manner: but they were so ill instructed, that they did not obey God; for which reason they fell into calamities, and were made sensible, be experience, of what sin they had been guilty; for when they flourished with a numerous youth, God admonished them again to send out colonies; but they, imagining the prosperity they enjoyed was not derived from the favor of God, but supposing that their own power was the proper cause of the plentiful condition they were in, they did not obey him. Nay, they added to this their disobedience to the Divine will, the suspicion that they were therefore ordered to send out separate colonies, that, being divided asunder, they might the more easily be oppressed.

Now it was Nimrod who excited them to such an affront and contempt of God....He persuaded them not to ascribe it to God, as if it was through his means they were happy, but to believe that it was their own courage which procured their happiness. He gradually changed the government into tyranny, -seeing no other way to turn men from the fear of God, but to bring

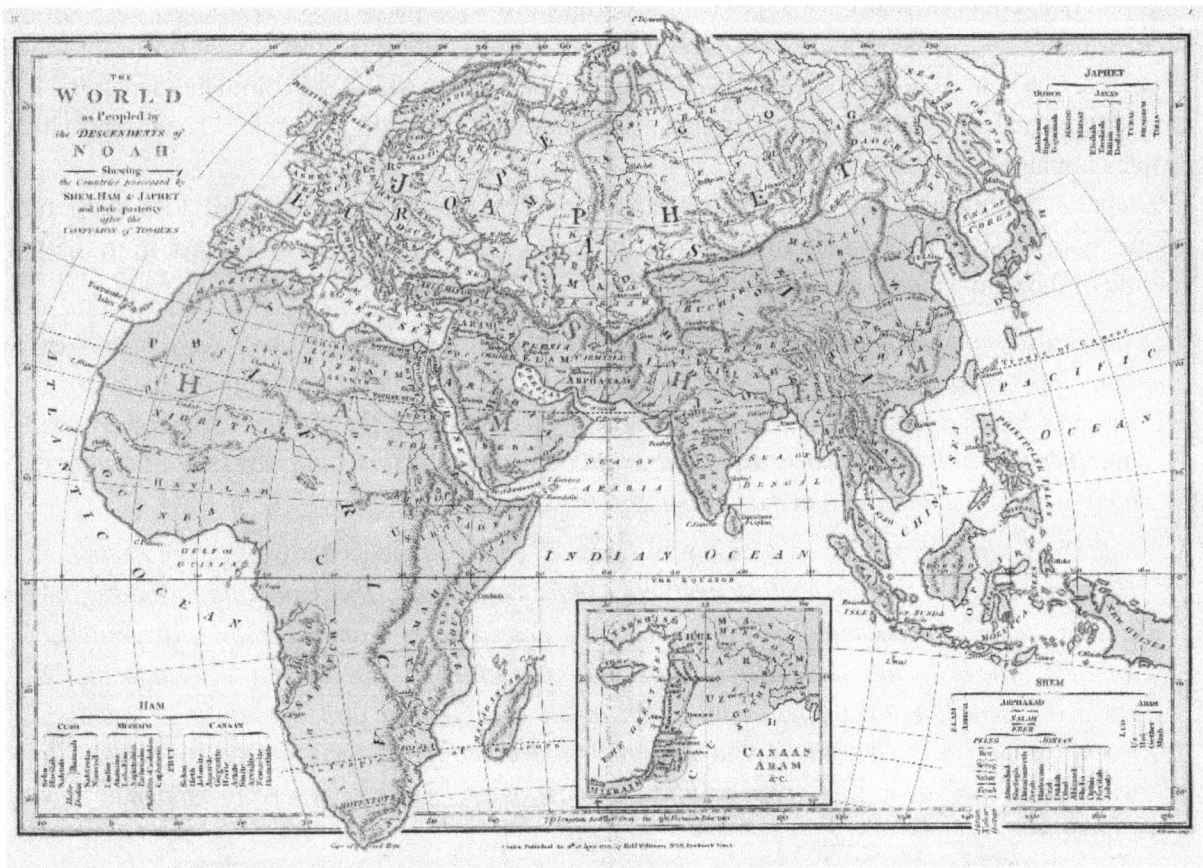

Figure 25: Map of The World as Peopled by the Descendants of Noah (1818)

them into a constant dependence upon his power. He also said he would be revenged on God, if he should have a mind to drown the world again; so that he would build a tower so high for the waters to be able to reach! And that he would avenge himself on God for destroying their forefathers. [Ant I:IV:1-2]

God thus determined to overthrow this Tower of Babel, and to confuse their language "*...that they may not understand one another's speech.*" [Gen 11:7] Then Gen 11:8-9 tells us:

So the LORD scattered them abroad from there over the face of all the earth, and they ceased building the city. Therefore its name is called Babel, because there the LORD confused the language of all the earth; and from there the LORD scattered them abroad over the face of all the earth.

Here again we have evidence for the supercontinent. God scattered mankind "*...over the face of all the earth.*" In these two verses that phrase is repeated, I believe to emphasize that it was indeed the *whole* earth. Most of the maps I've seen developed to show the dispersion of the nations show only three continents (Africa, Asia, and Europe). See an example in Figure 25. They notably neglect the Americas, and I believe this to be a serious deficiency, most probably because they failed to recognize the full scope of God's actions and methods described herein. Now God, in His omnipotence, could indeed have supernaturally transported people across the oceans, but I do not believe there is adequate evidence for this. On the contrary, these people moved on foot to their respective, designated geographic regions and settled there, after which the continents separated in a rapid continental shift, as previously detailed. Why did the shift need to be rapid? To ensure that the peoples remained separated.

Zecharia Sitchin, the twentieth-century author of *The Earth Chronicles*, provides supporting testimony of the Biblical account of the Tower of Babel. The following is an excerpt from the first volume of the Chronicles series, *The Twelfth Planet*:

The Babylonian historian-priest Berossus, who in the third century BC compiled a history of Mankind, reported that the "first inhabitants of the land, glorying in their own strength...undertook to raise a tower whose 'top' should reach the sky." But the tower was overturned by the gods and heavy winds, "and the gods introduced a diversity of tongues among men, who till that time had all spoken the same language."

*George Smith (*The Chaldean Account of Genesis*) found in the writings of Greek historian Hestaeus a report that, in accordance with "older traditions," the people that escaped the Deluge came to Senaar in Babylonia but were driven away from there by a diversity of tongues. The historian Alexander Polyhistor (first century BC) wrote that all men formerly spoke the same language. Then some undertook to erect a large and lofty tower so that they might "climb up to heaven." But the chief god confounded their design by sending a whirlwind; each tribe was given a different language. "The city where it happened was Babylon."*

*There is little doubt by now that the biblical tales, as well as the reports of Greek historians of 2,000 years ago and of their predecessor Berossus, all stem from earlier – Sumerian – origins. A. H. Sayce (*The Religion of the Babylonians*) reported reading on a fragmentary tablet in the British Museum "the Babylonian version of the building of the Tower of Babel." In all instances, the attempt to reach the heavens and the ensuing confusion of tongues are basic elements of the version. There are other Sumerian texts that record the deliberate* *confusion of Man's tongue by an irate god.* [*The Twelfth Planet* by Zecharia Sitchin published by Inner Traditions International and Bear & Company, ©1991. All rights reserved. Reprinted with permission of the publisher. http://www.Innertraditions.com.]

In his *Chronicles*, Sitchin propounds a theory of ancient astronauts from a twelfth planet based on his interpretation of the Sumerian and Akkadian tablets. To be clear, I do not subscribe to this interpretation, but his translation of these tablets is nonetheless accepted as accurate, and very enlightening when read through the lens of Scriptural truth.

Lastly on the subject of the Tower of Babel, I've often wondered how large it was. If one has hope of ascending to the heavens, it would have to be a structure so large that its height would have to exceed even the tallest mountains. Did these people have any idea of how large a structure it would have to be? The Book of Jasher provides an interesting detail in regard to its size:

> *And as to the tower which the sons of men built, the earth opened its mouth and swallowed one third part thereof, and a fire also descended from heaven and burned another third, and the other third is left to this day, and it is of that part which was aloft, and its circumference is three days' walk.* [Jash 9:38]

I suspect that a days' walk would have been about 25-30 miles. I can walk 10 miles in just over 2 hours, but that is speed-walking. If you're walking all day, the pace would be slower, but faster than a leisurely pace, say between 15 and 20 minutes per mile; but you wouldn't do that all day, either…probably no more than 8 hours. So, a circumference of 80 miles would imply a diameter of about 25 miles. And that is only the top third of it. I assume it to be a pyramidal structure making the original base about three times 25 miles, thus requiring angelic power to construct!

The Dispersion of Nations

According to my chronology, the dispersion of nations takes place in 1948 BC (1996 AM). Among the secondary sources I used is a book entitled *The Chaldean Account of Genesis*, by George Smith, first published in 1876, the same year that the author died. Smith was the noted Assyriologist who discovered and translated the *Epic of Gilgamesh* into the English language. In the second chapter of his *Chaldean Account of Genesis*, he wrote the following:

> *Before the time of Hammurabi, there ruled several races of kings, of whom we possess numerous monuments. These monarchs principally reigned at the cities of Ur, Karrak, Larsa, and Akkad. Their inscriptions do not determine the length of their rule, but they probably covered the period from B.C. 2000 to 1550.*

Thus, he places the beginning of the most ancient Mesopotamian cultures (Sumerian, Akkadian, and Babylonian) at about the same time as I've placed the dispersion of nations, which confirmation is reassuring. While Smith places the date of rule of Urukh, the then-known earliest monarch in the region, at 2000 BC, he admits that other scholars place his rule "*at a much earlier date*." Obviously, I regard Smith's estimate to be correct. While it is possible that Noah's progeny could have populated that area prior to the dispersion, it is unlikely, and could not in any event have been more than about 200 years earlier. The very existence of the distinct Sumerian language is supporting evidence that it had to be the later date.

Chapter 10 of Genesis is commonly termed the Table of Nations. It provides the genealogy of the sons of Noah to the time of the dispersion of these nations. I will refrain from inserting the Scripture here, but instead insert a table of the names. Now this table delineates 71 names. I find it intriguing that the Book of Jasher relates in the story of Joseph the proposition that seventy languages comprised

Ham (Cham)	aka	Shem (Sem)	aka	Japheth	aka
Cush	Chus	Aram		Gomer	Gamer
.Seba	Saba	.Uz		.Ashkenaz	Aschanaz
.Havilah	Evila	.Hul	Ul	.Riphath	Diphath
.Sabtah	Sabatha	.Gether	Gater	.Togarmah	Thorgama
.Sabteca	Sabathaca	.Meshech	Mosoch	Magog	Magog
.Raamah	Rhegma	Arphaxad		Madai	Madoi
..Sheba	Saba	.Shelah	Sala	Javan	Jovan
..Dedan	Dadan	..Eber	Heber	.Elishah	Elisa
.Nimrod	Nebrod	...Peleg	Phaleg	.Tarshish	Tharseis
Put	Phud, Phut	...Joktan	Yoktan	.Kittim	Cetians
Mizraim	Mesrain	....Almodad	Elmodad	.Rodanim	Dodanim
.Ludim	Ludiim, Lud	....Sheleph	Saleth	Tubal	Thobel
.Anamim	Enemetiim	....Hazarmaveth	Sarmoth	Meshech	Mosoch
.Lehabim	Labiim	....Jerah	Yerach	Tiras	Thiras
.Naphtuhim	Naphthalim	....Hadoram	Odorrha		
.Pathrusim	Patrosoniim	....Uzal	Aibel		
.Casluhim	Chasmoniim	....Diklah	Declah		
..Philistines	Phylisitiim	....Obal	Eval, Ebal		
.Caphtorim	Gaphthoriim	....Abimael			
Canaan	Chanaan	....Sheba	Saba		
.Sidon	Zidon	....Ophir	Uphir		
.Heth	Hittite	....Havilah	Evila		
.Jebusites		....Jobab			
.Amorites	Amori	Elam			
.Girgashites	Gergashi	Lud			
.Hivites	Evites	Asshur	Assur		
.Arkites	Arukites				
.Sinites	Assennites				
.Arvadites	Aradians				
.Zemarites	Samareans				
.Hamathites	Amathites				

Table 4: Table of Nations (Genealogy of the Sons of Noah)

all those then spoken in the world. Joseph entered the service of Pharaoh about 233 years after the dispersion of nations, so it is reasonable to believe that most or all of the languages were still in use. The excerpt from Jasher is as follows:

> *And the king said to all the officers: I have thought that since God has made known to the Hebrew man all that he has spoken, there is none so discreet and wise in the whole land as he is; if it seem good in your sight I will place him over the land, for he will save the land with his wisdom.*

And all the officers answered the king and said, But surely it is written in the laws of Egypt, and it should not be violated, that no man shall reign over Egypt, nor be the second to the king, but one who has knowledge in all the languages of the sons of men. Now therefore our lord and king, behold this Hebrew man can only speak the Hebrew language, and how then can he be over us the second under government, a man who not even knoweth our language? Now we pray thee send for him, and let him come before thee, and prove him in all things, and do as thou see fit.

And the king said, It shall be done tomorrow, and the thing you have spoken is good; and all the officers came on that day before the king.

And on that night the Lord sent one of his ministering angels, and he into the land of Egypt under Joseph, and the angel of the Lord stood over Joseph, and behold Joseph was lying in the bed at night in his master's house in the dungeon, for his master had put him back in the dungeon on account of his wife. And the angel roused him from his sleep, and Joseph rose up and stood upon his legs, and behold the angel of the Lord was standing opposite to him; and the angel of the Lord spoke with Joseph, and he taught him all the languages of man in that night, and he called his name Jehoseph. [Jash 49: 8-14]

Whether the number of languages is correctly 70 or 71 is of little concern to me. I believe that on the basis of Scriptural symmetry, the number is more likely to be 70, a recurrent indication of completeness. This would then imply that two of the nations delineated in Gen 10 shared a single tongue, which is not in itself so problematic.

What we will attempt to do is to create a list of the nations from the Genesis account, augmenting this with geographic information from our extra-Biblical sources, and then add languages from these and other source materials. By the process of elimination, we may be able to identify candidate nations that populated the Americas, Oceania, and perhaps even the island nations around the globe.

The Descendants of Ham

We'll start with the Hamitic tribes one by one, starting with Cush. Josephus tells us that

"The children of Ham possessed the land from Syria and Amanus, and the mountains of Libanus, seizing upon all that was on its seacoasts and as far as the ocean, and keeping as their own. Some, indeed, of its names are utterly vanished away; others of them being changed, and another sound given them, are hardly to be discovered; yet a few there are which have kept their denominations entire: for of the four sons of Ham, time has not at all hurt the name of Chus; for the Ethiopians, over whom he reigned, are even at this day, are by themselves and by all men in Asia, called Chusites. [Ant I:VI:2]

According to Wikipedia, the Kingdom of Kush was an ancient kingdom in Nubia, centered along the Nile Valley in what is today northern Sudan, southern Egypt, Somalia, and Ethiopia. The people there have spoken Cushitic languages of the Afroasiatic language family. The map in Figure 25 shows the land of Cush to extend across the Red Sea into Arabia. Thus, we'll assign the Cushitic language and northeastern Africa to the Cushites.

With regard to the Egyptian nation, Jospehus tells us:

> *The memory also of the Mesraites is preserved in their name; for all we who inhabit this country [of Judea] call Egypt Mestre, and the Egyptians Mestreans.* [Ant I:VI:2]

Thus, we can certainly assign the Egyptian language and country to this son of Ham.

Ezekiel 27:10 reads in part, *"Those from Persia, Lydia and Libya were in your army as men of war...."* The NKJV Study Bible footnote on this verse states that Lydia and Libya are literally Lud and Put, usually understood to be in western Asia Minor (Lud) and Africa (Put). Once again, Josephus continues his dissertation on the sons of Ham:

> *Phut was also the founder of Libyia, and called the inhabitants Phutites, from himself: there is also a river in the country of the Moors which bears that name; whence it is that we may see the greatest part of the Grecian historiographers mention that river and the adjoining country by the appellation of Phut: but the name it has now has been by change given it from one of the sons of Mesraim, who was called Lybyos.* [Ant I:VI:2]

The map in Figure 25 shows that the region of Phut includes modern day Mauritania, Tunisia, Algeria, and Morocco. Linguists assign the Berber language to this region in antiquity. To be clear, the mention of Libyia here should not be confused with Libya, which Josephus tells us later was settled by Labim (aka, Lehabim, Labiim) and that the name "Libya" was derived from his name.

There is an interesting account of Canaan, the last son of Ham, in the Book of Jubilees. It reads as follows:

> *And Ham and his sons went into the land which he was to occupy, which he acquired as his portion in the land of the south. And Canaan saw the land of Lebanon to the river of Egypt that it was very good, and he went not into the land of his inheritance to the west (that is to) the sea, and he dwelt in the land of Lebanon, eastward and westward from the border of Jordan and from the border of the sea. And Ham, his father, and Cush and Mizraim, his brothers, said unto him: "Thou hast settled in a land which is not thine, and which did not fall to us by lot: do not do so, thou and thy sons will fall in the land and (be) accursed through sedition; for by sedition ye have settled, and by sedition will thy children fall, and thou shalt be rooted out for ever. Dwell not in the dwelling of Shem; for to Shem and his sons did it come by their lot. Cursed art thou, and cursed shalt thou be beyond all the sons of Noah, by the curse by which we bound ourselves by an oath in the presence of the holy judge, and in the presence of Noah our father." But he did not hearken unto them, and dwelt in the land of Lebanon from Hamath to the entering of Egypt, he and his sons to this very day. And for this reason that land is named Canaan.* [Jub x: 28-34]

Josephus simply says that Canaan occupied the land called Judea (in Jospehus' day) and called it Canaan after himself. Now within the whole land of Canaan we have both the Canaanite tribe and the tribes of his sons: Sidonians, Hittites, Jebusites, Amorites, Gergashites, Hivites, Arkites, Sinites, Arvadites, Zemarites, and Hamathites. The Bible provides ample description of the locations of each of these mostly during the Canaanite wars with the Jews in the books of Numbers, Deuteronomy, and Joshua.

Sidon is widely acknowledged as a principal city of ancient Phoenicia, which also had its own language. Thus we can complete this entry in the table.

The Hittites (sons of Heth, son of Canaan) are also well established as an Anatolian people (Asia Minor, modern day Turkey) whose language may have been Hittite cuneiform, Luwian, Hattic, as well as Akkadian. Each of these four are separately included in lists of the oldest languages.

While most scholars agree that the city of Jebus is Jerusalem, a few dispute this. However, in chapter 15 v8 of the Book of Joshua, the Jebusite city is identified directly as the city of Jerusalem during the Israelite conquest of Canaan. Apparently, there are no remaining records outside of the Old Testament that refer to the city of Jebus or the Jebusites. Thus, unless or until further archaeological evidence is uncovered, assignment of a unique language by name to this Canaanite sub-tribe will remain unachievable.

Shifting now to the Amorites, archaeological records of the Sumerians, Akkadians, and Egyptians (dated to the 21st century BC which is reasonably close to my calculation of the dispersion in the 20th century BC) make references to these people, but just as with the Jebusites, there are no early records of their language that remain extant. There are later records written by Amorites in Akkadian, but these occur sufficiently later than the conquest by the Israelites that there was likely a change in the primary language of these peoples, as civilizations were conquered and assimilated. There are Sumerian texts which apparently make reference to these people as speaking "a different language."

Now there is an interesting passage in the Biblical Book of Amos (Ch. 2 v 9-10) that reads as follows:

> *Yet it was I who destroyed the Amorite before them,*
> *Whose height was like the height of cedars,*
> *And he was as strong as the oaks;*
> *Yet I destroyed his fruit above*
> *And his roots beneath.*
> *Also it was I who brought you up from the land of Egypt,*
> *And led you forty years through the wilderness,*
> *To possess the land of the Amorite.*

It would seem that God is describing the Amorites as powerful giants. We know that when Moses sent Joshua and Caleb and others to spy out the land of Canaan before the forty years of wandering in the desert, that some of the others spread doubt and fear among the Israelites saying that there were giants in the land. Specifically, in Num 13:33 (NKJV), it says:

> *There we saw the giants (the descendants of Anak came from the giants); and we were like grasshoppers in our own sight, and so we were in their sight.*

It thus appears that the second fall of angels occurs at least a generation before the Exodus. I find it fascinating that the name "Annunaki," designating deities in the ancient Sumerian, Akkadian, Babylonian, and Assyrian cultures, is so similar to the name of "Anak" in this passage. Given that the Annunaki were regarded as lesser gods (in contrast to the twelve major deities), it is a likely affirmation of the association of these with the fallen angels. In his *Chronicles*, Sitchin says the following:

> *The ancient texts described the Annunaki as the rank-and-file gods who had been involved in the settlement of Earth – the gods "who performed the tasks." The Babylonian "Epic of Creation" credited Marduk with giving the Annunaki their assignments." [The Twelfth*

Planet by Zecharia Sitchin published by Inner Traditions International and Bear & Company, ©1991. All rights reserved. http://www.Innertraditions.com. Reprinted with permission of the publisher.]

As with the Amorites, we essentially have similar circumstances that prevent us from positively identifying the languages of the Girgashites, Hivites, Arkites, Sinites, Arvadites, Zemarites, and Hamathites.

Let's now turn our attention to Nimrod, son of Cush. Gen 10:8-12 provides details as to the cities established by Nimrod:

Cush begot Nimrod; he began to be a mighty hunter before the LORD; therefore it is said, "Like Nimrod the mighty hunter before the LORD." And the beginning of his kingdom was Babel, Erech, Accad, and Calneh, in the land of Shinar. From that land he went to Assyria and built Nineveh, Rehoboth Ir, Calah, and Resen between Nineveh and Calah (that is the principal city).

The first three of these cities are readily identified with Babylon, Uruk, and Akkad, all found in Sumeria. Calneh has not been positively identified, but some have proposed the city of Nippur. The last four cities are identified as being Assyrian, and we certainly know the location of ancient Nineveh.

Calah is now broadly associated with the modern city of Nimrūd, located south of Mosul in present-day Iraq. Neither Rehoboth Ir nor Resen have been positively identified. Now as to the languages, according to the Cambridge University Department of Archaeology, the languages of ancient Mesopotamia ware considered collectively as 'Akkadian,' comprised of Sumerian, Babylonian, and Assyrian. Given Nimrod as the common founder of these three civilizations, it is not at all surprising that the three languages should be considered together, and thus we assign Akkadian as the root language of Nimrod and his descendants, in the region of Mesopotamia.

As to the offspring of Cush, son of Ham, Josephus has identified these peoples in terms of his day (i.e., Roman Empire). In his *Antiquities*, I:VI:2, he tells us:

The children of these [four] were these: Sabas, who founded the Sabeans; Evilas, who founded the Evileans, who are called Getuli; Sabathes founded the Sabatheans; they are now called by the Greeks, Astaborans; Sabactas founded the Sabactens; and Ragmus the Ragmeans; and he had two sons, the one of whom Jadadas, settled the Judadeans, a nation of the western Ethiopians, and left them his name; as did Sabas to the Sabeans.

I found a couple of maps showing the Getuli in the region of northern Africa south of the Atlas Mountains, in an area roughly comparable to that of modern Algeria. I show one such map in Figure 27.

The Sabeans are associated with the country of Sheba, elsewhere referenced in the Bible, most notably during the reign of Solomon, wherein the Queen of Sheba visits Solomon, presenting him with gifts of spices, gold, and precious stones (see 1Ki 10, 2Chr 9). This kingdom was located at the southern end of the Arabian Peninsula.

While I was able to find little information on the Sabatheans, I was able to find the Astaborans by languages of that name, with a regional association with present-day Sudan, Chad, and Eritrea.

Regarding the Sabactens and Ragmeans, I nearly struck out, but found an obscure reference in a book with a lengthy title: *Light and Truth; Collected from Ancient and Modern History, Containing the Universal History of the Colored and Indian Race, from the Creation of the World to the Present*

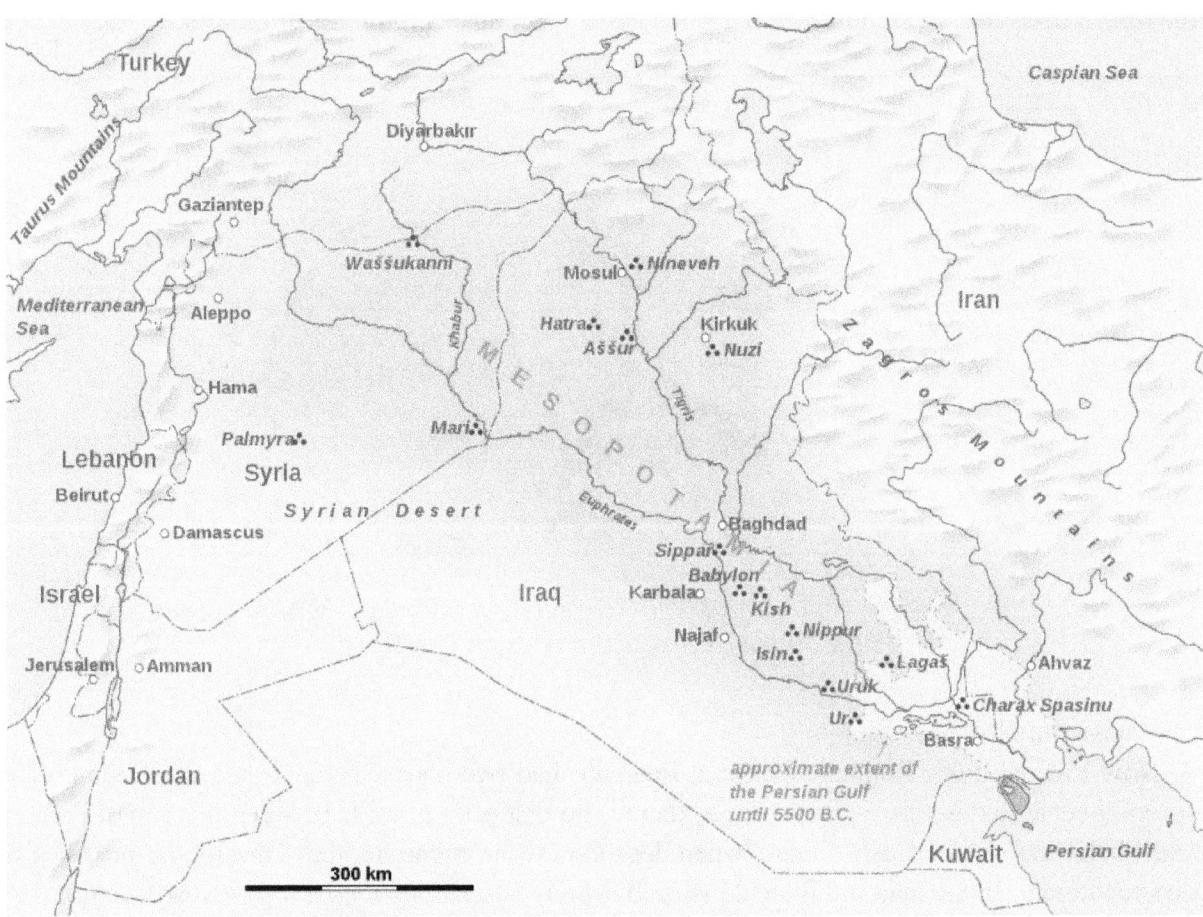

Figure 26: Ancient Mesopotamia. (By Goran tek-en, CC BY-SA 4.0; https://commons.wikimedia.org/w/index.php?curid=30851043)

Time, by R. B. Lewis, published in 1851. The citation has no footnotes or supporting references, although in the Introduction it says that the collection is "...*from sacred and profane history*...." The pertinent passage reads as follows:

> *The Sabactens, descendants of Sabtechah, (Sabactas,) settled likewise in Arabia, upon the borders of the Red Sea; and the Ragmeans, the descendants of Raaman, (Ragmus,) settled in Ethiopia.* [Public domain]

Thus, while we have now evidence that the Sabactens were in Arabia, their language is unknown, as is that of the Ragmeans. Arabic did not emerge as a language until about 500 AD. Whatever the languages were, they did not survive assimilation and are now almost certainly lost forever. Whatever may have been plainly identifiable to the reader of Josephus' *Antiquities* in the first century AD, is

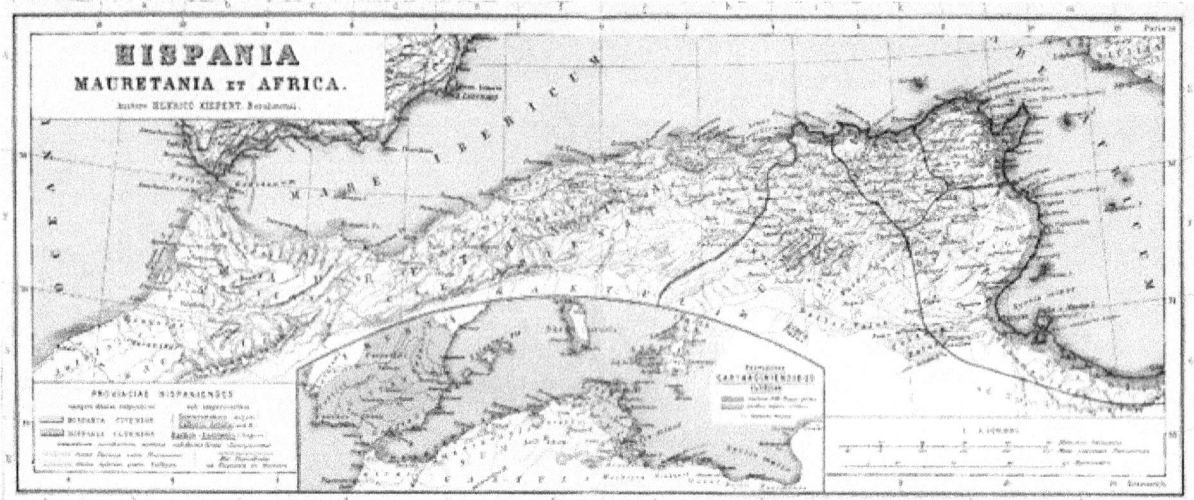

Figure 27: Map of Hispania showing the Getuli in N. Africa.
(Public domain, https://commons.wikimedia.org)

now apparently lost to antiquity.

Now Raamah (aka, Ragmus, Rhegma, Raaman) had two sons, Sheba (Saba) and Dedan. This second Sheba muddies the waters a bit, as there is no distinctions made between this son of Raamah and Sheba the son of Cush. Thus, when Josephus twice mentions the Sabeans, he provides no differentiation. In the map in Figure 25 (*The World as Peopled by the Descendants of Noah*), there are two distinct nations with similar names: Sheba and Seba, which would seem to be the very nations in question here. This map shows Sheba at the southwestern shore of India, and Seba at the southern tip of the Arabian Peninsula. The sources used for this are unspecified, so lacking further evidence, we are left with these sites as the best candidates I've been able to discover.

The most ancient language used in southern India is Tamil, deemed by some to be the oldest language in the world, and the only one of the most ancient languages surviving today. Given its most ancient dating, I believe we must assign Tamil as the language of the Sabeans in southern India.

Dedan, the other son of Raamah, is called by Josephus "Judadas," and says of him that he "...*settled the Judadeans, a nation of the western Ethiopians, and left them his name.*" Lacking further information, we'll simply call the language Judadean.

Josephus goes on to tell of the sons of Mizraim, as follows:

Now all the children of Mesraim, being eight in number, possessed the country from Gaza to Egypt, though it retained the name of one only, the Philistiim; for the Greeks call that part of the country Palestine. As for the rest, Ludieim, the Enemim, and Labim, who alone inhabited Libya, and called the country from himself, Nedim, and Phethrosim, and Chesloim, and

Cepthorim, we know nothing of them besides their names; for the Ethiopic war, which we shall describe hereafter, was the cause that those cities were overthrown. [Ant. I:VI:2]

The region "*from Gaza to Egypt*" is the Sinai Peninsula (Figure 28). While this peninsula is today part of Egypt, at the time of dispersion it was apparently considered to be separate. Shortly thereafter, however, it was assimilated into Egypt, and has remained so through most of history. During the expansion of the Roman Empire, the Romans allotted it to the province of Arabia, and it effectively remained so until the end of WWI (1914-1918 AD), at which time it was returned to Egypt. This land

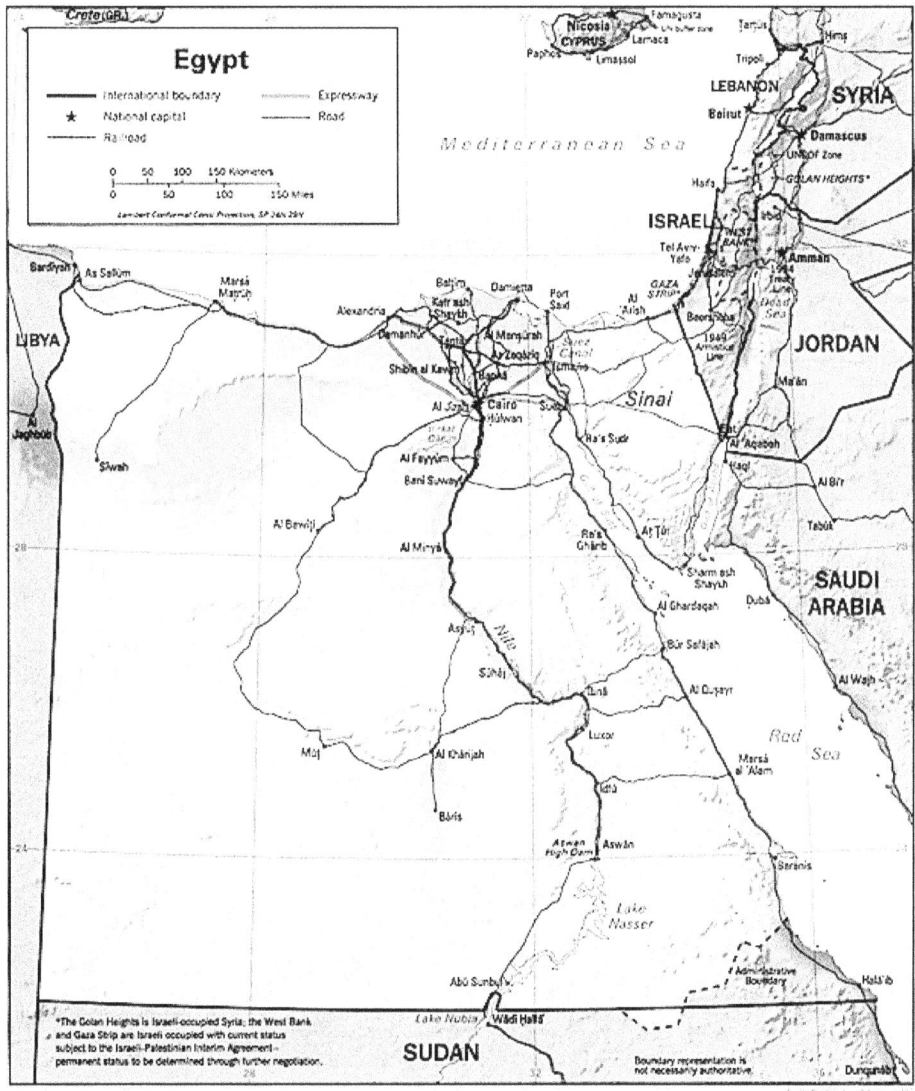

Figure 28: Sinai Peninsula. (commons.wikimedia.org)

was also occupied by Israel for a number of years in late 20th century. By the time of Josephus, all details of the fates of the offspring of Mizraim had been lost, save for the Philistines, mentioned enduringly throughout the OT. As Josephus points out, it was the Greeks who called the land of the Philistines "Palestine," which name survives to this day.

In summary, the descendants of Ham occupied the continent of Africa, as well as the Sinai Peninsula, Arabia, India, part of Asia Minor, and the land of Canaan extending through Phoenicia.

The Descendants of Shem

Genesis 10:21-31 delineates the posterity of Shem, and again, rather than inserting the Scripture here, I refer you to Table 4, where I have tabulated the names. As to the allotment of land to these nations, v30 says *"And their dwelling place was from Mesha as you go toward Sephar, the mountain of the east."* At first, I was uncertain as to whether or not the reference to "their" meant only the immediate antecedent in v29 (the sons of Joktan, son of Eber), or if it referred to the broader sense of all the children of Shem going back to v22. In the entire span of v21-31, only one destination is mentioned, and that is v30. Thus, while many assign the reference only to the sons of Joktan, it could be to all the progeny of Shem. I thought first to discover to what "Mesha" refers. According to Strong's Concordance, Mesha (Strong's 4852) is *"A place in southeastern Arabia."* And it also tells us that Sephar (Strong's 5611) is *"A mountain in Arabia."* These clues, as well as a search in the Book of Jasher, proved to be of no value, and my internet searches returned various proposed locations, none of which was particularly persuasive. I thus revisited Josephus' *Antiquities*, and this proved quite instructive:

> *Shem, the third son of Noah, had five sons, who inhabited the land that began at Euphrates, and reached to the Indian Ocean; for Elam left behind him the Elamites, the ancestors of the Persians. Ashur lived at the city Nineve; and named his subjects Assyrians, who became the most fortunate nation, beyond others. Arphaxad named the Arphaxadites, who are now called Chaldeans. Aram had the Aramites, which the Greeks call Syrians; as Laud founded the Laudites, which are now called Lydians. Of the four sons of Aram, Uz founded Trachonitis and Damascus; this country lies between Palestine and Celesyria. Ul founded Armenia; and Gather the Bactrians; and Mesa the Mesaneans; it is now called Charax Spasini. Sala was the son of Arphaxad; and his son was Heber, from whom they originally called the Jews, Hebrews. Heber begat Joctan and Phaleg: he was called Phaleg, because he was born at the dispersion of nations to their several countries; for Phaleg, among the Hebrews, signifies division. Now Joctan, one of the sons of Heber, had these sons, Elmodad, Saleph, Asermoth, Jera, Adoram, Aizel, Decla, Ebal, Abimael, Sabeus, Ophir, Euilat, and Jobab. These inhabited from Cophen, an Indian river, and in part of Asia adjoining to it. And this shall suffice concerning the sons of Shem.* [Ant. I:VI:4].

Josephus very clearly identifies many of the nations coming from the Shemites: Elam – Persia; Ashur – Assyria; Arphaxad – Chaldea; Aram – Syria; Laud – Lydia (Asia Minor); Uz – Trachonitis (SW Syria); Ul – Armenia; Gether – Bactria (Afghanistan); and Meshech – within Sumer. As for the progeny of Joktan, he refers to the Cophen River as Indian. Research reveals that this river is now called the Kabul River that runs mostly through modern-day Pakistan which borders India. The Indian Empire, prior to 1947, included what is today Pakistan, all the way to the border of Afghanistan. Thus, to identify the river as Indian would have been correct in any era prior. He ends his description of the nations from Joktan as spreading into part of Asia adjoining it. The limits to which this reach extended remain unclear. The map in Figure 23 shows this to extend all the way to the eastern limits of Asia, including the island nations of southeastern Asia and Oceania. I've not yet found sufficient evidence to substantiate this.

Recall that it was to Abraham's lineage that the land then occupied by the Canaanites was promised to him.

The Descendants of Japheth

The lineage of Japheth is clearly now my only remaining hope of finding nations that would occupy the continents beyond Asia and Africa. I was well aware that this would include Europe, but what about beyond? As I reviewed the Scriptures, I again read Gen 10:1-5. Beginning with v2, this deals with the genealogy of Japheth. Verses 2-5 read as follows:

> *The sons of Japheth were Gomer, Magog, Madai, Javan, Tubal, Meshech, and Tiras. The sons of Gomer were Ashkenaz, Riphath, and Togarmah. The sons of Javan were Elishah, Tarshish, Kittim, and Dodanim. From these the coastline peoples of the Gentiles were separated into their lands, everyone according to his language, according to their families, into their nations.*

I focused on the word "coastline." When I opened Strong's, this word was not there. Thus, I had to go back to the KJV to find the correct word. The KJV reads as follows:

> *The sons of Japheth; Gomer, and Magog, and Madai, and Javan, and Tubal, and Meshech, and Tiras. And the sons of Gomer; Ashkenaz, and Riphath, and Togarmah. And the sons of Javan; Elishah, and Tarshish, Kittim, and Dodanim. By these were the isles of the Gentiles divided in their lands; every one after his tongue, after their families, in their nations.*

The "isles" of the Gentiles...hmmm. This word (Strong's 339) is defined as:

> *A habitable spot (as desirable); dry land, a coast, an island: country, isle, island.*

With this, I realized that this is describing the separation of the supercontinent into the soon to be disconnected "islands" (continents!). *Indeed, the posterity of Japheth were being sent to the four corners of the globe.* Understanding that Josephus and Jasher delineate specific and identifiable nations in Europe, I had to continue to delve more deeply to obtain the certainty I sought.

Turning first to Josephus' *Antiquities*, I read the following account:

> *Japhet, the son of Noah, had seven sons: they inhabited so, that, beginning at the mountains of Taurus and Amanus, they proceeded along Asia, as far as the river Tanais, and along Europe to Cadiz; and settling themselves upon the lands which they light upon, which none had inhabited before, they called the nations by their own names; for Gomer founded those whom the Greeks call Galatians, [Galls,] but were then called Gomerites. Magog founded those that from him were called Magogites, but who are by the Greeks called Scythians. Now as to Javan and Madai, the sons of Japhet; from Madai came the Madeans, who are called Medes by the Greeks; but from Javan, Ionia and all the Grecians are derived. Thobel founded the Thobelites, who are now called Iberes; and the Mosocheni were founded by Mosoch; now they are Cappadocians. There is also a mark of their ancient denomination still to be shewn; for there is even now among them a city called Mazaca, which may inform those able to understand, that so was the entire nation once called. Thiras also called those*

whom he ruled over, Thirasians, but the Greeks changed the name to Thracians. And so many were the nations that had the children of Japhet for their inhabitants. Of the three sons of Gomer, Aschanax founded Aschanaxians, who are now called by the Greeks Rheginians. So did Riphath found the Ripheans, now called Paphlagonians; and Thrugramma the Thrugammeans, who, as the Greeks resolved, were named Phrygians. Of the three sons of Javan also, the son of Japhet, Elisa gave name to the Eliseans, who were his subjects; they are now the Aeolians. Tharsus to the Tharsians; for so was Cilicia of old called; the sign of which is this, that the noblest city they have, and a metropolis also, is Tarsus, the tau being by change put for theta. Cethimus possessed the island of Cethima; it is now called Cyprus: and from that it is that all islands, and the greatest part of the sea coasts, are named Cethim by the Hebrews: and one city there is in Cyprus that has been able to preserve its denomination; it is called Citius by those who use the language of the Greeks, and has not, by the use of that dialect, escaped the name of Cethim. And so many nations have the children and grand-children of Japhet possessed. [Ant I:VI:1]

Josephus knew not of the Americas, Australia, or Antarctica. His scope for the posterity of Japheth stopped at the limits of Europe and Asia. Is there still room for other continental nations? Let's work through the list. Gomer = Galls (France). This is confirmed in the Book of Jasher where it says:

And the children of Gomer, according to their cities, were the Francum, who dwell in the land of Franza, by the river Franza, by the river Senah. [Jash 10:8]

It couldn't be any clearer; the Senah is clearly the river Seine. The Magogites are described as being Scythians. The Scythian Empire included parts of Iran and extended both eastward and northward from there into what is today the Ukraine. The language spoken by these nomadic peoples is recognized as Indo-Iranian. The Madai are plainly identified as the Medes, which kingdom was also centered in modern-day Iran. And the descendants of Javan are explicitly identified as the Ionians, that is, Greeks. The Greek language has been spoken in this European region since the second millennium BC. Tubal (Thobel) is said to be the founder of the Iberes. The Iberian Peninsula comprises Spain and Portugal. Spanish and Portuguese are very similar languages, and share a common origin in Latin. As Latin did not come into being until the 6th century BC, the language of the Iberes is said to be Iberian, but so little is known about it that it remains an unclassified language. Meshech (Mosoch) founded Cappadocia, which is a region of Anatolia, or what is today eastern Turkey. Little is known of the language of the ancient Cappadocians, but the Greek historian Strabo (1st century BC) said that it was not Greek. Tiras ruled over the Thracians, which is in present day southern Bulgaria. As with so many other of the extinct languages of ancient times, there is precious little evidence of this remaining today.

Ashkenaz, a son of Gomer, founded what Josephus says to be the Rheginians. While no one is certain about these peoples, many identify them with the Scythians. However, there is another school of thought that places them in northern France and western Germany. I tend to favor this view for two reasons: first, the Scythians have already been associated with Magog; and secondly, Ashkenaz' brother is Gomer who settled France and this latter scheme would place them in close proximity. Riphath is associated with Paphlagonia, which lies in Asia Minor (modern day Turkey) centered on the southern shore of the Black Sea. Apparently, this region of Asia Minor was quite isolated and of insufficient strategic location to have played much of a role in ancient history, and thus the language is obscure. The historian Strabo did say that the language was differentiated from the others in the region. Phrygia, founded by Togarmah (Jospehus' Thrugramma) was a kingdom in central Asia Minor, lying roughly between Lydia and Galatia, south of Paphlagonia and west of Cappadocia. The language spoken in ancient times was Phrygian, although Strabo apparently considered the Phrygians a Thracian tribe. The Eliseans, or Aeolians, are associated with Elishah, son of Javan. Aeolis was a part of Thessaly, considered one of the Greek city-states. Their language is considered a dialect of Greek, but their Biblically ancient origin infers that the Greek dialect probably developed by proximity and/or assimilation. Cilicia is on the southeastern shore of Asia Minor, bordering on Syria. There is indeed a city of Tarsus there, so the association with Tarshish (Tharsus) is most probable. The Luwian language was spoken here in ancient times, and is, in fact, one of the oldest languages known. Eteocypriot is the ancient language of Cyprus before the influence of the Greeks, Cyprus being the identity of the land settled by Kittim (Cethimus), son of Javan.

This completes the Biblical table of nations. The Book of Jasher delineates another generation: the ten children of Togarmah, who all "...*spread and rested in the north and built themselves cities.*" (Jash 10:10) With names such as Tarki, Balgar, and Ongal, it is tempting to immediately associate these with the nations of Turkey, Bulgaria, and Mongolia. The author of Jasher says further of these that they "...*abide by the rivers Hithlah and Italac unto this day.*" (Jash 10:11) These names are now lost to antiquity, so connections would be highly speculative. There are also conflicts between Josephus and Jasher, so it is difficult to establish ultimate truth here.

Now, since I've run out of possibilities for peopling of the Americas among the 71 nations outlined in the Bible, there are certainly many nations on the earth not identified within this list, meaning that other members of these nations would have migrated, sooner or later. I can thus still opine that the Americas, Australia, and possibly Antarctica were populated very shortly after the dispersion of nations. As the continents were still connected during this migration, it would have been a simple matter to step beyond the borders described and thus to find some of the peoples of this generation edging into adjacent, yet unascribed regions.

Remember, it was 340 years after the Deluge that this dispersion takes place. We're not just dealing with the two, three, or four generations here. It is only in the line of Shem that the list goes to the fifth generation, but those later generations also existed in the lines of Shem and Japheth, as well, but consisted in the various specified nations. The line of Japheth is only enumerated to the second generation, and in Ham's line only three names are given in the third generation. These 71 nations were not just handfuls of people each, but thousands upon thousands.

I'd like to close this section out with one additional evidence that the nations populated the other continents. I will jump ahead exactly 1000 years to the time of Solomon. Let's look at the passage in 1Ki 10:22:

For the king had merchant ships at sea with the fleet of Hiram. Once every three years the merchant ships came bringing gold, silver, ivory, apes, and monkeys.

While the ivory, apes, and monkeys might indicate that these ships were bringing forth goods from Africa or India, I would venture to say that it does not take three years for a round trip from the shores of the Red Sea to the African or Indian coast. But a round trip to South America could be accomplished in such time. Don't forget that God imbued Solomon with wisdom beyond all men, and that he built a fleet of ships (1Ki 9:26). Given his God-given wisdom, these ships were surely engineered to traverse the high seas, and Solomon would have understood the spherical geography of the earth, and how to navigate to distant shores. So, yes, he would have shipments from Africa, but probably the Americas, as well. But little of his knowledge survived him.

On a closing note, I found it amusing that linguistics authorities place the dates of the oldest languages ALL at 5000 years old. These languages were fully developed with complex vocabulary covering the broadest range of disciplines, emotions, ideas, philosophical notions, and complex abstractions, along with well-established syntax, tenses, voices, and cases. All out of nowhere, all at the same time. Coincidence? Clearly, a better date is 4000 years old (1948 BC, to be precise).

CHAPTER 11: Mythology

We now turn our attention to the subject of mythology. After all that I've presented, do you still think that mythology is a myth? I'm a firm believer that all myths have at least a grain of truth to them. Is it so difficult, now understanding the fall of the angels, how they would have easily been regarded as gods? Not only that, but that the angels would have relished the power and encouraged such regard? They were supernatural beings, but with weaknesses of the flesh. And that their offspring by human women were the so-called demigods…the heroes of old!? Hercules was an historical person, but the mythical Hercules was based on a more ancient being, but just as real. The mythical creatures that were cross-breeds were likely also real creatures, at some point past.

The subject of ancient mythologies occupies volumes, and even the briefest overview would require the equivalent of several chapters that I really cannot delve into here. However, the biggest issue that has concerned me is that of the female gods, or goddesses. If the angels are all truly male beings, where did the goddesses in mythology arise? In my research, I found a commentary stating that it was long accepted by many that the ancient goddesses were actually demigods…the offspring of gods and women. I've not been able to rediscover this avowal to document the source, and for this lapse in my rigor you have my apologies. It is well known that the Greek god Zeus consorted with over forty human women, who then bore him about fifty demigod children.

Now I present on the next page (Figure 29) a "Family Tree of the Ancient Greek Gods," that presents a graphic summary of the Greek mythology as derived from Hesiod's *Theogony* (i.e., "birth of the gods"). This poem, written in the 7th or 8th century BC, is largely a cosmogony (i.e., "birth of the cosmos"), and there are striking parallels between the Genesis creation account and that in the Theogony. I find the first couple of lines in the chart fascinating, as they reflect the Genesis account of creation. Hesiod essentially personifies created things (both physical and conceptual) associating each with one of the various gods. Recall that the fallen angels each had specific disciplines to govern and/or to teach.

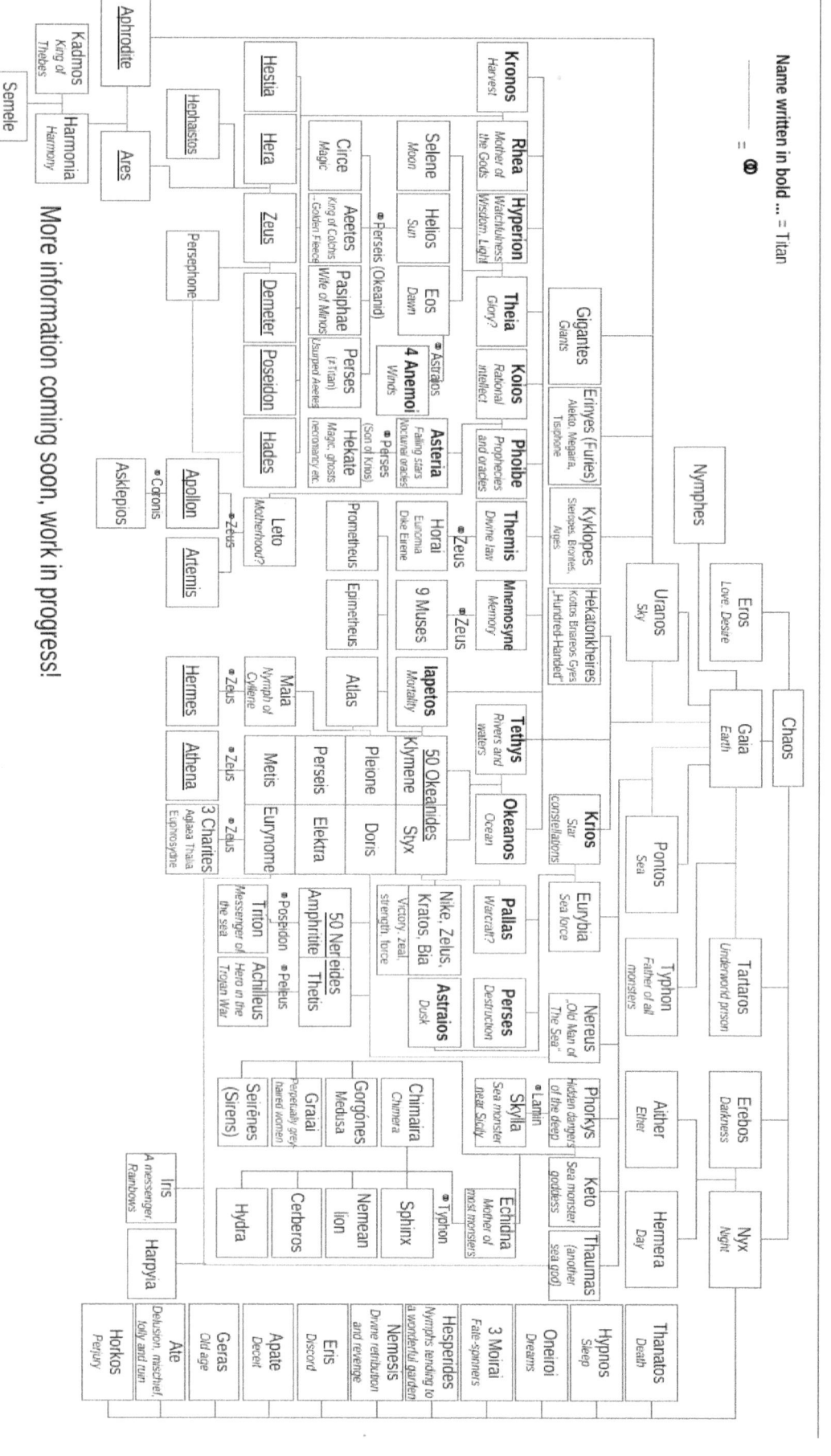

Figure 29: *Family Tree of the Ancient Greek Gods (from ju-te.neocities.org; reprinted with permission from Matt Kõiv)*
(Sources: Handout from the Ancient Greek Gods and Mythology lecture by Mait Kõiv, Wikipedia and theoi.org)

The poem also distinguishes three classes of created beings: gods, humans, and "powerful giants." Specifically, it all starts with the god "Chaos," and there is a footnote on the webpage below this image that reads, *"Note: 'Chaos' means nothingness in this case."* Hearkening back to Gen 1:2, it says, *"The earth was without form, and void; and darkness was on the face of the deep."* The footnote in the NKJV Study Bible reads *"The two words **without form…void express one concept – chaos**."* [Taken from NKJV Study Bible. Copyright ©1997, 2007 by Thomas Nelson. Used by permission of Thomas Nelson. www.thomasnelson.com; emphasis mine.] The Scripture definitely conveys a sense of great disorder, or chaos (high entropy). God imparts increasing order with each day (reducing entropy, or imparting negative entropy on the universe) as creation proceeds. The diagram then shows on the second rank the subsequent gods that arise out of the chaos: Gaia (earth), Erebos (darkness), Nyx (night), etc. On the third tier we have Uranos (sky), Pontos (sea), Hermera (day), etc. On the fourth rank we have Krios (star constellations), on the fifth we have Okeanus (waters), on the sixth we see Selene (moon), Helios (sun), Eos (dawn), and Astraios (dusk), not having delineated the various creatures and other personifications. There is a compelling parallel between the Scriptural creation and the Greek "gods." What I see is evidence of a corruption of the Genesis account of creation into the Greek mythology. And from the Greek mythology, we have the Roman and Norse derivatives, as well as ancestral (most notably Hittite) versions.

In 2Pet 2:4a we find the fate of the fallen angels:

"For if God did not spare the angels who sinned, but cast them down to hell and delivered them into chains of darkness, to be reserved for judgment."

Their destiny is echoed in Jude 6:

"And the angels who did not keep their proper domain, but left their own abode, He has reserved in everlasting chains under darkness for the judgment of the great day."

This place of darkness, or "hell," is the Greek word "Tartarus." Strong's Concordance tells us that this word (Strong's 5020) is the name for *"The deepest abyss of Hades."* In Greek mythology we have "Tartaros" as an underworld prison in which the Greek Titans (the "former gods") were confined after their defeat by the Olympian gods, and where, in the Biblical account, the disembodied, fallen angels are being held until their judgment. The same word "Tartaros" for this dark abyss is used in the Bible and mythology, which underscores their common origin.

Here is where we connect the dots. Could it thus be that the Titans were in fact the antediluvian fallen angels, defeated by the faithful angels, and then that the Olympian gods were the postdiluvian fallen angels, some of which may also have been among the virtuous, victorious army of angels? Very interestingly, Zeus is the leader of the Olympian gods, and is the god of the sky. Recall that in Eph 2:2, Satan is depicted as *"…the prince of the power of the air."* The NIV translation renders this same phrase as *"…the ruler of the kingdom of the air…."*

In the Biblical Book of Revelation, we have another interesting passage in chapter 2, verses 12 & 13:

And to the angel of the church in Pergamos write, 'These things says He who has the sharp two-edged sword: "I know your works, and where you dwell, where Satan's throne is."

In Pergamos, there is an acropolis on the city's highest point. One of the most impressive structures on that acropolis was the Temple of Zeus, with an accompanying feature known as the Great Altar of Pergamon, also referred to as the Altar of Zeus. The foregoing passage in Revelation makes the association between Zeus and Satan. The altar itself was removed from the acropolis in Pergamon by the Russians in 1948 as the spoils of war, and was later moved to Berlin in 1958, where it resides today. I've inserted an image of this (see Figure 30).

If that is not enough to persuade you, I provide the tale of the Flood of Deucalion. In Figure 29, you will find the Greek god Prometheus; while not shown in this graphic, Prometheus had a son named Deucalion. There are several versions of the account, but within these various accounts we have Zeus determining to flood the world because of man's wickedness, Prometheus telling his son Deucalion to build an ark that carries him and his wife through the flood, after which it comes to rest on one of various named mountains, he sacrifices to Zeus, and finally he and his wife repopulate the earth.

Again, the parallels are extraordinary. I conclude that mythology is not a complete myth, and is indeed founded upon the Biblical creation and the fall of angels.

Figure 30: The Altar of Zeus in Pergamum
(© Raimond Spekking / CC BY-SA 4.0 (via Wikimedia Commons)

CHAPTER 12: The Lost City of Atlantis

As I was reading Newton's *Chronicles* in the course of research for my Bible chronologies (see Appendix), I read a passage that so struck me that I nearly fell out of my chair. I've never been a believer in a real Atlantis, considering it only a mythical construct of Plato's imagination. I was often amused by television shows presenting present-day, educated men searching for archaeological evidence of this lost city in all imaginable locations around the globe. The subject passage in Newton's own words starts as follows:

> *The Atlantides, a people upon mount Atlas conquered by the Egyptians in the Reign of Ammon, related that* **Uranus was their first King**, *and reduced them from a savage course of life, and caused them to dwell in towns and cities, and lay up and use the fruits of the earth, and that he reigned over a great part of the world, and by his wife Titoea* [aka Gaia] *had eighteen children, among which were Hyperion and Basilea the parents of Helius and Selene; that the brothers of Hyperion slew him, and drowned his son Helius, the Phaeton of the ancients, in the Nile, and divided his kingdom amongst themselves; and* **the country bordering upon the Ocean fell to the lot of Atlas**, *from whom the people were called Atlantides. By Uranus or Jupiter Uranius, Hyperion, Basilea, Helius and Selene, I understand Jupiter Ammon, Osiris, Isis, Orus and Bubaste; and by sharing of the Kingdom of Hyperion amongst his brothers the Titans, I understand the* **division of the earth among the Gods mentioned in the poem of Solon**.
>
> *For Solon having travelled into Egypt, and conversed with the Priests of Sais; about their antiquities, wrote a Poem of what he had learnt, but did not finish it; and this Poem fell into the hands of Plato who relates out of it, that* **at the mouth of the Straits near Hercules's Pillars there was an island called Atlantis**, *the people of which nine thousand years before the days of Solon, reigned over Libya as far as Egypt; and over Europe as far as the Tyrrhene sea; and all this force collected into one body invaded Egypt and Greece, and whatever was contained in the Pillars of Hercules, but was resisted and stopt by the Athenians and other Greeks, and thereby the rest of the nations not yet conquered were preserved: he saith also that* **in those days the Gods, having finished their conquests, divided the whole earth amongst themselves**, *partly into larger, partly into smaller portions, and instituted Temples and Sacred Rites to themselves; and that the* **Island Atlantis fell to the lot of Neptune, who made his eldest Son Atlas King of the whole Island**, *a part of which was called Gadir....* [Isaac Newton, *Chronicles*, Ch. II; public domain]

Newton goes on to say that the Egyptians exaggerated the extent of their ancient history to 9000 years to make themselves to be the most ancient of civilizations. Specifically, he says,

> *...but the Priests of Egypt in those 400 years had magnified the stories and antiquity of their Gods so exceedingly, as to make them 9000 years older than Solon,* **and the Island Atlantis bigger than all Afric and Asia together, and full of people; and because in the days of Solon this great Island did not appear, they pretended that it was sunk into the sea with all its people**.... [Isaac Newton, *Chronicles*, Ch. II; public domain; boldface mine]

Starting at the end of the first paragraph, Newton describes the "*...division of the earth among the Gods mentioned in the poem of Solon.*" What is the poem of Solon? Well, the Greek philosopher

Plato (c428-348 BC) wrote, among many other things, a pair of "dialogues" entitled *"Timaeus"* (c360 BC) and its sequel, *"Critias,"* (c348 BC). These two comprise the only primary sources describing Atlantis. Any other writing about Atlantis should be considered embellished, and therefore unreliable. In *Timaeus*, the character Critias provides an introduction for the character Timaeus' monologue on the origin of the universe, the elements, etc. In that introduction he describes the journey of a more ancient Greek statesman, Solon (an actual, historical figure living c630 - 560 BC), to Egypt where he hears the story of Atlantis from the Egyptian priests as Solon makes inquiry about their ancient history. This story is passed down and Critias hears it from an aged man of 90 when he is but ten years old.

Sir Isaac Newton does a very good job in summarizing the pertinent part of the story of Atlantis in *Timaeus*. For the more curious, you can read the full English translation of this at http://classics.mit.edu/Plato/timaeus.html.

In the sequel *Critias*, Plato retells the tale told by Solon, providing additional details regarding the accomplishments of the nation of Atlantides. Critias starts with the following introduction:

> *Let me begin by observing first of all, that nine thousand was the sum of years which had elapsed since the war which was said to have taken place between* ***those who dwelt outside the Pillars of Heracles and all who dwelt within them****; this war I am going to describe.* [Public domain; emphasis mine]

Again, this establishes the location of the city and greater associated land mass. The next section begins with the following narrative:

> ***In the days of old the gods had the whole earth distributed among them by allotment.*** *There was no quarrelling; for you cannot rightly suppose that the gods did not know what was proper for each of them to have, or, knowing this, that they would seek to procure for themselves by contention that which more properly belonged to others.* ***They all of them by just apportionment obtained what they wanted, and peopled their own districts****; and when they had peopled them they tended us, their nurselings and possessions, as shepherds tend their flocks....* [Public domain; emphasis mine]

This provides us with the foundational parallel to the fallen angels of Genesis 6. They divided the earth among themselves for kingdoms, and governed the people benevolently, as a shepherd over his flock.

Critias goes on, intending to outline the war between the Atlantides and the Athenians, but he never gets to this in the unfinished dialogue *Critias* that Plato left. In his still preliminary monologue, he notes the following with regard to the land mass to the west of the Pillars of Hercules:

> *...and during all this time and through so many changes, there has never been any considerable accumulation of the soil coming down from the mountains, as in other places,* ***but the earth has fallen away all round and sunk out of sight****. The consequence is, that in comparison of what then was,* ***there are remaining only the bones of the wasted body, as they may be called, as in the case of small islands****....* [Public domain; emphasis mine]

As was perceived by the ancient Egyptians, this land mass had "fallen away," leaving only pieces behind, those being Atlantic islands. I propose to you that what happened in this time was the very catastrophic plate tectonics, separating the supercontinent into the seven continents we have today. I submit to you what Albert Einstein termed a *"gedanken* experiment"…that is, a thought experiment, such as he employed in developing his theory of relativity. Imagine yourself standing on the western shores of the Iberian Peninsula, witness to the rapid continental separation following the division of languages and nations. As you watched the eastern shores of the Americas fade into the distance, it would have the appearance of sinking, especially to someone ignorant of the spherical form of the earth. It would indeed constitute the only logical conclusion if one believed the earth to be flat. The island itself most probably disintegrated and/or sunk into the Atlantic Ocean in the course of this continental separation.

Continuing in the next section he opens with the following:

> *I have before remarked in speaking of the **allotments of the gods, that they distributed the whole earth into portions differing in extent, and made for themselves temples** and instituted sacrifices. And **Poseidon, receiving for his lot the island of Atlantis, begat children by a mortal woman**….* [Public domain; emphasis mine]

The gods built for themselves temples. Here we have evidence of the rationale for construction of the pyramids on the various continents, as well as the other ancient stone structures found, whose means of construction cannot be easily explained, even with the advantages of modern machinery (e.g., Puma Punku, Sacsayhuaman, Ollantaytambo, Chand Baori, Baalbek, the Sun Temple at Modhera, not having mentioned the Great Pyramid at Giza, and others). In addition, we have Poseidon begetting children by a mortal woman…precisely as described in Genesis 6.

Critias goes on to address the reason for Poseidon's construction of the unique harbor so often associated with Atlantis:

> *Poseidon fell in love with her and had intercourse with her, and breaking the ground, inclosed the hill in which she dwelt all round, making alternate zones of sea and land larger and smaller, encircling one another; there were two of land and three of water, which he turned as with a lathe, each having its circumference equidistant every way from the centre, so that **no man could get to the island, for ships and voyages were not as yet**.* [Public domain; emphasis mine]

It seems that he built this harbor as a gift for his bride. He built it around the mountain on which she lived, thus placing her home in the center. It is striking that he says that at this time *"…ships and voyages were not as yet."* In a previous comment within this monologue, Critias says that this took place before the *"great destruction of Deucalion."* I have doubt of this, in part. First, while Uranos was among the antediluvian fallen angels, Poseidon was not. On the contrary, Poseidon was among the second group of (postdiluvian) Olympian gods who overcame the (antediluvian) Titans.

As previously noted, Deucalion is the Greek-mythological counterpart to the historical Noah, who navigated and survived the global flood. I suspect that the antediluvian and postdiluvian histories were both conflated and corrupted by the Egyptians.

Now Poseidon, being a god (fallen angel), his offspring by his human wife (Cleito) were thus demigods, or Titans (not to be confused or conflated with the Titans that were the "old gods" of Greek mythology…an unfortunate association in name), the eldest of which was Atlas, who received the Atlantic continent as his kingdom. Atlas had nine brothers by the same parents, each of whom received other portions of the earth as kingdoms.

Critias says that there were elephants on this land mass where the City of Atlantis was. Seeing as there are no elephants native to the Americas today, I searched the internet for information on elephant and/or wooly mammoth remains found in the Americas, and indeed, I found first that *National Geographic* published an article in 2014 telling of an ancient tribe (the Clovis) in the region of the Sonoran Desert in North America who ate an ancient, tusked relative of the elephant ("Gomphotheres"). Similarly, there is an article from the *BBC* (bbc.com) dated November 2019 that describes the remains of wooly mammoths found in Mexico. These reports thus lend credence to Solon's story.

The work is unfinished, as you will see clearly from the closing lines, which themselves are telling of the true origin of the story:

> *Zeus, the god of gods, who rules according to law, and is able to see into such things, perceiving that an honourable race was in a woeful plight, and wanting to inflict punishment on them, that they might be chastened and improve,* **collected all the gods into their most holy habitation, which, being placed in the centre of the world, beholds all created things***. And when he had called them together, he spake as follows-* [public domain; emphasis mine]

Thus closes the completed portion of this tale. Recall that in the chapter on Mythology, I proposed that the antediluvian fallen angels were defeated by virtuous angels, and that some among the virtuous victors may have also been among the postdiluvian fallen ranks. Given the destiny of the fallen antediluvian angels (i.e., disembodied and cast into Tartarus until the last days), the tale of Atlantis provides a compelling parallel account.

(As with *Timaeus*, you can read the whole of an English translation of the original at http://classics.mit.edu/Plato/critias.html. It is a quick read.)

Appendix A: Chronology of Biblical History

As noted in the narrative of this book, Biblical chronology is not perfectly established. Not only are there vacancies in the Biblical narrative, but there are also apparent inconsistencies. As I have complete confidence in Biblical inerrancy, I cannot abide any belief that inaccuracies have been propagated in Scripture. Thus, while some such inconsistencies are admittedly difficult to reconcile, and consequently require significant mathematical contrivance to resolve, the ultimate truth is established, even if our proposed machinations may not be correct. In fact, if my interpretation of temporal prophetic Scripture is errant, my misconstruction would result in my pounding the proverbial square peg into its counterpart round hole. I am equally committed to discovering the accuracy of the chronology and cannot rest easy until I've persuaded myself that congruence of the times can be soundly established.

Now another matter that deserves comment regards the length of a year. The Hebrews used a lunar calendar, but with the lunar cycle being nominally 30 days (closer to 29.5 days), 12 months of this length is 360 days. The Egyptians, with their mastery of observational astronomy, appear to have been the first civilization to determine that the twelve lunar months were not synchronized with the solar year. The following is an extract from an article entitled *History of the Egyptian Calendar* from https://www.infoplease.com/calendars/history/history-egyptian-calendar:

> *The ancient Egyptians used a calendar with 12 months of 30 days each, for a total of 360 days per year.* **About 4000 B.C. they added five extra days** *at the end of every year to bring it more into line with the solar year. These five days became a festival because it was thought to be unlucky to work during that time.*
>
> *The Egyptians had calculated that the solar year was actually closer to 365¼ days, but instead of having a single leap day every four years to account for the fractional day (the way we do now), they let the one-quarter day accumulate. After 1,460 solar years, or four periods of 365 years, 1,461 Egyptian years had passed. This means that as the years passed, the Egyptian months fell out of sync with the seasons, so that the summer months eventually fell during winter. Only once every 1,460 years did their calendar year coincide precisely with the solar year.*
>
> *In addition to the civic calendar, the Egyptians also had a religious calendar that was based on the 29½-day lunar cycle and was more closely linked with agricultural cycles and the movements of the stars.* [Emphasis mine]

Astronomy was one of the disciplines taught by the fallen angels. So one has to wonder if generations back to the time of Noah knew to add intercalary days to synchronize with the solar year. And if perhaps that knowledge was lost for many generations before it was rediscovered.

Nonetheless, once this practice of adding intercalary days was instituted by the Egyptians, most other civilizations around the Mediterranean would also have adopted this practice soon after. As for the Greek civilization, they also knew to use intercalation of days and/or months. The following excerpt is from an article entitled *"The Athenian Calendar,"* written by Christopher Planeaux in 2015, and published to the Ancient History Encyclopedia website [https://www.ancient.eu/article/833/the-athenian-calendar/]:

Athenians, especially from the 3rd Century BCE forward, could consult any one of five separate "calendars:" Olympiad, Seasonal, Civil, Conciliar, and finally Metonic – depending on what event or type of event they wished to chronical. Athenians, furthermore, either created these calendars for specific purposes or adopted them from others.

All Athenian calendars, however, used lunar cycles and/or solar events (typically solstices and equinoxes but also certain stars or constellations) to affix dates. ...

Lunar (synodic) months each contain 29.53 days (one lunar cycle). A twelve month lunar year thus contains 354.36 days. A solar astronomical year, however, counts 365.24 days. Athenians understood from a very early time, especially with the advent of farming, that a lunar year fell 11 days short of a solar year. Any strict lunar calendar would therefore gain just over one synodic month in 3 years and drift through the seasons in 33 year cycles.

Nevertheless, Athenians did not abandon their lunar reckoning, because most of their annual festivals had become fixed by the phases of the moon (Geminus 8.7-8) – thus began the Athenian practice of ongoing periodical intercalations (deleting/inserting days and inserting months) designed to align the lunar and solar cycles. Athenians sought simply to keep these oscillations to a minimum. Scholars therefore refer to Athenian Calendars as "lunisolar."

The Romans took almost 300 years, to the first century AD, to come to the same conclusion as the Egyptians. If the previous errors would have remained uncorrected, then the accumulated error would be roughly 4000 years multiplied by the annual error of about 5.25 days, or about 57 years. If the lunar year were the measure, then we've already surpassed the preordained 6000-year term of history. I thus conclude that when the Bible marks events using the word "year," that a full solar year is intended. (Note that the meaning of the Hebrew word rendered as "year" does not provide any clarification or inference of lunar vs solar.)

The Rev. James Ussher shared this opinion. In *The Epistle to the Reader* (i.e., preface) from his *Annals of the World*, he writes:

"...we find that the years of our forefathers, the years of the ancient Egyptians and Hebrews were the same length as the Julian Year. It consisted of 12 months containing 30 days. (It cannot be proved that the Hebrews used lunar months before the Babylonian captivity.) 5 days were added to the 12th month each year. Every 4 years, 6 days were added to the 12th month." [Public domain]

Lastly, I return to *The Chaldean Account of Genesis*. As referenced earlier, in the fifth tablet of the creation legend, it reads in part:

It was delightful, all that was fixed by the great gods. Stars their appearance [in figures] of animals he arranged. To fix the year through the observation of their constellations, twelve months (or signs) of stars in three rows he arranged, from the day when the year commences unto the close. [Poetic lines concatenated.]

With this most ancient account telling us that it was known from antiquity that the span of a year was not determined by the lunar months, but by the stars, there is little foundation left to argue that the years accounted in the Bible are anything less than a true solar year. Remember, God knows how long a year really is, even if men did not. The Bible is the inspired word of God, so if the Bible says "year," a true solar year is intended. It is only in the case of secular histories that years might be different, but certainly not after the first century AD. The Bible itself tells us in Gen 1:14 that:

> *Then God said, "Let there be lights in the firmament of the heavens to divide the day from the night; and let them be for signs and seasons, and for days and years...."*

The sun was for the demarcation of days, the moon for the holy days, festivals, and signs (eclipses), and the stars for seasons and years.

Now this foundational deduction holds firmly up until the time of the exile of Jerusalem following the siege by Nebuchadnezzar in 3320 AM (624 BC). After this, the Biblical references to years are virtually all in regnal years of the Babylonian, Persian, and Median monarchs. This continues to about the year 3495 AM, near the end of Artaxerxes' reign.

With a lunar year of 12x29.5 = 354 days, the temporal lapse rate is about 11.24 days per lunar year. This was recognized by the Babylonians and they added intercalary months at the rate of about once every three years. They actually followed the so-called "Metonic cycle" that adds the intercalary month in the 3rd, 6th, 8th, 11th, 14th, 17th and 19th years. This methodology had apparently been instituted in the 8th century BC, so was already in place when the Jews were exiled. Thus, although the day/month synchronicity requires calculation, since absolute synchronization with the solar calendar is virtually never achieved due to the imprecision of the intercalation, the differential for my chronology is negligible. Real chronologists invest serious effort to track this, but such precision is well beyond the scope of this work.

The Enigma of the Period of the Judges

Certain portions of the Biblical chronology are quite clear with resultant broad agreement and consistent understanding. I would argue that the Biblical chronology from creation to the Deluge is seamlessly delineated, and that most scholars would probably agree to extend this chronological surety at least to the time of the Exodus (i.e., from 1 to 2448 AM, or about 40% of the total span of mankind's history). It is after this that some difficulties set in. The first enigma occurs from the time of Joshua through the time of the Judges.

The problems with this portion of Biblical chronology are multiple. The first is that the Bible does not disclose the exact number of years that Joshua led Israel after Moses' death, to his own death at the age of 110. It is after Joshua's death that the period of the Judges, and the Biblical book of the same name, begin. Secondly, we have no Biblical passage that establishes when the period of the Judges actually starts. While the Book of Judges opens with the phrase "*After the death of Joshua...,*" that does not necessarily mean 'immediately after;' it might instead mean 20, 30 or even 50 years after his death, particularly if nothing significant happened in that span. That there *is* a lapse in time here is alluded to in Jgs 2:8-10, which in the Septuagint (LXX) reads as follows:

> "*And Joshua the son of Naue, the servant of the Lord, died, a hundred and ten years old. And they buried him in the border of his inheritance, in Thamnathares, in mount Ephraim, on the north of the mountain of Gaas. And all that generation were laid to their fathers:* **and another generation rose up after them, who knew not the Lord***, nor yet the work which he wrought in Israel.*" (Emphasis mine)

Thus, it seems we have about the span of a generation from the death of Joshua to the beginning of the chronicle of the Judges. And the third issue in this time period is that the numbers of years do not seem to rightly add up to align with other verses of Scripture. Specifically, if we sum all the episodes in the sequence delineated in the Book of Judges, as presented in Table 5 on the next page, it should not conflict with any other passage of Scripture that deals with this era. The difficulty, however, arises when the account in the Book of Judges is juxtaposed with 1Ki 6:1 [NIV], which reads:

> *In the four hundred and eightieth year after the Israelites came out of Egypt, in the fourth year of Solomon's reign over Israel, in the month of Ziv, the second month, he began to build the temple of the LORD.*

To illustrate the issue, I've included in Table 5 the Biblical chronology of the complementary periods that complete the 480 year span delimited in 1Ki 6:1 (i.e., the reigns of Moses and Joshua and the *interregnum* before the period of the judges, and the reigns of Eli, Samuel, Saul, Ish-Bosheth, David, and Solomon, after the period of the judges). Upon doing this, the temporal discrepancy becomes clear. The subtotal for the period of the Judges (i.e., from the subjugation of Israel by Cushan-Rishathaim to the death of Samson) totals 410 years. Amending this span with the pertinent preceding and subsequent intervals in the 1Ki 6:1 sequence, the total then exceeds the cited 480 years by 163 years.

Be assured that no matter what we manipulate within the period of the Judges, it does not alter the comprehensive integrity of Biblical chronology. The lynchpin of so certain a declaration of timespan given in 1Ki 6:1 ensures the certainty and continuity of the timeline up to the time of Solomon's rule. Given that we already have confidence in the integrity of the first 2448 years of history, 1Ki6:1 extends this by another 480 years to the year 2928 AM, or about 49% of history to present day. Thus, while the episodes within this 410-year period of the judges may be entangled in incongruities, it is ultimately not a crucial matter. At the same time, though, I am compelled to find an arrangement of these events compliant with the balance of facts, if for no other reason than to satisfy my somewhat obsessive-compulsive nature when dealing with numbers, but also to confirm Biblical inerrancy.

Starting at the top of Table 5, the span of 40 years from the Exodus to the entry into the so-called Promised Land is well established in the Bible. Exo12 tells us that Passover was established the day before the Israelites left Egypt. Joshua takes them over the Jordan into Canaan 4 days prior to the 40th anniversary of this event (Jos 4:19, 5:10).

The term of Joshua's leadership is not disclosed in the Bible, but Jasher tells us in Ch. 90 v 47 that he judged Israel for 28 years. Josephus says that he judged Israel for 25 years. That the Canaanite wars ended after 5 years under Joshua is established in the fourteenth chapter of the book of Joshua,

Judge/King	Oppressor/Enemy	Years	Reference
Moses	Egypt, Moab, Midian, Edom, Arad, Amorites, Ammonites, Bashan	40	Exo 7:7; Deu 34:7
Joshua	Canaanites	25	Jash 90:47 Ant V:I:29
[*Interregnum*]	Canaanites	17	Jash 91:12
	Cushan-Rishathaim king of Aram	8	Jdg 3:8
Othniel	Peace	40	Jdg 3:11
	Eglom the Moabite	18	Jdg 3:14
Ehud/Shamgar	Peace	80	Jdg 3:30-31
	Canaan	20	Jdg 4:3
Deborah	Peace	40	Jdg 5:31
	Midian	7	Jdg 6:1
Gideon	Peace	40	Jdg 8:29
Abimelech	Abimelech	3	Jdg 9:22
Tolah	Philistines	23	Jdg 10:2
Jair	Philistines	22	Jdg 10:3
	Philistines and Ammonites	18	Jdg 10:8
Jephthah	Peace	6	Jdg 11:7
Ibzan	Peace	7	Jdg 12:9
Elon	Peace	10	Jdg 12:11
Abdon	Peace	8	Jdg 12:14
	Philistines	40	Jdg 13:1
Samson	Philistines	20	Jdg 16:31
Eli	Philistines	40	1Sam 4:18
Ark at Kiriath Jearim		20	1Sam 7:2
Samuel	Philistines	12	Ant VI:XIII:5
Samuel	Peace		
Samuel/Saul	Philistines	18	Ant VI:XIII:5
Saul	Philistines	22	Act 13:21
Is-Bosheth	Philistines	2	
David	Philistines	33	2Sa 5:4-5
Solomon	Peace	4	1Ki 6:1
	TOTAL	**643**	

Table 5: Chronology from the Exodus to Solomon

where in v10, as the conquered land is being divided among the tribes, Caleb says that God kept him alive for 45 years while Israel moved about in the desert. As an aside, Caleb and Joshua were contemporaries, so Caleb would be 105 at the time of Joshua's death at age 110.

As set forth previously, the book of Judges tells us that there was a wayward generation that grew up after Joshua's death that instigates the period of the Judges. Jospehus says that this "interregnum" lasts for 18 years, while the Book of Jasher says 17.

After having made several unsuccessful (and very frustrating…see preceding admission to being somewhat OCD) attempts to identify the resolution that has eluded so many before me, I thought to apply mathematics to help resolve the matter. We have the 480-year figure from 1Ki 6:1 and can set up an equation for that. Are there other verses of Scripture that can provide additional, constraining equations? The answer is yes. The first one we have can be found within the Book of Judges itself. Jephthah, one of the Judges, makes an interesting statement, addressed to the Ammonite king under whose oppression Israel was then suffering

> *For three hundred years Israel occupied Heshbon, Aroer, the surrounding settlements and all the towns along the Arnon.* [Jgs 11:26; NIV].

If this statement is accurate, we should be able to determine the approximate year in which Jephthah asserts this. An examination of the Book of Numbers (notably Ch. 20-33) reveals that the Israelites dispossessed the inhabitants of this region (east of the Jordan, or so-called "Transjordan") in the 40th year after the Exodus. This was the same year in which Miriam, Aaron, and Moses all died, or 2488 AM (1456 BC). Now, some argue that Israel's occupation of the Transjordan did not start until after the campaigns led by Joshua were completed, about five or six years later. However, the tribes of Reuben, Gad, and Manasseh left their wives and children there while the men went on to participate in the Canaanite wars on the west side of the Jordan, after which they returned to the Transjordan. This point is legitimately debatable and creates an uncertainty (and/or accounting latitude) in the chronology. However, the anchor should either be 2488 AM or 2493 AM, but no year in between.

Before we set up our two equations, I should note that many regard Jephthah's reference to 300 years as a "round number." They have done so because they cannot find agreement within the numbers with this constraint, and have thus assigned to it a more figurative status. I have to admit that the textual support for this is not without merit. The Book of Judges tells us what Jephthah said, not that what he said was precise or accurate. We can find numerous instances in the Bible where someone says something that is not accurate. For example, I reference the account in Genesis when Eve tells the serpent what God told her about the fruit from the Tree of Knowledge, but she adds to what God is therein recorded to have said by amending it with the phrase "*…and you shall not touch it….*" Bearing this in mind, I may also discover that I have to employ this escape, but we'll see if we cannot first make the numbers work without using this ploy.

Thus, we have two equations, but we need a common element in each in order to accomplish a solution. The common period to these spans is the time from the end of the Israelite campaigns in Canaan (which we'll label "EIC"), to the year of Jephthah's confrontation with the Ammonites (which we'll designate "JCA"), which is 300 years. To complete the equations, we also must factor in the 45 years from the Exodus to the end of the campaigns; that is, the 40 years wandering in the desert plus the 5 years of the campaigns themselves. Lastly, we'll designate the fourth year of Solomon's reign as "FSR." Setting up the equations, we have:

$$JCA - EIC = 300$$
$$FSR - (EIC + 45) = 480$$

Solving these simultaneously to eliminate the EIC term, we end up with the equation:

$$FSR - JCA = 135$$

If we had used just 40 years to the possession of the Transjordan, our final equation would be FSR - JCA = 140. Thus, we hope to find a solution using one or the other. Now referring back to Table 3 and summing the years from the start of Jephthah's judgeship through the fourth year of Solomon's reign, we have 242 years. Since we know that the total excess in the entire span from the Exodus to Solomon is 163 years, and now that this part of the table is specifically 107 years too long, we know that the solution must be in two parts: the first part from the Exodus to Jephthah, and the second part from Jephthah to Solomon. We'll start with the latter segment.

So, the first question is whether or not there is sufficient syntactic flexibility in the Biblical narrative of the second period to allow us to compress this by the necessary 107 years. I believe that there is, as I propose herein. First, I want to deal with the tenures of Samson and Eli. Regarding Samson, Jdg 15:20 says, *"Samson led Israel for twenty years in the days of the Philistines."* Thus, his twenty years coincide, at least in part, with the Philistine rule, so we can reckon those together, gaining us a portion of 20 years.

Similarly, we can construe that Eli's 40 years of leadership are also within the Philistine oppression since he dies immediately after the Philistines capture of the Ark of the Covenant…that is, the Philistines oppressed Israel for 40 years and there is no clear lapse between Samson and Eli. This means that Eli must have been leading concurrently with the judgeship of Samson. I believe that this, in part, disqualifies Eli from being one of the judges. To start, the passage about Eli is not found in the book of Judges, but rather in the book of 1Sam. While this in itself is not sufficient evidence to discount his status as a judge, it is notable that Eli is introduced in the book of 1Sam as a priest, as contrasted with the judges of the period. Furthermore, in Jgs 2:16 we are provided with a definition of judges in the context of this era:

> *Nevertheless, the LORD raised up judges, who delivered them out of the hands of those who plundered them.*

Eli did not save the Israelites from anyone. He was no warrior. Thus, I must conclude that he led Israel (per 1Sam 4:18) in a *priestly* capacity only, and not as a judge in the sense of what Scripture describes in the book of *Judges*. So, while others include Eli as a judge, I find absolutely no justification for this. In either case, we can eliminate his 40 years (or 20, as per the Septuagint, but this difference between the versions is moot in our analysis) of leadership from the table. Thus, we have picked up almost 60 of the 107 years that must be eliminated.

Now, let's examine when Samuel becomes "judge" over Israel. This event is described in 1Sam 7:6. Eli had died about 7 months earlier when the Ark of the Covenant was taken by the Philistines in a battle with Israel. The Israelites had imprudently brought the Ark up from Shiloh where it then resided. After its capture, the Philistines were beleaguered with plagues, and consequently returned it to Israel very obligingly, and it was then placed at Kiriath Jearim, specifically in the house of Abinadab. 1Sam 7:2 says that the ark remained there 20 years, and then Samuel is referred to for the first time as leading Israel on that day. Samuel was clearly regarded as a Prophet prior to that time, even before the death of Eli (1Sa 3:19 - 4:1); but his ascendency to official leadership (or judgeship) only starts upon the death of Eli. Samuel goes on to take on a role as a quasi-military leader at Mizpah, at the end of these 20 years. Does this make him a "judge" as Scripturally defined? Well, yes and no. While the incident at Mizpah ends the 40-year Philistine oppression, my interpretation is that he is not a judge, and I base this upon Acts 13 where the Apostle Paul is speaking at a synagogue in Pisidia Antioch. In v20 [NIV] of said chapter, he says,

After this, God gave them Judges until the time of Samuel the Prophet.

Clearly, the word "until" infers that Paul does not include Samuel with the judges. Whether or not Samuel is a judge is immaterial to the chronology, but I think it is a point worthy of clarification. Having reached this conclusion, I confidently construe the period of the judges to end with Samson's death.

We'll now move back to the time of Jephthah's confrontation of the Ammonites, which punctuates the 300-year span of Israelite occupation of the Transjordan territory. Unlike most of the language in the first part of the Judges account, which seems quite constraining, the interval from Jephthah through Abdon lacks this same syntactic constraint. This is an era of both Philistine and Ammonite incursions into Israeli territory, and is recounted in Judges Chapters 10 through 12. Chapter 10 is brief, and only a preamble to the story of Jephthah. Verses 7-9 read as follows:

So the anger of the LORD was hot against Israel; and He sold them into the hands of the Philistines and into the hands of the people of Ammon. From that year they harassed and oppressed the children of Israel for eighteen years - all the children of Israel who were on the other side of the Jordan in the land of the Amorites, in Gilead. Moreover the people of Ammon crossed over the Jordan to fight against Judah also, against Benjamin, and against the house of Ephraim, so that Israel was severely distressed.

Jephthah then comes and defeats the Ammonites, and then we have a very short narrative at the end of Chapter 12, vv7-14, that reads as follows:

And Jephthah judged Israel six years. Then Jephthah the Gileadite died and was buried in among the cities of Gilead. After him, Ibzan of Bethlehem judged Israel. He had thirty sons. And he gave away thirty daughters in marriage, and brought in thirty daughters from elsewhere for his sons. He judged Israel seven years. Then Ibzan died and was buried at Bethlehem. After him, Elon the Zebulunite judged Israel. He judged Israel ten years. And Elon the Zebulunite died and was buried at Aijalon in the country of Zebulun. After him, Abdon the son of Hillel the Pirathonite judged Israel. He had forty sons and thirty grandsons, who rode on seventy young donkeys. He judged Israel eight years.

The most interesting observation is that while chapter 10 introduces to us the episode referring to an 18 year oppression by the Philistines and the Ammonites, Jephthah only confronts (and defeats) the Ammonites. I believe that this implies that the Philistines were being dealt with separately by Ibzan (7 years), and subsequently held at bay by Elon (10 years), then concluding with Abdon (8

	Ammonites - 0
	Jephthah - 6
Philistines - 18	Ibzan - 7
	Elon - 10
	Abdon - 8
Samson - 20	

years). With this arrangement, we pick up a portion of the 18 year oppression by the Philistines and Ammonites. The chart below illustrates this graphically:

We will have to wait to ascertain the appropriate number of years for the Ammonite incursion, and we set this aside for the moment as a "TBD" in the chronology. [As it turns out, the Ammonites must be defeated immediately after their incursion in order to get the years in alignment, making the correct number 0.]

Now we turn our attention back to the span of 300 years from EIC to JCA. As noted previously, we are constrained here by the specific language pertaining to the start and finish of judgeships in most every case. Specifically, the language consistently states that (1) an enemy oppresses Israel, so (2) God raises up a judge, who puts down the incursion, and then (3) the land has rest for so many years; then the cycle repeats. Wiggle room is hard to find here.

Oppressor	*Duration*	*Judge*	*Rest*
Aram	8	*Othniel*	40
Moab	18	*Ehud*	80
Canaan	20	*Deborah*	40
Midian	7	*Gideon*	40
Midian	na	*Abimelech*	3
Unspecified	na	*Tolah*	23
Unspecified	na	*Jair*	22
TOTAL	**53**		**248**

There is an odd interlude of 3 years (detailed in Judges Ch. 9) during which Gideon's son Abimelech, upon the death of his father, attempts to establish himself king of the city of Shechem. However, the rise of the next real Judge only starts "*After the time of Abimelech....*" (Jgs 10:1). Within the period under consideration, the only exceptions to this established pattern and language occurs in Jgs 10:1-5, wherein the judgeships of Tolah and Jair are described briefly, without mention of an opposing nation. However, the language is still sufficiently limiting to understand that there is no concurrency of judgeships before or during their leadership. Scripture clearly states that "*After Abimelech, there arose to save Israel Tolah....*" Two verses later it says "*After him arose Jair...and he judged Israel twenty-two years.*"

Now before I could proceed further, I realized I had a compounding problem with the years of King Saul. So now let's briefly digress to examine the problematic reign of Saul and the issues it creates in the chronology.

Samuel anoints Saul as king, but continues to function as God's prophet until his own death during Saul's reign. We'll start by looking at various translations of 1Sa 13:1-2a:

Saul reigned one year; and when he had reigned two years over Israel, Saul chose for himself three thousand men of Israel. [NKJV]

Saul was thirty years old when he began to reign, and he reigned forty two years over Israel. Now Saul chose for himself 3,000 men of Israel,... [NASB]

And Saul chooses for himself three thousand men of the men of Israel:... [LXX; public domain]

Saul was [forty] years old when he began to reign; and when he had reigned two years over Israel, Saul chose him three thousand men of Israel,.... [ASV; public domain]

Saul was 30 years old when he began to reign, and he ruled for 42 years over Israel. [ISV; Scripture taken from the Holy Bible: International Standard Version® Release 2.0. Copyright ©1996-2013 by the ISV Foundation. Used by permission of Davidson Press, LLC. ALL RIGHTS RESERVED INTERNATIONALLY.]

Sha'ul was — years old when he began his reign, and he had ruled Isra'el for two years,.... [The Complete Jewish Bible, by David H. Stern. Copyright ©1998. All rights reserved. Used by permission of Messianic Jewish Publishers, 6120 Day Long Lane, Clarksville, MD 21029. www.messianicjewish.net.]

Saul was a young man when he became king, and he ruled Israel for two years." [Contemporary English Version®. Copyright ©1995 American Bible Society. All rights reserved. Reprinted content within the *gratis* use guidelines of the Publisher.]

Each of these excerpts is appropriately footnoted in the respective versions, essentially telling us that the numbers "one," "thirty," and "forty" are only found in later manuscripts, and thus would appear to have been inserted speciously. *In the oldest manuscripts of the Septuagint (LXX), this verse is simply non-existent.* In later versions of the LXX, it appears, but the number after "*Saul was…*" or "*Saul reigned…*" is simply not there; the ASV shows the number forty in brackets, thus indicating its (arbitrary) insertion. The ASV adds the number "forty" while the ISV adds the number "thirty." And that's just the first issue. The number at the end of the verse has similar issues. In some manuscripts, the number is missing, while in others it shows only the number "two." When such issues arise, I usually fall back to the Septuagint, which means here that I dismiss the verse entirely as a later addition from less reliable manuscripts. My fallback upon the Septuagint is not infallible since later manuscripts of the LXX are not without this conflict. As previously noted, the earliest versions of the Septuagint omit verse 1 altogether, and I believe this is the only valid account. So, how old was Saul when crowned, and how long did he reign?

Turning back to the book of *Acts*, in Ch. 13 we again examine Paul's discourse to those at the synagogue in Pisidia Antioch. We'll start at verse 16 as there is also an overarching contextual point to be made here:

Then Paul stood up, and motioning with his hand said, "Men of Israel, and you who fear God, listen: The God of this people Israel chose our fathers, and exalted the people when they dwelt as strangers in the land of Egypt, and with an uplifted arm He brought them out of it. Now for a time of about forty years He put up with their ways in the wilderness. And when He had destroyed seven nations in the land of Canaan, He distributed their land to them by allotment.

After that He gave them judges for about four hundred and fifty years, until Samuel the prophet. And afterward they asked for a king; so God gave them Saul the son of Kish, a man of the tribe of Benjamin, for forty years. [Act 13: 16-21]

It seems apparent that Paul is assigning 40 years to the reign of Saul. He also seems to say that the period of the Judges spans about 450 years, which, after review, creates an entirely new inconsistency with regard to the overall chronology of this period. In his *Antiquities*, Josephus says that the span from Eli's death to Saul's death is only 32 years, and that after the death of Samuel, Saul only reigned another 2 years. The Seder Olam also puts Saul's reign after Samuel's death at 2 years. Assuming Paul is right, and reckon that Saul reigned 38 years while Samuel was alive, I must add 20 years to my chronology. Even if I take all the years of the Ammonite oppression in Jephthah's days out (making their defeat at his hand immediately after their incursion), my chronology ends up being 8 years too long, and without any further means apparent to compress what remains. Is there any deliverance from this dilemma? There is a footnote in the 1599 Geneva Bible, which, in reference to verse 21, states the following:

Acts 13:21 In this space of forty years must the time of Samuel be reckoned with the days of Saul: for the kingdom did as it were swallow up his government. [public domain]

At first I thought this a mere contrivance. However, as I read the whole of Acts 13, I realized that Paul is presenting eras of the Israelite history, in sequence, and attaching spans of years to each.

Paul lived in the first century AD, and the Septuagint had already been in existence for over three centuries. So, was he basing his figure of 40 years on either a variant copy of the Torah, a tainted Septuagint, or was he arriving at this figure otherwise, perhaps from oral tradition? After thorough review of these verses, I came to the conclusion that the NKJV is an unfortunate translation, as is that in the NIV, and others that I read. A much better translation is given in the ASV, which reads as follows:

And Paul stood up, and beckoning with the hand said, Men of Israel, and ye that fear God, hearken: The God of this people Israel chose our fathers, and exalted the people when they sojourned in the land of Egypt, and with a high arm led he them forth out of it. And for about the time of forty years as a nursing-father bare he them in the wilderness. And when he had destroyed seven nations in the land of Canaan, he gave them their land for an inheritance, for about four hundred and fifty years: and after these things he gave them judges until Samuel the prophet. And afterward they asked for a king: and God gave unto them Saul the son of Kish, a man of the tribe of Benjamin, for the space of forty years. [Acts 13:16-21, ASV; public domain]

In Paul's summary history, the first element is when "*...God...chose our fathers...*" and ends with the destruction of the seven nations in Canaan. <u>This</u> is the span of "*...about four hundred and fifty years.*" According to my chronology, the span from the covenant of circumcision with Abraham ("*chose our fathers*") to the end of the Israelite conquests in Canaan is precisely 446 years, and is thus highly compliant (within less than 1% error) with Paul's assertion of "*about 450 years.*" The second element of Paul's historical summary runs from the period of the Judges <u>until</u> Samuel the prophet, but he regrettably fails to specify the years for this stretch. Then, the last element would seem to consist of either (a) the span of Samuel and Saul, or (b) the reign of Saul alone. As previously noted, one footnote says that the passage must be rendered using the former framework. Now understanding the context of this passage and the unfortunate punctuations and translations, I can confidently disregard any assignment of the 450 years to the period of the Judges. However, we are still left with the conundrum of Saul's age at his anointing and the term of his reign.

In an attempt to unmuddle these waters, I searched the Scriptures for other clues. The first such clue is provided in 2Sam 2:10a:

> *Ishbosheth, Saul's son, was forty years old when he began to reign over Israel, and he reigned two years. Only the house of Judah followed David.*

Turning back to 1Sa 13:1-2, you can see the further problem this presents. If Saul is 30 or even 40 when he becomes king and reigns only 2 years, Ish-Bosheth could not be 40 when Saul dies. Both 1Sa 9:2 and Josephus, in his *Antiquities*, describe Saul at the time of his anointing as a "young man," which expression is somewhat nebulous. But, this makes the absence of 1Sam13:1 in the Septuagint even more convincingly appropriate. Even if the Apostle Paul is right about Saul reigning 40 years, Ish-Bosheth's age of 40 at Saul's death is possible, but unlikely, if Saul is crowned as a young man. With every attempt to resolve the chronology of this period, I could not do so with Saul as a young man at his coronation. But as the word "young" is comparative, and relative to some reference, it is not determinant. That is, a man of 40 years might, to some, be considered a young man. Not only do we have Ish-Bosheth at 40 when Saul dies, but we have his son Jonathan joining him in battle against the Philistines (1Sam 13:2) immediately after his confirmation as king (1Sam 11:12-15). Does a man 30 years old have a son old enough to be a soldier? Possible, but unlikely. It is far more likely that Saul was 40 when crowned. Note that as soon as this engagement with the Philistines is complete, 1Sam14:49 says,

> *The sons of Saul were: Jonathan, Jishui, and Malchishua. And the names of his two daughters were these: the name of the firstborn Merab, and the name of the younger Michal.*

Ish-Bosheth is **not** named here, so is presumably yet to be born. If he is born *immediately* thereafter, then his age of 40 at Saul's death would coincide directly with Saul's reign. Thus, the figure of 40 years for both Saul's age and the term of his reign are virtually inescapable. This conclusion has a rigorous and compound impact on the chronology of this period: it not only disqualifies Josephus' figures, but may also constitute cause to reassess Jephthah's figure of 300 as approximate.

Now, with all these adjustments made to the chronology, we still end up about 40 years too long, both in Jephthah's 300 years and the 480 years of 1Ki 6:1. That means that the final resolution must be in the chronology prior to Jephthah's appearance. There are thus two possibilities: (1) that the 40 years is in a single correction, or (2) that the subtractions must be distributed in some way throughout the upper half. Clearly, the former option would be more appealing since it requires less work, and fewer contrivances. An examination of the upper half of the chronology only gives us one viable option for the single correction, and that is in the judgeship term of Ehud & Shamgar. Noting that Gideon, Deborah, and Othniel all had terms of 40 years, not having mentioned Saul, David, and Solomon, I thought that perhaps the 80 year figure in the Bible was wrong. I diligently searched every translation, attendant footnotes, and commentaries, believing that at least one would say that the number should be 40, but that resolution eluded me. Frustrated, I began to question if the Bible could indeed be in error. At wits' end, I prayed to the LORD for revelation, and the answer came to me almost immediately. Like the proverbial light bulb illuminating, I realized that the 80 years of rest in Jgs 3:30b was *cumulative*! That is, the 80 years consists of 40 years during Othniel's leadership and another 40 during Ehud's. The better translation would be "And the land had *had* rest for eighty years." *Through this understanding, the inerrancy of the Bible is upheld*! Suddenly, the last piece of the puzzle fell into place and the resultant picture was elegant and thereby gratifying. It did not take complex contrivances or machinations. We had the 480 years, exactly, and Jephthah's 300 years as 298. Now, if we shift the starting point of this latter era back by 5 years to the time that the Transjordan was won, the 298 becomes 303 years. So, did Jephthah realize this 5-year tolerance and use the number 300 as a median? Maybe. Was he rounding up or down? More likely. We'll probably never know, but I am quite confident that my final chronology is correct, though I concede that it is possible that other chronologies may provide alternate, equally defensible reconciliations.

So, by this model, we have the span of the Judges being established as 299 years. I would have found greater satisfaction had this number been 300, as this is also a number used repetitively in Scripture, and the LORD loves order and symmetry. While there is almost always a scheme to be found or fabricated to manipulate numbers to force a preconceived notion, such undertakings are generally dishonest. I want to discover truth…let the chips fall where they may.

So, in its final form, I present in Figure 31 the graphic tool I created in Microsoft Excel. It helped me visualize events and allowed me to move things around as I worked through the process. The cells heights are not sized to scale, but provide a general picture of the timespans.

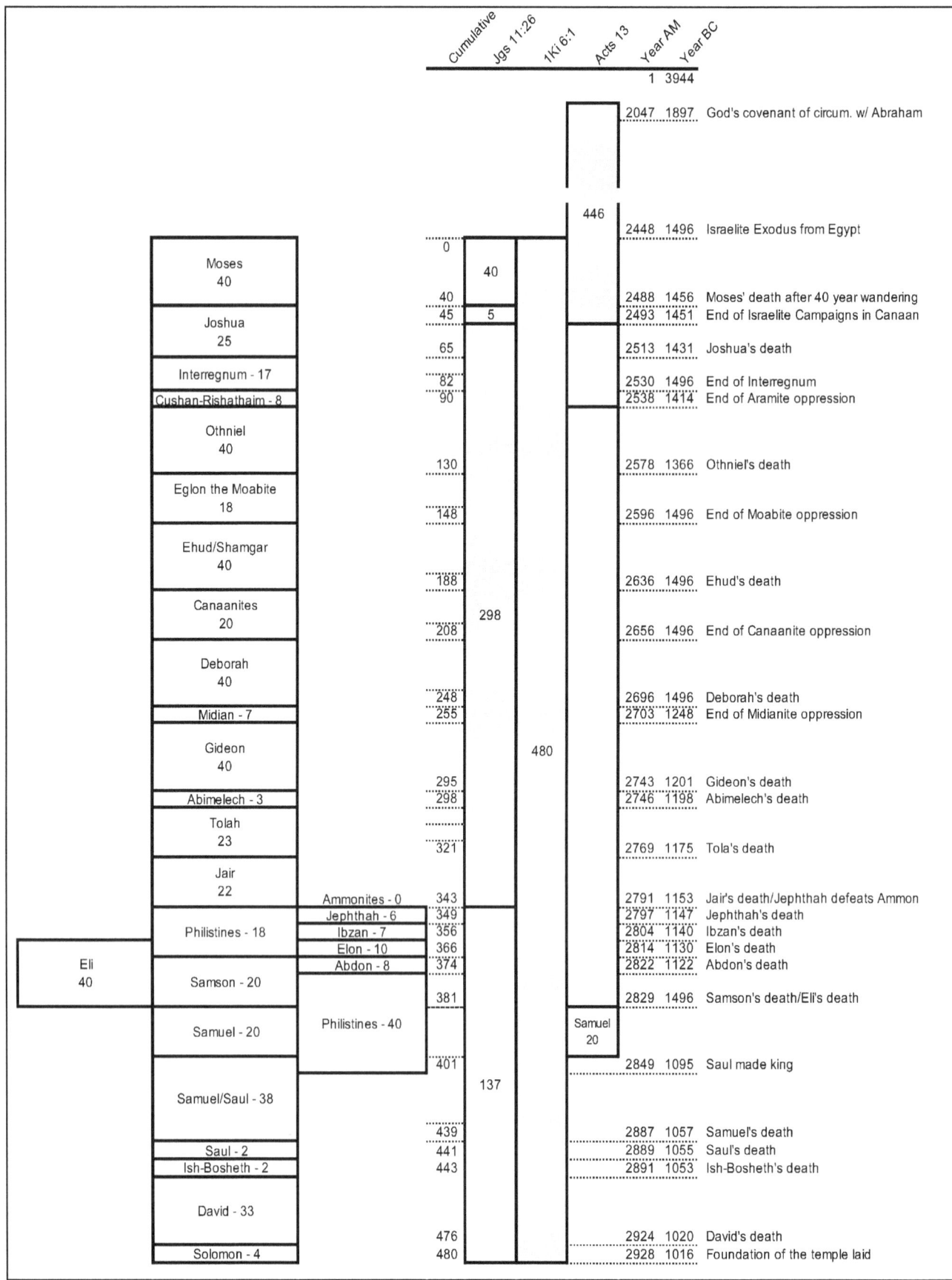

Figure 31: Reconciled Chronology of the Period of the Judges

The Mysterious Numbers of the Hebrew Kings

I borrowed the title of this section from the book of the same name by Edwin Thiele (first published in 1951), who therein provides much rationale for reconciliation, and whose conclusions are now broadly accepted. With all sincere and due respect for Thiele, I have difficulty accepting the complex instruments and dismissals he employs to seemingly achieve resolution.

Many dismiss the integrity of the Bible based on the paradoxes contained in the books of Judges, Kings, and Chronicles. Being myself committed to their veracity, I was compelled to find the resolutions. While I did review other sources in these efforts, my reliance on the truth of Scripture meant that for these investigations, it ultimately did not matter what other sources expressed. If such other accounts were completely reconciled but hinged upon any inconsistency with the Biblical record, I knew that they would thereby be rendered invalid. Similarly for the employment of convoluted devices.

Let's start with an abbreviated summary of the Scripture covering this period. After the last Judge (Samson), Israel is led by Eli the priest, and then by Samuel the prophet (some esteem Samuel also to be a judge, and while I do not, he certainly did function as both judge and Prophet). It is during Samuel's leadership that God accedes to the pleas of the misguided Hebrews who ask Samuel to appoint for them a king, to be like the other nations in the region. Samuel inquires of God, Who determines that Saul is to be their first King. With the death of Saul, David ascends to the throne. And just before David dies, he appoints Solomon as king which punctuates contention between him and at least one other brother as to who would inherit the throne. Upon the death of Solomon, and as a judgment from the LORD for his sins (see 1Ki 11:1-13), Israel is split immediately into two kingdoms. The southern kingdom ("Judah") consists of the tribes of Judah and Benjamin, while the northern kingdom ("Israel") consists of the other ten tribes. The first king of the southern kingdom is Rehoboam, son of Solomon and legitimate heir by birthright. In the northern kingdom, the first king is Jeroboam, a servant of Solomon, but elevated to regency by God Himself. (Note that during the 17-year reign of Rehoboam, the Levites depart from their cities in the northern kingdom, relocating to Judah; thus, in the time of the divided kingdom, the southern kingdom is actually comprised of three tribes. See 2Ch 11:13-17.)

The book of 1st Samuel provides the historical account from the birth of Samuel to the death of Saul, with 2nd Samuel taking us from the accession of David to his last days. The first book of Kings opens with the fraternal contention for David's throne through about the first 80 years of the divided kingdom, while the second book of Kings completes the era of the divided kingdom. The 1st and 2nd books of Chronicles are complementary to the books of Samuel and Kings, duplicating much of the record, but with a central focus on Judah, being mostly silent on concurrent events in Israel. Many passages in Chronicles are taken word-for-word from Kings (it being generally agreed that the books of Chronicles were written after the books of Kings).

What is the essential problem with the Biblical account? Generally speaking, we have apparent disparities within the books of Kings, as well as some between the accounts in Kings and those in Chronicles, that are problematic. While Thiele's reconciliation appears to resolve the issues, I found that he uses complicated or specious maneuverings (e.g., the assumption that the methods for reckoning years was different between the two kingdoms) to achieve his resolution. *To be clear, I am not dismissing Thiele's approach or resolution.* I simply sought a solution that employed fewer schemes applied consistently throughout the Scriptural text.

Now one part of this resolution presented itself shortly after I started my research. Specifically, it was the realization that there is a consistent "rounding up" of regnal years. I submit the following Scriptural references to support my conclusion:

> *In the eighteenth year of King Jeroboam the son of Nebat, Abijam became king over Judah. He reigned three years in Jerusalem.* [1Ki 15:1-2]

> *In the twentieth year of Jeroboam king of Israel, Asa became king over Judah.* [1Ki 15:9]

Since Asa succeeds Abijam, the two verses are directly related. First, it says that Abijam reigned 3 years, but he comes to power in the 18th year of Jeroboam, and after his death, is succeeded by Asa in the 20th year of Jeroboam. The difference between these years of Jeroboam's reign is only two years. Recognizing this pattern elsewhere, the clear conclusion is that when a king reigned for *x* full years plus any portion of the next year, he was credited as having ruled *x+1* years. The repetitive pattern is established with Elah king of Israel in 1Ki 16:8 and 1Ki 16:15, and again with Asa king of Judah in 1Ki 15:10 and 2Ch 16:13. In the latter case, Asa dies in the 41st year (i.e., 40 years plus a fraction) of his reign, but is credited with a full 41 years. And there are additional supporting verses I could cite, but these are sufficient to establish the authors' consistent observance of this rule. Thus, to account for the rounding up, I typically started by subtracting 0.5 year to get to the mean of all possibilities. So, if a ruler was said to have reigned 12 years, it could have been anywhere from 11.003 (11 years plus one day) to 12.000 years, and thus I generally began in the middle of the 'tolerance band,' or 11.5 years.

The most notable exceptions to this rounding rule are when reigns are six months or less; in these cases, the reigns are specified in days, weeks, or months. The shortest of these is the reign of Zimri at just 7 days; the longest is that of Zechariah, being six months. Ahaziah reigned just one year, and it is unclear from the germane verses alone whether this is a full year, or perhaps a span as short as 7 months.

As I was building my table of the chronology for the period of the divided kingdom, I started to notice another pattern emerging, particularly in the years of the nation of Israel. Specifically, I found myself moving the numbers of years to the very margins of the tolerance band in order to make the synchronisms work. At first, this was disconcerting because almost all were skewed to the bottom of the band, and I found myself concerned for the validity of my initial assumptions. However, as my eyes were directed down the columns of the table, I realized that what I saw was more than coincidence, and quite contrary to my worries. Suddenly, the purposeful intent in the reading of the Scripture was revealed to me. I understood that when verses were written as "*In the nth year of [king's name] reign…,*" it is almost always intended that we should read this as "*At the beginning of the nth year of [king's name] reign…!*" This astonishing revelation provided a most significant key to resolving the chronology (God is indeed great!). It also reveals that the lengths of the reigns were not a matter of happenstance, but rather that they were truly ordained by God…that is, if Scripture says that a king reigned, say, 20 years, it almost always means *exactly* twenty years.

Once this was made clear to me, I thought to look into the Hebrew word for "in" to determine if the actual wording was determinant: I wanted to discern if in cases where this rule could not be made to work, that the word used for "in" might actually be another that would be translated as something like "within." When I turned to Strong's Concordance, I discovered that there is apparently no Hebrew word for "in." Thus, the better translation would simply be *"The nth year of [king's name] reign…,"* which might seem at first to make matters worse, but upon reflection it actually seems to bring more clarity and certainty to my conclusion; the introduction of the word "in" appears to have muddied the waters ever so slightly. To investigate this further, I would need to employ the services of someone that can read the ancient Hebrew, but I'll defer on this point to a future revision of this book.

The next recurrent circumstance I found was that of co-regencies. That is, it happens more than once that specific kings assumed the throne before their predecessors met their demise. For an explicit example, we examine what Scripture says about the reigns of Omri and his son Ahab:

> *In the thirty-first year of Asa king of Judah, Omri became king over Israel, and reigned twelve years. Six years he reigned in Tirzah.* [1Ki 16:23]

> *In the thirty-eighth year of Asa king of Judah, Ahab the son of Omri became king over Israel; and Ahab the son of Omri reigned over Israel in Samaria twenty-two years.* [1Ki 16:29]

These two verses cannot both be true unless Ahab's regency overlaps that of his father. Thus, we cannot avoid the conclusion that Ahab started as co-regent or viceroy to his father, ensuing in Omri's seventh year. Scripture never tells us explicitly that two kings ruled in the same kingdom at the same time; it is always inferred, and from the 'conflicts' the years of overlap can be deduced. There is only one instance I found where Scripture provides anything more than inference. The particular case is during the reign of Jehoshaphat where his son Jehoram is his co-regent. 2Kin 8:16 tell us:

> *Now in the fifth year of Joram the son of Ahab, king of Israel,* **Jehoshaphat having been king of Judah***, Jehoram the son of Jehoshaphat began to reign as king of Judah.* [Emphasis mine]

I searched for other occurrences of such unequivocal confirmation of co-regencies and found only one (less explicit) candidate in the reign of Amaziah. 2Ki 14:13-14 states:

> *Then Jehoash king of Israel captured Amaziah king of Judah, the son of Jehoash, the son of Ahaziah, at Beth Shemesh; and he went to Jerusalem, and broke down the wall of Jerusalem, from the Gate of Ephraim to the Corner Gate, - four hundred cubits. And he took all the gold and silver, all the articles that were found in the House of the LORD and in the treasury of the king's house, and hostages, and returned to Samaria.*

Thus, it is clear that Amaziah was alive after his capture. His son Azariah would be crowned king of Judah about 10½ years later, at the age of 16. So there was nobody ceremoniously appointed to govern the nation of Judah for this decade, as Azariah would have only been about 5 years old at the time of his father's capture. His age alone would not preclude his having been crowned, as Joash king of Judah had previously been made king at the age of seven. However, since Amaziah was still alive, there was perhaps hope of his return, so Azariah was the figurehead, or place-holder of the throne, until his father's return or demise was established.

It is important to mention here that when reconciling parallel kingdoms, we have the constraint that we cannot add years to bring the shorter-termed up to the longer. Such would require introduction of a lapse between reigns, and since there are no specific Scriptural incidences of such within the period of the divided kingdom, I would consider such contrivance as "cooking the books." It is always the case that we are constrained to compress the longer to match the shorter, and the only mechanism we have to do such is through co-regency.

Now I found it absolutely necessary to use fractional years to reconcile the accounts. That is, we cannot achieve reconciliation with only whole numbers of years. As one example, I refer to the reigns of Hoshea (Israel) and Hezekiah (Judah). Specifically, we examine 2Ki 18:1 and 2Ki 18:9, which read as follows:

In the third year of Hoshea son of Elah king of Israel, Hezekiah son of Ahaz king of Judah began to reign. [2Ki 18:1]

In King Hezekiah's 4th year, which was the 7th year of Hoshea son of Elah king of Israel, Shalmaneser marched against Samaria and laid siege to it. [2Ki 18:9]

If we do not account for such offsets of regnal years, we end up with conflict. In this case, it would at first seem a simple matter of adding 4 years to get from the third year of Hoshea to his seventh, and adding the same four years to the first year of Hezekiah. However, the latter puts us in the fifth

Figure 32: Requirement for Fractional Years

year of Hezekiah instead of the fourth. In order to reconcile these, it is necessary to consider that Hoshea was partly into his first year when Hezekiah starts his rule. See the graphic above.

Here you can see why it is necessary to introduce fractional years to find the full agreement with the Scriptural text. As with the several examples of rounding up, there are many other examples I could provide where fractional years are required, but this should be adequate for demonstration of the point. With regard to the (granular) resolution within each year, the smallest fraction I used was 0.003 year, which is approximately one day (1/365 = 0.002739...). As it turns out, this was both necessary and, for the most part, sufficient.

Now, for a contrary example, we look at 1Ki 15:1 and 2Ch 12:13:

In the eighteenth year of the reign of Jeroboam son of Nebat, Abijah became king of Judah.... [1Ki 15:1]

Now Rehoboam was forty-one years old when he became king; and he reigned seventeen years in Jerusalem.... [2Ch 12:13]

Now, since Rehoboam and Jeroboam started their reigns at virtually the same time (there is Scriptural support for a lapse of a month or so, but there is also evidence for an implied reset to a coincident start), King Rehoboam would have had to reign exactly 17 full years for both verses to be true. While Scripture does infer a short lapse after the beginning of Rehoboam's reign before Jeroboam starts his, if this were any more than a matter of days, it would work against reconciliation of these two verses.

Next, Biblical inerrancy must be upheld. 2Ki 1:17 precipitated an irreconcilable problem. The verse itself reads:

So Ahaziah died according to the word of the LORD which Elijah had spoken. Because Ahaziah had no son, Joram succeeded him as king in the second year of Jehoram son of Jehoshaphat king of Judah.

The problem becomes apparent when we compare this to 2Ki 3:1:

Joram son of Ahab became king of Israel in Samaria in the eighteenth year of Jehoshaphat king of Judah, and he reigned twelve years.

At first, I reasoned that the paradox might be addressable through the co-regency of Jehoshaphat with Jehoram. But my efforts to align the two verses cited here produced inconsistencies elsewhere. Multiple iterations finally convinced me that I was dealing with an inescapable conflict. But which verse was the root cause, or was my analysis deficient? Did this indeed threaten Biblical inerrancy? Once again I resorted to the Septuagint and stepped through the relevant verses in the chronology until I got to 1Ki 1:17, whereupon I found that the second sentence in the verse was completely absent! Thus, I thus disqualified this verse and removed it completely from the table.

During my work on this chronology, I started to see a trend in the difference between the time when someone was made eligible to be king and the day such was acknowledged. I was sufficiently far along in my chronology when I discovered this trend that I chose not to go back and make the changes for each accession to the throne. But it seems that most typically, there is a lapse of one day, sometimes two. This can easily be rationalized, for example, as the time taken to bury or mourn one's father before the transfer of regency.

With these procedures, I believe I have completely reconciled the period of the divided kingdom with a singular exception. In my worksheet, I use fractional years of various lengths, sufficiently assigned to achieve reconciliation, but not necessarily refined to the extent that they should be deemed absolute. The work was quite tedious, and it frankly got befuddling after a couple of weeks. I cannot even tell you how many times I thought I was finished, only to find errors that caused me to throw nearly everything out and start over. The "rules" delineated above were not all revealed before commencement of the work, but rather as the result of the work itself.

As previously noted, out of my concern for harmony, I did read Jospehus' account of the divided kingdom. His narrative uses the same counts of years as specified in the Bible in every case with two exceptions: he records Jehu's reign as 27 years instead of 28, and Jeroboam's rule as 40 years instead of 41 in the Biblical account. And while his accounts add particulars, none of these details has any impact on the chronology, which was my sole concern in this segment of history, at the time of this writing and within the scope of this book.

With all this said, I've inserted a copy of the worksheet I created for this analysis. Space constraints dictated that I break it into two parts.

Year AM	Year BC	King (Judah)	Ordinal	Proposed	Cardinal	Subtot.	Cumulative	Subtot.	King (Israel)	Ordinal	Cardinal	Proposed	Ref.
2964.000	-980	Rehoboam					0.000		Jeroboam				
2981.000	-963	~~Rehoboam~~		17.000	17		17.000		Jeroboam				2Chr 12:13
2981.003	-963	Abijah		0.003			17.003		Jeroboam	18th		17.003	1Ki 15:1
2984.000	-960	~~Abijah~~		2.997	3	22.000	20.000	22.000	Jeroboam				1Ki 15:2
2984.000	-960	Asa	1st				20.000		Jeroboam	20th		20.000	1Ki 15:9
2985.003	-959	Asa	2nd	1.003			21.003		Jeroboam/Nadab				1Ki 15:25
2986.000	-958	~~Asa~~					22.000		~~Jeroboam/Nadab~~		22	22.000	1Ki 14:20
2986.006	-958	Asa					22.006		~~Nadab~~		2	1.003	1Ki 15:25
2986.006	-958	Asa	3rd	2.006			22.006		Baasha				1Ki 15:28
2986.006	-958	Asa	3rd	2.006			22.006		Baasha				1Ki 15:33
3009.009	-935	Asa					45.009		~~Baasha~~		24	23.003	1Ki 15:33
3009.009	-935	Asa	26th	25.009			45.009		Elah				1Ki 16:8
3010.012	-934	Asa					46.012		~~Elah~~		2	1.003	1Ki 16:8
3010.012	-934	Asa	27th	26.012		39.000	46.012	39.000	Zimri				1Ki 16:15
3010.031	-934	Asa	27th	26.022			46.031		~~Zimri~~		0.019	0.019	1Ki 16:15
3010.031	-934	Asa					46.031		Omri v Tibni				1Ki 16:21
3014.003	-930	Asa					50.003		Omri v ~~Tibni~~			3.972	1Ki 16:21
3014.003	-930	Asa	31st	30.003			50.003		Omri				1Ki 16:23
3021.003	-923	Asa	38th	37.003			57.003		Omri/Ahab				1Ki 16:29
3025.000	-919	Asa		41.000			61.000		Omri/Ahab				1Ki 15:10
3025.000	-919	~~Asa~~	41st	41.000	41		61.000		Omri/Ahab				2Chr 16:13
3025.003	-919	Jehoshaphat					61.003		Omri/Ahab	4th		4.000	1Ki 22:41
3026.003	-918	Jehoshaphat					62.003		~~Omri~~/Ahab		12	12.000	1Ki 16:23
3041.006	-903	Jehoshaphat	17th	16.003			77.006		Ahab/Ahaziah				1Ki 22:51
3042.006	-902	Jehoshaphat	18th	17.003			78.006		Ahab/~~Ahaziah~~				2Ki 3:1
3043.003	-901	Jehoshaphat					79.003		~~Ahab~~/Joram		22	22.000	1Ki 16:29
3043.009	-901	Jehoshaphat					79.009		Joram				na
3047.006	-897	Jehoshaphat/Jehoram				30.009	83.006	30.009	Joram	5th		4.003	2Ki 8:16
3050.003	-894	~~Jehoshaphat~~/Jehoram		25.000	25		86.003		Joram				1Ki 22:42
3054.003	-890	Jehoram/Ahaziah					90.003		Joram				2Ch 21-22
3054.009	-890	~~Jehoram~~/Ahaziah		7.003	8		90.009		Joram				2Ki 8:17
3054.009	-890	Ahaziah					90.009		Joram	11th		11.000	2Ki 9:29
3054.006	-890	Ahaziah					90.006		Joram	12th		11.003	2Ki 8:25
3055.003	-889	Ahaziah					91.003		Joram		12	12.000	2Ki 3:1
3055.009	-889	~~Ahaziah~~		1.000	1		91.009		~~Joram~~				2Ki 8:26
3055.009	-889	Athaliah					91.009		Jehu				2Ki 9:13
3061.009	-883	~~Athaliah~~		6.000	6		97.009		Jehu				2Chr 22:12
3061.012	-883	Joash	7th	6.003			97.012		Jehu				2Ki 11:4-12
3061.012	-883	Joash					97.012		Jehu	7th		6.003	2Ki 12:1
3083.009	-861	Joash					119.009		~~Jehu~~		28	28.000	2Ki 10:36
3083.015	-861	Joash	23rd	22.003			119.015		Jehoahaz				2Ki 13:1
3097.015	-847	Joash	37th	36.003		61.006	133.015	61.006	Jehoahaz/Jehoash				2Ki 13:10
3100.015	-844	Joash					136.015		~~Jehoahaz~~/Jehoash		17	17.000	2Ki 13:1
3101.012	-843	~~Joash~~		40.000	40		137.012		Jehoash				2Chr 24:1
3101.018	-843	Amaziah					137.018		Jehoash	2nd		1.003	2Ki 14:1
3104.015	-840	Amaziah					140.015		Jehoash/Jeroboam II				2Ki 15:1
3108.006	-836	Amaziah/Azariah					144.006		Jehoash/Jeroboam II				2Ki 15:8
3116.015	-828	Amaziah/Azariah					152.015		~~Jehoash~~/Jeroboam II		16	16.000	2Ki 13:10
3116.015	-828	Amaziah/Azariah	15th	14.997			152.015		Jeroboam II				2Ki 14:23

Figure 33a: Chronology of the Divided Kingdom - Part I

Hidden in Genesis

Year AM	Year BC	King (Judah)	Ordinal	Proposed	Cardinal	Subtot.	Cumulative	Subtot.	King (Israel)	Ordinal	Cardinal	Proposed	Ref.
3116.015	-828	Amaziah/Azariah					152.015		Jeroboam II				na
3131.015	-813	Amaziah/Azariah	15	15.000			167.015		Jeroboam II				2Ki 14:17
3130.018	-814	Amaziah/Azariah		29.000	29		166.018		Jeroboam II				2Ki 14:2
3130.018	-814	Azariah				29.994	166.018	29.994	Jeroboam II				2Chr 26:1
3130.018	-814	Azariah					166.018		Jeroboam II	27th		26.003	2Ki 15:1
3145.015	-799	Azariah					181.015		Jeroboam II		41	41.000	2Ki 14:23
3145.509	-798	Azariah	38th	37.503			181.509		Zechariah				2Ki 15:8
3146.009	-798	Azariah	38th				182.009		Zechariah		0.5	0.500	2Ki 15:8
3146.009	-798	Azariah	39th	38.003			182.009		Shallum				2Ki 15:13
3146.092	-798	Azariah	39th				182.092		Shallum		0.083	0.083	2Ki 15:13
3146.092	-798	Azariah	39th	38.086			182.092		Menachem				2Ki 15:17
3157.009	-787	Azariah				13.997	193.009	13.997	Menachem		10	10.917	2Ki 15:17
3157.009	-787	Azariah	50th	49.003			193.009		Pekahiah				2Ki 15:23
3159.009	-785	Azariah/Jotham					195.009		Pekahiah		2	2.000	2Ki 15:23
3159.009	-785	Azariah/Jotham	52nd/x	51.003			195.009		Pekah				2Ki 15:27
3160.006	-784	Azariah/Jotham		52.000	52		196.006		Pekah				2Chr 26:3
3160.006	-784	Azariah/Jotham					196.006		Pekah				
3160.012	-784	Jotham					196.012		Pekah	2nd		1.003	2Ki 15:32
3168.012	-776	Jotham/Ahaz					204.012		Pekah				2Ki 16:2
3175.009	-769	Jotham/Ahaz		16.000	16		211.009		Pekah				2Chr 27:8
3175.012	-769	Ahaz					211.012		Pekah	17th		16.003	2Ki 16:1
3179.009	-765	Ahaz					215.009		Pekah		20	20.000	2Ki 15:27
3179.015	-765	Ahaz	20th	19.003			215.015		Hoshea				2Ki 15:30
3179.015	-765	Ahaz	12th	11.003		27.012	215.015	27.012	Hoshea				2Ki 17:1
3181.018	-763	Ahaz/Hezekiah					217.018		Hoshea	3rd		2.003	2Ki 18:1
3184.012	-760	Ahaz/Hezekiah		16.000	16		220.012		Hoshea				2Ki 16:2
3185.018	-759	Hezekiah	4th				221.018		Hoshea	7th			2Ki 18:9
3185.018	-759	Hezekiah	4th				221.018		Hoshea	7th		6.003	2Ki 18:9
3187.018	-757	Hezekiah					223.018		Hoshea	9th		8.003	2Ki 17:6
3187.018	-757	Hezekiah	6th				223.018		Hoshea				2Ki 18:10
3187.018	-757	Hezekiah	6th				223.018		Hoshea	9th		8.003	2Ki 18:10
3194.021	-750	Hezekiah	14th	13.003			230.021						2Ki 18:13
3209.021	-735	Hezekiah	29th	28.003			245.021						2Ki 18:2
3210.018	-734	Hezekiah		29.000	29		246.018						2Chr 29:1
3210.021	-734	Manasseh					246.021						2Ki 21:1
3265.021	-679	Manasseh		55.000	55		301.021						2Chr 33:1
3265.024	-679	Amon					301.024						2Ki 21:19
3267.024	-677	Amon		2.000	2		303.024						2Chr 33:21
3267.027	-677	Josiah					303.027						2Chr 34:1
3298.027	-646	Josiah		31.000	31		334.027						2Ki 22:1
3298.030	-646	Jehoahaz				133.545	334.030	133.545					2Ki 23:31
3298.280	-646	Jehoahaz		0.250	0.25		334.280						2Chr 36:2
3298.283	-646	Johoiakim					334.283						2Chr 36:5
3309.283	-635	Jehoiakim		11.000	11		345.283						2Ki 23:36
3309.286	-635	Jehoiachin					345.286						2Chr 36:9
3309.563	-634	Jehoiachin		0.277	0.277		345.563						2Ki 24:8
3309.563	-634	Zedekiah					345.563						2Ki 24:18
3317.566	-626	Zedekiah	9th	8.003			353.566						2Ki 25:1
3319.566	-624	Zedekiah	11th	10.003			355.566						2Ki 25:2
3320.563	-623	Zedekiah		11.000	11.000		356.563						2Chr 36:11
						356.563		356.563					

Figure 33a: Chronology of the Divided Kingdom - Part II

Explanatory Notes for Figures 33a & b: *Chronology of the Divided Kingdom*:

1. I divided the chronology into seven arbitrary subsections to compartmentalize analysis and isolate conflicts. The subtotals for each section are shown in the merged cells to the right of the column titled "Cumulative."
2. For each kingdom (Judah on the left and Israel on the right) I created columns to note which Bible verses specifically use the ordinal term "n^{th} year," (e.g., sixth, seventh, eleventh, etc.) for the reasons identified in the narrative, with the ordinal numbers specified in these columns. The numbers in the columns to the right of "n^{th}" columns contain the number of years I assigned while working the model. As discussed, the rule for these occurrences is that this syntax typically denoted the beginning of the nth year.
3. In contrast with syntax using the 'ordinal' terminology 'n^{th},' when years are written 'cardinally' (e.g., 41 years, 3 years, 17 years, etc.) for the reign of a king, it is typically to be understood as completed, integer numbers of years (i.e., 41.000, 3.000, 17.000 years, etc.), and the figures I used are specified in the "Proposed Data" columns.
4. The center column designated "Cumulative" represents the cumulative total of years from the start of the division of the kingdom. The cells in the Cumulative column almost always have an underlying formula utilizing the data in the columns designated "Proposed Data." Where numbers in the Cumulative column should agree (for example, the end of the reign of one king and the accession of his successor), I have added a border around the pair.
5. The cells in the last column on the right contain the Biblical reference for the source data. Those cells highlighted in gray indicate those for which the associated verse is a 'synchronism' (synchronizing an event in one kingdom with an event in the other…e.g., "*In the third year of Asa king of Judah, Baasha son of Ahijah became king of all Israel….*"). Where more than one verse provided confirming data (e.g., one in Kings and another in Chronicles), I typically deleted the second reference only to condense the chart.
6. In the Proposed Data column for Israel, I placed a border around the only cell with unresolved conflict. The model I show here represents my best efforts, within the established rules, over the development period of about 4 weeks, and still results in the one conflict. This occurs between the years 3145 AM and 3156 AM, and results in a violation of about 11 months. Thus, my final figure for the term of the divided kingdom is 356.563 years. Given that I have an unresolved conflict, I am uncertain as to the tolerance band on this figure.

As noted in my narrative regarding the period of the Judges, I always look for numerical symmetry. The span of 356.56 years is close enough to 360 to make this significant. God's division of the kingdom was a judgment of Solomon (1Ki 11:11-13). Thus, it would seem suitable that the span of this period would be a multiple of 40 years; 356 is not, but 360 is (3x3x40). My first priority is to be faithful to the facts. Sometimes, though, the process of discovery in search of truth can be enhanced through recognition and application of symmetries. Thus, there is reason to believe that the divided kingdom lasted 360 years: the vision of Ezekiel chapter 4. In this chapter, God tells the prophet Ezekiel to portray the years of Israel's iniquity by lying on his left side for 390 days, and Judah's iniquity by lying on his right side for 40 days. God explains the symbolism to Ezekiel instructing him that each day on his side represents one year of their iniquity. The total of days/years is 430. The period must apply to the divided kingdom because God specifies periods for the houses of Israel and of Judah, notably not including the years of Solomon's iniquity (nor those of Saul or David). Some include these years in order to synthesize a reconciliation. (I'm not dismissing such attempts, for they may be correct.) If the total term of the divided kingdom is indeed 360 years, then if you add the 70 years of their captivity under Nebuchadnezzar, which starts at the end of the divided kingdom, then the total years of their iniquity is 430. But even if 360 years is the right number for the divided kingdom, the only problem I have with this application of the Scripture is that there is an overlap of 20 years between the divided kingdom and the 70-year exile.

One other interesting candidate for the 390 years is the span from the year of Ezekiel's vision, 3314 AM. Subtracting 390 years gets us to 2924 AM which is exactly the first year of Solomon's reign. In this relation, though, I cannot find a corresponding period for the 40 years of Judah's iniquity.

Complete Biblical Chronology to the Time of Christ

Once I had completed my reconciliations of the periods of the Judges and the Divided Kingdom, I was able to integrate these into a more comprehensive chronology from Creation to the death of Jesus Christ. This also facilitated understanding when the end of history will be, as well as the extent to which my chronology is deficient.

I integrated the relevant Scripture citations, the years in AM and BC, as well as the correlated dates in Ussher, Newton, Josephus, Jubilees, Seder Olam, and Jasher. However, in consideration of readability, I have hidden some of these from the view here. I also included columns that provided the names of the rulers in the various kingdoms interacting with the nation of Israel (Babylonia, Assyrian, Persian, Median, and Egyptian), where available and when appropriate, but again space did not permit this more complete view. This is probably a moot point for most readers anyway, as I had not yet completed these entries since it was not consequential to my objective...I only completed it sufficiently to accomplish my intended goals. (It is my hope to set up a website following publication where I can make this more complete work available in the Excel format.)

Now I did notice an interesting trend as I went through the Bible: dates and continuities are very precisely and completely established in Genesis, and as I moved through the books, I discovered that these data became increasingly cryptic. The very first riddle is that of the interregnum at the end of Joshua's life, which gets no explicit mention in the Bible, but is inferred. It is by employment of the clues in Jgs 11:26 and 1Ki 6:1 that we can actually figure this out. And the time of the Kings is even more perplexing, but with diligent effort, we discover co-regencies and discern the rules of interpretation employed that resolve all but one of the paradoxes. *I concluded that Biblical numerology is actually set up as a type of challenge, and the LORD indeed built into us a desire to win games. God is enticing us to use increasing scrutiny to ferret out the details.* And there are intentional gaps. While I've come to believe that all the gaps can probably be reconciled through understanding of prophecies, I also believe that God may have purposely included such gaps to hinder us from ascertaining precisely the day and hour of his return. Nonetheless, He yet intrigues us with the symmetries and prophecies that we might desire to solve these riddles.

So as it turned out, I had thought to surrender with the acknowledgment that my chronology was deficient. At that time, my timeline was long by about 7 years without an avenue apparent to resolve it. I understood the error of my chronology from the prophetic verses in Daniel chapter 9; specifically, the prophecy of 69 weeks in Dan 9:25-26. The prophecy is given to Daniel in the first year of the reign of Darius the Mede (Dan 9:1); the person speaking to Daniel is the archangel Gabriel (Dan 9:21). Verses 25 and 26 read as follows:

> *Know therefore and understand,*
> **That from the going forth of the command**
> **To restore and build Jerusalem**
> *Until Messiah the Prince,*
> **There shall be seven weeks and sixty-two weeks;**
> *The street shall be built again, and the wall,*
> *Even in troublesome times.*
>
> **And after the sixty-two weeks**
> **Messiah shall be cut off**, *but not for Himself;*

And the people of the prince who is to come
Shall destroy the city and the sanctuary.
The end of it shall be with a flood,
And till the end of the war desolations are determined.

The "weeks" in these verses are almost universally accepted to be weeks of years. Given that Jesus Christ would not be born for another, roughly, 450 years, this has to be the case. Thus, the 69 weeks of years would be 69 x 7 = 483 years from the command to rebuild Jerusalem.

Here we have another of God's cryptographs. You see, there are four times in the Bible where commands were issued to restore Jerusalem: (1) by the proclamation of Cyrus king of Persia (Cyrus II) in the first year of his reign as detailed in 2Ch 36:23, repeated in Ezr 1:1-4, and again in Ezr 6:3-5; (2) by the decree of Darius King of Persia (Darius I; not to be confused with Darius the Mede, a contemporary of Cyrus II) found in Ezra 6:6-12; (3) by the letter to Ezra from Artaxerxes I in the seventh year of his reign containing his decree, as cited in Ezr 7:12-26; and (4) by the letters from Artaxerxes I, in the twentieth year of his reign, to Nehemiah described in the second chapter of the book bearing his name. Thus, I set out to examine each to determine which could be the most appropriate.

For this exercise, I thought it best to work backwards. Specifically, I started with the date of the crucifixion and subtracted 483 years to see which of the four candidates would be determined. The predicament here is that scholars do not all agree on when this pivotal event occurred. In spite of the fact that the designation of *anno domini* (AD) is supposed to indicate the years since the birth of Christ Jesus, the synchronicity was incorrectly established when the dating system was instituted 525 years after the crucifixion by Dionysius Exiguus, a Scythian monk. As it is, the range of dates most broadly accepted for His death runs from 29 AD to 36 AD. I had previously consulted a number of sources for the date of Christ's birth, and recalled that 4 BC was, by far, the most commonly proffered, and I had grown to accept this. Revisiting this issue, my more recent research turned up a slightly broader range between 6 BC and 1 BC, with 4 BC still being the most accepted. Understanding that a difference a couple of years would probably not have enough impact to change the result, I elected to use 4 BC.

Working now forward, Jesus began his ministry at age 30 (Luke 3:23), and ended when He was 33…or so I thought. This is a second source of some controversy, with figures for the term of His ministry spanning two to four years. Again, presuming that this differential would still not significantly alter the result, I elected to utilize the 3-year figure. Integrating all of these figures, we have the death of Jesus occurring in about 30 AD, with a tolerance band of roughly -4 years to +6 years. According to my chronology, Christ's crucifixion would thus be in the year 3944 + 30 - 1 = 3973 AM. (There is a 1 year adjustment to the subtraction since there is no year 0. Note also that I believe 30 AD is the correct year of the crucifixion, as the Temple was destroyed in 70 AD, implying a 40-year judgment on the Jews…recall that the number 40, in Biblical numerology, is a number signifying judgment.) Consequently, subtracting 483 years we end up at 3490 AM, or 454 BC. This left me with only one candidate, if my chronology is otherwise correct. As I have it, the decree by Artaxerxes in his twentieth year is the closest, with the inescapable conclusion that my total chronology was long by seven years for my timeline to be in perfect alignment. Given the tolerance band, I could be off by as little as 3 years, but as much as 13 years, *assuming the secular histories are correct*. Since I have yet to undertake an in-depth study of Biblical prophecy, I have had to resort to the use of secular histories in order to establish the year of Artaxerxes' reign.

You'll note that in the column entitled "Bk:ch:v," I have the Biblical and extra-Biblical references that establish the years for the events delineated in the chronology. However, there are over twenty lines where these cells are empty. In most of these cases, I have used secular histories to establish continuity, and while broadly accepted, they are not universally so, nor inerrant as is the Biblical account. (The same can be said about the extra-Biblical sources referenced, but these I generally esteem to be more reliable than profane accounts.)

This meant that my 7 extra years would necessarily have to be deleted between Artaxerxes' decree and Christ's crucifixion. That does not, though, dismiss the possibility that my chronology has problems earlier than the subject decree. And let's not forget that this presumes that the decree referenced in Daniel's prophecy of 69 weeks is, in fact, the second of Artaxerxes. If it were any of the others, the error would increase significantly.

Once again, I turned to Josephus. Book XI of the Antiquities is headed with the descriptive phrase *"Containing the interval of two hundred and fifty-three years five months"* (*"From the First of Cyrus to the Death of Alexander the Great"*). I checked the dates in my chronology and found the difference between these events was just 248 years; such would seem to make matters worse, and unfortunately, Josephus fails to provide the detail for his summation, and it was at this point that I once more thought to forfeit the game, leaving me with this unsettled gap.

Being again at wit's end, I prayed for help. I had thought this to come as I searched for confirmation of the dates of Artaxerxes' reign. Specifically, I discovered a paper written by Gerard Gertoux, a modern-day chronologist whose work I found to be most excellent. The paper is entitled *"Dating the Reigns of Xerxes and Artaxerxes,"* published in 2015. Gertoux's methodology is exceptionally rigorous and comprehensive, using archaeological evidence, astronomical simulations, and secular histories to establish the synchronisms with the Biblical account. Gertoux concludes that the death of Xerxes is actually in 475 BCE, as contrasted with the otherwise established, and quite broadly accepted, date of 465 BC. I was firmly persuaded that Gertoux is correct, and started to integrate his dates for the reigns of Xerxes and Artaxerxes into my chronology, and further adopted this as a firm anchor point. Gertoux also determined that Xerxes was co-regent with Darius I for a span of 10 years, which had a more profound effect on my timeline. Given this domino effect, the entire chronology began to unravel, and I had to dig more deeply. I found that Gertoux has published many chronographic papers on various periods, and most notably a book entitled *"Absolute Chronology of the Ancient World from 1533 BCE to 140 BCE,"* published in 2016. As I awaited its arrival, I was quite concerned that I would have to disassemble and reassemble my entire timeline, but hoped at the same time that the conformance of Biblical prophecies would be confirmed. I still seek truth, even if that truth is that of my error.

The first opportunity I had to look at Gertoux's chronology, I went immediately to the period of the Judges to see if his reconciliation was the same as mine…it was not, and he had Ehud judging for 80 years, which meant that other parts of his chronology for the Israelites had to be called into question. (I am thus certain that for this challenge there will be blowback, but it was my sincere hope that Gertoux's work would help me. I must, however, exercise the utmost caution to ensure that I do not once more cast out the baby with the bathwater. Thus, I must examine his work more closely.)

In closing, I submit the following convincing partial correction. Remember that Daniel's prophecy of 9:24-27 starts off in 9:24 with 70 weeks, and then goes on in 9:25 with only 7+62 weeks from *"the command to restore Jerusalem until Messiah the Prince."* In 9:26 it continues with *"And after the sixty-two weeks Messiah shall be cut off...."* Most, myself included, assume that the 7+62 can be summed giving us 69 weeks (483 years)…but, to the crucifixion? The passage in 9:26 only says *"…after the sixty-two weeks…"* but not "immediately after." We had a similar issue with the start of the period of the Judges after Joshua's death, whereupon we discovered an *interregnum* of 17 years. If the phrase *"until Messiah the Prince"* means the start of Jesus' ministry, and He is "cut off" at the close of a 3-year ministry, I'm only long by 4 years. I believe this to be the correct interpretation.

Other considerations include: (1) that the reigns of the Persian kings from Cyrus to Artaxerxes (collectively about 94 years) were actually just a couple of years less; and/or (2) that my date for Creation in 3944 BC requires correction by a couple of years.

Secular historians place the death of Xerxes at 465 BC, and I have 480 BC; Gertoux places it at 475 BC. If I use Gertoux's figure, my total error is reduced to just 1 year. However, the problem of the 4 year correction is then simply shifted the period preceding Xerxes' death. I do believe Gertoux is right, but I cannot implement this without identifying where the 4 or 5 year error is.

With all of this, I conclude the prelude to the (mostly) complete chronology from Creation to Christ.

Hidden in Genesis

Chronology of the Patriarchs from 1 to 2047 AM

Ussher	Joseph.	Joseph. (rev.)	Seder Olam	Jasher	Year AM	Year BC	Bk ch:v	Description of Event	Patriarch
1	1	1	1	1	1	-3944	Ge 1:1	Creation	Adam
130	230	130	130	130	130	-3814	Ge 5:3	Birth of Seth	Adam
235	435	235	235	235	235	-3709	Ge 5:6	Birth of Enosh	Adam
325	625	325	325	325	325	-3619	Ge 5:9	Birth of Kenan	Adam
395	795	395	395	395	395	-3549	Ge 5:12	Birth of Mhalalel	Adam
460	960	460	460	460	460	-3484	Ge 5:15	Birth of Jared	Adam
622	1122	622	622	622	622	-3322	Ge 5:18	Birth of Enoch	Adam
687	1287	687	687	687	687	-3257	Ge 5:21	Birth of Methuselah	Adam
874	1474	874	874	874	874	-3070	Ge 5:25	Birth of Lamech	Adam
930	930	930	930	930	930	-3014	Ge 5:4	Death of Adam	Enoch
930	930	930	930	930	930	-3014	Ge 5:5	Death of Adam	Enoch
987	1587	987	987	987	987	-2957	Ge 5:22	Assumption of Enoch	Enoch
987	1487	987	987	987	987	-2957	Ge 5:23	Assumption of Enoch	Methuselah
1042	1242	1042	1042	1042	1042	-2902	Ge 5:7	Death of Seth	Methuselah
1042	1142	1042	na	1042	1042	-2902	Ge 5:8	Death of Seth	Methuselah
1056	1656	1056	1056	1056	1056	-2888	Ge 5:28	Birth of Noah	Methuselah
1140	1340	1140	1140	1140	1140	-2804	Ge 5:10	Death of Enosh	Methuselah
1140	1340	1140	1140	1140	1140	-2804	Ge 5:11	Death of Enosh	Methuselah
1235	1535	1235	1235	1235	1235	-2709	Ge 5:13	Death of Kenan	Methuselah
1235	1535	1235	1235	1235	1235	-2709	Ge 5:14	Death of Kenan	Methuselah
1290	1690	1290	1290	1290	1290	-2654	Ge 5:16	Death of Mahalalel	Methuselah
1290	1690	1290	1290	1290	1290	-2654	Ge 5:17	Death of Mahalalel	Methuselah
1422	1922	1422	1422	1422	1422	-2522	Ge 5:19	Death of Jared	Methuselah
1422	1922	1422	1422	1422	1422	-2522	Ge 5:20	Death of Jared	Methuselah
1536	na	na	1536	1536	1536	-2408	Ge 6:3	God foretells the Deluge	Noah
1556	2556	1656	1556	1556	1556	-2388	Ge 5:32	Birth of Noah's children	Noah
1558	2556	1556	1558	1558	1558	-2386	Ge 11:10	Birth of Shem	Noah
1651	2251	1651	1651	1651	1651	-2293	Ge 5:30	Death of Lamech	Noah
1651	2251	1651	1651	1651	1651	-2293	Ge 5:31	Death of Lamech	Noah
1656	2256	1656	1656	1656	1656	-2288	Ge 5:26	Death of Methuselah	Noah
1656	2256	1656	1656	1656	1656	-2288	Ge 5:27	Death of Methuselah	Noah
1656	2656	1656	1656	1656	1656	-2288	Ge 7:6	Deluge commences	Noah
1656	2656	1656	1656	1656	1656	-2288	Ge 7:11	Deluge commences	Noah
1657	na	na	na	1657	1657	-2287	Ge 8:13	Deluge waters recede	Noah
1658	2658	1668	1658	1658	1658	-2286	Ge 11:10	Birth of Arphaxad	Noah
1693	2793	1703	na	1693	1693	-2251	Ge 11:12	Birth of Shelah	Noah
1723	2923	1733	na	1723	1723	-2221	Ge 11:14	Birth of Eber	Noah
1757	3057	1767	na	1757	1757	-2187	Ge 11:16	Birth of Peleg	Noah
1787	3187	1797	na	1787	1787	-2157	Ge 11:18	Birth of Reu	Noah
1819	3317	1827	na	1819	1819	-2125	Ge 11:20	Birth of Serug	Noah
1849	3449	1859	na	1849	1849	-2095	Ge 11:22	Birth of Nahor	Noah
1878	3478	1878	na	1878	1878	-2066	Ge 11:24	Birth of Terah	Noah
na	na	na	na	1916	1916	-2028	Jash 7:22	Birth of Haran & Nahor	Noah
1948	3548	1948	1948	1948	1948	-1996	Ge 11:26	Birth of Abram	Noah
2008	3548	1948	1948	1948	1948	-1996	Jash 8:51	Birth of Abram	Noah
1996	na	na	na	1996	1996	-1948	Ge 11:19	Death of Peleg	Noah
na	na	na	1996	1996	1996	-1948	Sed Ol 1	Division of languages	Noah
na	na	na	na	1996	1996	-1948	Jash 10:1-3	Death of Peleg	Noah
1997	na	na	na	1997	1997	-1947	Ge 11:25	Death of Nahor	Noah
na	na	na	na	1998	1998	-1946	Jash 11:13	Abram returns from Noah's house	Noah
na	na	na	na	1998	1998	-1946	Jash 12:37	Death of Haran	Noah
2006	2996	2006	2006	2006	2006	-1938	Ge 9:28	Death of Noah	Noah
2006	na	na	2006	2006	2006	-1938	Ge 9:29	Death of Noah	Noah
2006	na	na	na	2006	2006	-1938	Jash 13:9	Death of Noah	Abraham
na	na	na	2018	2018	2018	-1926	Jash 13:17	God appears to Abram 1st time	Abraham
2083	3623	2023	2023	2023	2023	-1921	Ge 12:4	Abram departs Haran	Abraham
2084	na	na	2023	2023	2023	-1921	Jash 15:1-2	Abram departs Canaan for Egypt	Abraham
2026	na	na	na	2026	2026	-1918	Ge 11:21	Death of Reu	Abraham
2093	na	na	2033	2033	2033	-1911	Ge 16:3	Abram seeds Hagar	Abraham
2094	3634	2034	2034	2034	2034	-1910	Ge 16:16	Birth of Ishmael	Abraham
2107	3647	2047	na	2047	2047	-1897	Ge 17:1	God appears to Abram 2nd time	Abraham
2107	3647	2047	na	2047	2047	-1897	Ge 17:17	God foretells Isaac's birth	Abraham
2107	3647	2047	2047	2047	2047	-1897	Ge 17:24	Rite of circumcision instituted	Abraham

Chronology of the Patriarchs from 2048 to 2531 AM

Ussher	Joseph.	Joseph. (rev.)	Seder Olam	Jasher	Year AM	Year BC	Bk ch:v	Description of Event	Patriarch
2108	3648	2048	2048	2048	2048	-1896	Ge 21:5	Birth of Isaac	Abraham
2049	na	na	na	2049	2049	-1895	Ge 11:23	Death of Serug	Abraham
2083	3683	2083	2083	2083	2083	-1861	Ge 11:32	Death of Terah	Abraham
2083	na	na	na	2083	2083	-1861	Sed Ol 1	Death of Terah	Abraham
2133	3673	2073	2085	2085	2085	-1859	Jash 22:41+	God tells Abram to sacrifice Isaac	Abraham
2145	3685	2085	2085	2085	2085	-1859	Ge 23:1	Death of Sarah	Abraham
na	na	na	na	2087	2087	-1857	Jash 24:22	Death of Lot (Isaac 39 yrs. old)	Abraham
2148	3700	2088	na	2088	2088	-1856	Ge 25:20	Isaac marries Rebecca	Abraham
2093	na	na	na	2096	2096	-1848	Ge 11:13	Death of Arphaxad	Abraham
2168	na	na	2108	2108	2108	-1836	Ge 25:26	Birth of Jacob & Esau	Abraham
2183	3723	2123	na	2123	2123	-1821	Ge 25:7	Death of Abraham	Abraham
2126	na	na	na	2126	2126	-1818	Ge 11:15	Death of Shelah	Isaac
2208	3748	2148	na	2148	2148	-1796	Ge 26:34	Esau marries Judith & Basemath	Isaac
2158	na	na	na	2158	2158	-1786	Ge 11:11	Death of Shem	Isaac
2231	na	na	2172	2171	2171	-1773	Ge 25:17	Death of Ishmael	Isaac
2187	na	na	na	2187	2187	-1757	Ge 11:17	Death of Eber	Isaac
na	na	na	na	na	na	na	Jub 27:19	Jacob departs for Haran	Isaac
2246	na	na	na	na	na	na	Jub 28:11	Birth of Reuben (by Leah)	Isaac
2247	na	na	na	na	na	na	Jub 28:13	Birth of Simeon (by Leah)	Isaac
2248	na	na	na	na	na	na	Jub 28:14	Birth of Levi (by Leah)	Isaac
2249	na	na	na	na	na	na	Jub 28:15	Birth of Judah (by Leah)	Isaac
na	na	na	na	na	na	na	Jub 28:18	Birth of Dan (by Bilhah)	Isaac
na	na	na	na	na	na	na	Jub 28:19	Birth of Naphtali (by Bilhah)	Isaac
na	na	na	na	na	na	na	Jub 28:20	Birth of Gad (by Zilpah)	Isaac
na	na	na	na	na	na	na	Jub 28:21	Birth of Asher (by Zilpah)	Isaac
na	na	na	na	na	na	na	Jub 28:22	Birth of Issachar (by Leah)	Isaac
na	na	na	na	na	na	na	Jub 28:23	Birth of Zebulun & Dinah (by Leah)	Isaac
2259	na	na	na	na	2199	-1745	Jub 28:24	Birth of Joseph (by Rachel)	Isaac
2276			2216	2216	2216	-1728	Ge 37:2	Joseph sold into slavery	Isaac
2288	3833	2228	2228	2228	2228	-1716	Ge 35:28	Death of Isaac	Isaac
2296	na	na	2228	2229	2229	-1715	Ge 41:46	Joseph enters Pharaoh's service	Jacob
2300	na	na	2238	2238	2238	-1706	Ge 47:9	Jacob before Pharaoh (age 130)	Jacob
2317	na	na	2255	2255	2255	-1689	Ge 47:28	Death of Jacob (age 147)	Jacob
2369	na	na	2309	2309	2309	-1635	Ge 50:22	Death of Joseph (age 110)	Joseph
2385	na	na	2331	2331	2331	-1613	Ex 6:16	Death of Levi (age 137)	na
na	na	na	na	na	na	na	Ex 6:18	Death of Kohath (age 133)	na
na	na	na	na	2368	na	na	Jub 47:1	Amram departs Canaan	na
na	na	na	na	na	na	na	Ex 6:20	Death of Amram (age 137)	na
2513	na	na	2448	2448	2448	-1496	Ex 7:7	Moses & Aaron before Pharaoh	Moses
2513	na	na	2448	2448	2448	-1496	Ex 12:40	Exodus from Egypt	Moses
2513	4053	2448	2448	2448	2448	-1496	Ex 12:41	Exodus from Egypt	Moses
2513	4053	2448	2448	2448	2448	-1496	Gen 15:13	Exodus from Egypt	Moses
2514	4054	2449	2449	na	2449	-1495	Num 1:1	Second year in wilderness	Moses
na	na	na	na	2484	2484	-1460	Jash 84:14	Thirty-sixth year in the wilderness	Moses
2552	4093	2488	2488	2488	2487	-1457	Nu 14:33	Fortieth year in the wilderness	Moses
2552	4093	2488	2488	2488	2487	-1457	Nu 14:34	Fortieth year in the wilderness	Moses
2552	4093	2488	2488	2488	2487	-1457	Nu 32:13	Fortieth year in the wilderness	Moses
2552	4093	2488	2487	2488	2487	-1457	Nu 33:38	Death of Aaron (age 123)	Moses
2552	4093	2488	2488	2488	2487	-1457	Nu 33:39	Death of Aaron (age 123)	Moses
2552	4093	2488	na	2488	2487	-1457	De 1:3	Fortieth year in the wilderness	Moses
2552	4093	2488	na	2488	2487	-1457	De 2:14	Fortieth year in the wilderness	Moses
2552	4093	2488	2488	2488	2487	-1457	De 31:2	Moses prohibited from Canaan	Moses
2552	4093	2488	2488	2488	2487	-1457	De 34:7	Moses at age 120	Moses
2553	4094	2489	2488	2489	2488	-1456	Jos 4:19	Israelites cross into Canaan	Joshua
2559	na	na	na	na	2494	-1450	Jos 14:10	Caleb at 85 years old	Joshua
2560	4099	2494	na	2493	2493	-1451	Jash 90:1	End of the Canaanite wars under Joshua	Joshua
2560	4099	2494	2495	2494	2494	-1450	Ant V:I:19	End of the Canaanite wars under Joshua	Joshua
na	na	na	na	na	2514	-1431	Jash 90:32	Joshua 26 years after crossing Jordan	Joshua
2561	4118	2513	2516	2516	2514	-1430	Jash 90:47	Death of Joshua (age 110)	Joshua
2561	4118	2513	2516	2516	2514	-1430	Jos 24:29	Death of Joshua (age 110)	Joshua
2561	4118	2513	2516	2516	2514	-1430	Ant V:I:29	Death of Joshua (age 110)	Joshua
na	na	na	2533	2533	2531	-1413	Jash 91:12	End of Interregnum	
na	4136	2531	2533	2533	2531	-1413	Ant 5:4	Interregnum	

Hidden in Genesis

Chronology of the Judges and Monarchs

Ussher	Joseph.	Joseph. (rev)	Seder Olam	Year AM	Year BC	Bk ch:v	Description of Event	Judge	King
na	4136	2531	2533	2531	-1413	Ant 5:4	Interregnum		
2599	na	na	2541	2538	-1406	Jdg 3:8	End of oppression by Aram		
2661	na	na	2573	2578	-1366	Jdg 3:11	Death of Othniel	Othniel	
2679	na	na	2584	2596	-1348	Jdg 3:13	End of oppression by Moab: Eglon		
2699	na	na	2654	2636	-1308	Jdg 3:30	End of Ehud and Shamgar judging Israel	Ehud	
2719	na	na	na	2656	-1288	Jdg 4:3	End of oppresson by Canaan		
2752	na	na	2694	2696	-1248	Jdg 5:31	Deborah completes judgment of Israel	Deborah	
2759	na	na	na	2703	-1241	Jdg 6:1	End of oppression by Midian		
2768	na	na	2734	2743	-1201	Jdg 8:28	Gideon completes judgment of Israel	Gideon	
2772	na	na	2737	2746	-1198	Jdg 9:22	Abimelech's death	Abimelech	
2795	na	na	2760	2769	-1175	Jdg 10:2	Tolah ends judgment of Israel	Tolah	
2817	na	na	2780	2791	-1153	Jdg 10:3	Death of Jair	Jair	
2823	na	na	2785	2797	-1147	Jdg 12:7	Death of Jephthah	Jephthah	
2830	na	na	2792	2804	-1140	Jdg 12:9	Death of Ibzan	Ibzan	
2817	na	na	2782	2809	-1135	Jdg 10:8	End of oppression by Philistines		
2840	na	na	2802	2814	-1130	Jdg 12:11	Death of Elon	Elon	
2848	na	na	2810	2822	-1122	Jdg 12:14	Death of Abdon	Abdon	
2887	na	na	2830	2862	-1082	Jdg 13:1	End of oppression by Philistines	Eli	
2887	na	na	2830	2829	-1115	Jdg 15:20	Death of Samson	Samson	
na	na	na	2830	2829	-1115	Jdg 16:31	Death of Samson	Samson	
2888	4569	2964	2870	2829	-1115	1Sa 4:18	Death of Eli the priest	Eli	
2909	na	na	na	na	na	1Sa 7:2	The Ark at Kirlath Jearim	Samuel	
na	4599	2994	na	2849	-1095	Ant VI:XIII:5	Death of Samuel the prophet		
2949	4601	2996	2882	2889	-1055	1Sa 13:1	End of Saul's reign		Saul
2949	4601	2996	2882	2889	-1055	Acts 13:21	End of Saul's reign		Saul
2951			na	2891	-1053	2Sa 2:10	End of Ish-Bosheth's reign		Ish-Bosheth
2989			2892	2891	-1053	2Sa 2:11	End of David's over Judah only		David
2989			2924	2924	-1020	2Sa 5:4	End of David's reign over all Israel		David
2989			2924	2924	-1020	2Sa 5:5	End of David's reign over all Israel		David
2989			2924	2924	-1020	1Chr 3:4	End of David's reign over all Israel		David
2989			2924	2924	-1020	1Ki 1:30	End of David's reign over all Israel		Solomon
2989			2924	2924	-1020	1Ki 2:11	End of David's reign over all Israel		Solomon
2992			2928	2928	-1016	1Ki 6:1	Foundation for the first Temple laid		Solomon
2992			2928	2928	-1016	2Chr 3:2	Foundation for the first Temple laid		Solomon
2992			2928	2928	-1016	1Ki 6:37	Foundation for the first Temple laid		Solomon
3000			2935	2935	-1009	1Ki 6:38	Completion of first Temple		Solomon
3012			na	2948	-996	1Ki 7:1	Completion of Solomon's palace		Solomon
3012			na	2948	-996	2Chr 8:1	Completion of Solomon's palace		Solomon
3029			2964	2964	-980	1Ki 11:42	End of Solomon's reign		Solomon
3029			2964	2964	-980	2Chr 9:30	End of Solomon's reign		Solomon

Chronology of the Divided Kingdom to the End of Amaziah's Reign

Ussher	Seder Olam	Year AM	Year BC	Bk ch:v	Description of Event	King-Judah	King-Israel
3033	2969	2969	-975	1Ki 14:25	Shishak attacks Jerusalem	Rehoboam	Jeroboam
3033	2969	2969	-975	2Chr 12:2	Shishak attacks Jerusalem	Rehoboam	Jeroboam
3046	2981	2981	-963	1Ki 14:21	End of Rehoboam's reign	Rehoboam	Jeroboam
3046	2981	2981	-963	2Chr 12:13	End of Rehoboam's reign	Rehoboam	Jeroboam
3046	2981	2981	-963	1Ki 15:1	Abijah accedes to the throne in Judah	Abijah	Jeroboam
3046	2981	2981	-963	2Chr 13:1	Abijah accedes to the throne in Judah	Abijah	Jeroboam
3049	2984	2984	-960	2Chr 13:2	End of Abijah's reign in Judah	Abijah	Jeroboam
3049	2984	2984	-960	1Ki 15:2	End of Abijah's reign in Judah	Asa	Jeroboam
3049	2983	2984	-960	2Chr 14:1	End of Abijah's reign in Judah	Asa	Jeroboam
3049	2983	2984	-960	1Ki 15:9	Asa accedes to the throne in Judah	Asa	Jeroboam
3050	2985	2985	-959	1Ki 15:25	Nadab accedes to the throne in Israel	Asa	Nadab
3050	2985	2985	-959	1Ki 14:20	Nadab accedes to the throne in Israel	Asa	Nadab
3051	2986	2986	-958	1Ki 15:28	End of Nadab's reign	Asa	Baasha
3051	2986	2986	-958	1Ki 15:33	Baasha accedes to the throne in Israel	Asa	Baasha
3063	2998	2998	-946	2Chr 15:10	Israelites assemble in Jerusalem	Asa	Baasha
3074	3009	3009	-935	1Ki 16:8	Elah accedes to the throne in Israel	Asa	Elah
3074	3010	3010	-934	1Ki 16:10	End of Elah's reign in Israel	Asa	Zimri
3074	3010	3010	-934	1Ki 16:21	Omri & Zimri contend for throne in Israel	Asa	Zimri
3079	3010	3014	-930	1Ki 16:23	Omri accedes to the throne in Israel	Asa	Omri
na	na	3018	-926	2Chr 15:19	No war until 35th year of Asa	Asa	Omri
na	na	3020	-924	2Chr 16:1	Israel attacks Judah in 36th year of Asa	Asa	Omri
3086	3021	3021	-923	1Ki 16:29	Ahab starts co-regency w/Omri in Israel	Asa	Omri/Ahab
3087	na	3023	-921	2Chr 16:12	Asa afflicted in his 39th year	Asa	Omri/Ahab
3090	3024	3025	-919	2Chr 16:13	End of Asa's reign in Judah	Asa	Omri/Ahab
3090	3024	3025	-919	1Ki 15:10	End of Asa's reign in Judah	Asa	Omri/Ahab
3090	3024	3025	-919	1Ki 22:41	Jehoshaphat accedes to the throne in Judah	Jehoshaphat	Omri/Ahab
3090	3024	3025	-919	1Ki 22:42	Jehoshaphat accedes to the throne in Judah	Jehoshaphat	Omri/Ahab
3090	3024	3025	-919	2Chr 20:31	Jehoshaphat accedes to the throne in Judah	Jehoshaphat	Omri/Ahab
na	na	3026	-918	1Ki 16:23	End of Omri's co-regency in Israel	Jehoshaphat	Ahab
3107	na	3027	-917	1Ki 22:2	Jehoshaphat visits Ahab in his 3rd year	Jehoshaphat	Ahab
3106	3041	3042	-902	1Ki 22:51	Ahaziah accedes to the throne in Israel	Jehoshaphat	~~Ahab~~/Ahaziah
3107	3043	3043	-901	2Ki 1:17	End of Ahaziah's reign in Israel	Jehoshaphat	Joram
3107	3043	3043	-901	2Ki 3:1	Joram accedes to the throne in Israel	Jehoshaphat	Joram
3106	3043	3047	-897	2Ki 8:16	Jehoram starts co-regency with Jehoshaphat	Jehoshaphat/Jehoram	Joram
3106	3043	3047	-897	2Ki 8:17	Jehoram starts co-regency with Jehoshaphat	Jehoshaphat/Jehoram	Joram
3115	3049	3050	-894	1Ki 22:42	End of Jehoshaphat's reign in Judah	Jehoram	Joram
3119	3055	3054	-890	2Ki 8:25	End of Jehoram's reign in Judah	Ahaziah	Joram
3119	3055	3054	-890	2Chr 21:5	End of Jehoram's reign in Judah	Ahaziah	Joram
3119	3055	3054	-890	2Chr 21:20	End of Jehoram's reign in Judah	Ahaziah	Joram
3119	3055	3054	-890	2Chr 22:2	Ahaziah accedes to the throne in Judah	Ahaziah	Joram
3120	3055	3054	-890	2Ki 8:26	Ahaziah accedes to the throne in Judah	Ahaziah	Joram
3120	3055	3054	-890	2Ki 9:29	Ahaziah accedes to the throne in Judah	Ahaziah	Joram
3120	3055	3055	-889	2Ki 3:1	End of Joram's reign in Israel	Ahaziah	Joram
3120	3055	3055	-889	2Ki 10:36	Jehu accedes to the throne of Israel	Jehoram/Athaliah	Jehu
3126	3061	3061	-883	2Ki 11:4	Joash accedes to the throne of Judah	Athaliah	Jehu
3126	3061	3061	-883	2Chr 23:1	Joash accedes to the throne of Judah	Athaliah	Jehu
3126	3061	3061	-883	2Chr 22:12	Joash accedes to the throne of Judah	Athaliah	Jehu
3126	3061	3061	-883	2Ki 11:21	Joash accedes to the throne of Judah	Joash	Jehu
3126	3061	3061	-883	2Chr 24:1	Joash accedes to the throne of Judah	Joash	Jehu
3126	3061	3061	-883	2Ki 12:1	Joash accedes to the throne of Judah	Joash	Jehu
3148	na	3083	-861	2Ki 12:6	End of Jehu's reign in Israel	Joash	Jehu
3148	3083	3083	-861	2Ki 13:1	Jehoahaz accedes to the throne of Israel	Joash	Jehoahaz
3163	3098	3097	-847	2Ki 13:10	Jehoash starts co-regency with Jehoahaz	Joash	Jehoahaz
3165	3100	3100	-844	2Ki 13:1	End of Jehoahaz' reign in Israel	Joash	~~Jehoahaz~~/Jehoash
3165	na	3101	-843	2Chr 24:23	Syria invades Judah ending reign of Joash	Joash	Jehoash
3165	3100	3101	-843	2Ki 14:1	Amaziah accedes to the throne in Judah	Amaziah	Jehoash
3165	3100	3101	-843	2Ki 14:2	Amaziah accedes to the throne in Judah	Amaziah	Jehoash
3165	3100	3101	-843	2Chr 25:1	Amaziah accedes to the throne in Judah	Amaziah	Jehoash
3179	3114	3116	-828	2Ki 13:10	End of Jehoash's reign in Israel	Amaziah/Azariah	~~Jehoash~~/Jeroboam II
3179	3115	3116	-828	2Ki 14:23	Jeroboam II accedes to the throne in Israel	Amaziah/Azariah	Jeroboam II
3179	3115	3130	-814	2Ki 14:17	End of Amaziah's reign in Judah	~~Amaziah~~/Azariah	Jeroboam II
3179	3115	3130	-814	2Ki 14:2	End of Amaziah's reign in Judah	~~Amaziah~~/Azariah	Jeroboam II
3179	3115	3130	-814	2Chr 25:25	End of Amaziah's reign in Judah	~~Amaziah~~/Azariah	Jeroboam II

Hidden in Genesis

Chronology of the Divided Kingdom from Azariah's Reign to Jehoiachin's Surrender

Ussher	Seder Olam	Year AM	Year BC	Bk ch:v	Description of Event	King-Judah	King-Israel
3179	3115	3130	-814	2Ki 14:21	Azariah accedes to the throne in Judah	Azariah	Jeroboam II
3179	3115	3130	-814	2Ki 15:1	Azariah accedes to the throne in Judah	Azariah	Jeroboam II
3179	3115	3130	-814	2Chr 26:1	Azariah accedes to the throne in Judah	Azariah	Jeroboam II
3179	3115	3130	-814	2Ki 15:2	Azariah accedes to the throne in Judah	Azariah	Jeroboam II
3179	3115	3130	-814	2Chr 26:3	Azariah accedes to the throne in Judah	Azariah	Jeroboam II
na	na	na	na	Zec 14:5	Earthquake in the days of Uzziah & Jeroboam	Azariah	na
3232	3153	3145	-799	2Ki 15:8	Zechariah accedes to the throne in Israel	Azariah	Zechariah
3232	3154	3146	-798	2Ki 15:13	Shallum accedes to the throne in Israel	Azariah	Shallum
3232	3154	3146	-798	2Ki 15:17	Menahem accedes to the throne in Israel	Azariah/Jotham	Menachem
3243	3164	3157	-787	2Ki 15:23	Pekahiah accedes to the throne in Israel	Azariah/Jotham	Pekahiah
3245	3166	3159	-785	2Ki 15:27	Pekah accedes to the throne in Israel	Azariah/Jotham	Pekah
3245	na	3159	-785	Isa 6:1	End of Azariah's reign in Judah	Azariah/Jotham	Pekah
na	3167	3160	-784	2Ki 15:32	Jotham accedes to the throne in Judah	Jotham	Pekah
na	3167	3160	-784	2Ki 15:33	Jotham accedes to the throne in Judah	Jotham	Pekah
na	3167	3160	-784	2Chr 27:1	Jotham accedes to the throne in Judah	Jotham	Pekah
na	3167	3160	-784	2Chr 27:8	Jotham accedes to the throne in Judah	Jotham	Pekah
na	3183	3168	-776	2Ki 16:2	Ahaz accedes to the throne in Judah	Jotham/Ahaz	Pekah
3262	3183	3175	-769	2Ki 16:1	Ahaz accedes to the throne in Judah	Jotham/Ahaz	Pekah
3262	3183	3175	-769	2Chr 27:8	End of Jotham's reign in Judah	Jotham/Ahaz	Pekah
3265	3187	3179	-765	2Ki 15:30	End of Pekah's reign in Israel	Ahaz	Hoshea
3265	3187	3179	-765	2Ki 17:1	Hoshea accedes to the throne in Israel	Ahaz	Hoshea
3277	3199	3181	-763	2Ki 18:1	Start of Hezekiah's co-reign in Judah	Ahaz	Hoshea
3277	3199	3181	-763	2Ki 18:2	Hezekiah accedes to the throne in Judah	Ahaz	Hoshea
3277	3199	3181	-763	2Chr 29:1	Hezekiah accedes to the throne in Judah	Ahaz	Hoshea
3278	3199	3181	-763	2Chr 29:3	Hezekiah repairs the Temple	Ahaz	Hoshea
3278	3199	3184	-760	2Chr 28:1	End of Ahaz' reign in Judah	Ahaz	Hoshea
3278	3199	3184	-760	Isa 14:28	End of Ahaz' reign in Judah	Hezekiah	Hoshea
3280	na	3185	-759	2Ki 17:5	Start of Assyrian siege of Samaria	Hezekiah	Hoshea
3280	na	3185	-759	2Ki 18:9	Start of Assyrian siege of Samaria	Hezekiah	Hoshea
3283	na	3187	-757	2Ki 17:6	End of Assyrian siege of Samaria	Hezekiah	Hoshea
3283	3205	3187	-757	2Ki 18:10	End of Assyrian siege of Samaria	Hezekiah	Hoshea
3291	3213	3194	-750	2Ki 18:13	Assyria attacks Jersalem under Hezekiah	Hezekiah	
3291	3213	3194	-750	Isa 36:1	Assyria attacks Jersalem under Hezekiah	Hezekiah	
3306	3228	3210	-734	2Ki 21:1	Mannaseh accedes to the throne in Judah	Manasseh	
3306	3228	3210	-734	2Chr 33:1	Mannaseh accedes to the throne in Judah	Manasseh	
3361	3283	3265	-679	2Ki 21:19	Amon accedes to the throne in Judah	Amon	
3361	3283	3265	-679	2Chr 33:21	Amon accedes to the throne in Judah	Amon	
3363	3285	3267	-677	2Ki 22:1	Josiah accedes to the throne in Jerusalem	Josiah	
3363	3285	3267	-677	2Chr 34:1	Josiah accedes to the throne in Jerusalem	Josiah	
3370	na	3274	-670	2Chr 34:3	Josiah seeks God	Josiah	
3374	na	3278	-666	2Chr 34:3	Josiah begins to purge idolatry in Judah	Josiah	
3375	na	3279	-665	Jer 1:2	God speaks to Jeremiah in Josiah's 13th yr	Josiah	
3380	3302	3284	-660	2Ki 22:3	Josiah sends Shaphan to the Temple	Josiah	
3380	3302	3284	-660	2Chr 34:8	Josiah sends Shaphan to the Temple	Josiah	
3381	3302	3284	-660	2Ki 23:23	Passover celebrated in Josiah's 18th yr	Josiah	
3381	3302	3284	-660	2Chr 35:19	Passover celebrated in Josiah's 18th yr	Josiah	
3394	3316	3297	-647	2Ki 23:31	Jehoahaz accedes to the throne of Judah	Jehoahaz	
3394	3316	3297	-647	2Chr 36:2	End of Jehoahaz' reign in Judah	Jehoahaz	
3394	3316	3297	-647	2Ki 23:36	Jehoiakim accedes to the throne in Judah	Joholakim	
3394	3316	3297	-647	2Chr 36:5	Jehoiakim accedes to the throne in Judah	Jehoiakim	
3398	3319	3299	-645	2Ki 24:1	Nebuchadnezzar beseiges Jerusalem	Jehoiakim	
3398	3319	3299	-645	Dan 1:1	Nebuchadnezzar beseiges Jerusalem	Jehoiakim	
na	na	3300	-644	Jer 25:1	Jeremiah prophesies against Judah	Jehoiakim	
na	na	3300	-644	Jer 25:11	Jeremiah's prophecy of 70 years desolation	Jehoiakim	
3399	na	3300	-644	Jer 46:2	Nebuchadnezzar defeats Egypt	Jehoiakim	
na	na	3300	-644	Jer 45:1	Prophecy of Jeremiah to Baruch	Jehoiakim	
3401	3320	3300	-644	Dan 2:1	Nebuchanezzar's dream of the statue (Dan 2)	Zedekiah	
na	na	3301	-643	Jer 25:3	Jeremiah's 23 years	Jehoiakim	
na	na	3301	-643	Jer 36:1	Jeremiah writes a prophetic scroll	Jehoiakim	
na	na	3302	-642	Jer 36:9	Scroll of Jeremiah read in the Temple	Jehoiakim	
3405	3327	3309	-635	2Ki 24:8	Jehoiachin accedes to the throne in Judah	Jehoiachin	
3405	3327	3309	-635	2Chr 36:9	Jehoiachin accedes to the throne in Judah	Jehoiachin	
3405	3327	3310	-634	2Ki 24:12	Jehoiachin surrenders to Nebuchanezzar	Jehoiachin	

Chronology of the Divided Kingdom from Jehoiachin's Surrender to the Exile of Jerusalem

Ussher	Seder Olam	Year AM	Year BC	Bk ch:v	Description of Event	King-Judah	Babylon
3405	3327	3310	-634	2Ki 24:18	Zedekiah accedes to the throne in Judah	Zedekiah	Nebuchadnezzar
3405	3327	3310	-634	Jer 52:1	Zedekiah accedes to the throne in Judah	Zedekiah	Nebuchadnezzar
na	na	3310	-634	Eze 29:17	Ezekiel prophesies Babylon's conquest of Egypt	Zedekiah	Nebuchadnezzar
3408	na	3312	-632	Jer 28:1	Hananiah's false prophecy	Zedekiah	Nebuchadnezzar
3409	na	3312	-632	Jer 51:59	Jeremiah records prophecies against Babylon	Zedekiah	Nebuchadnezzar
3409	na	3314	-630	Eze 1:1	Ezekiel's vision in the 5th year	Zedekiah	Nebuchadnezzar
3409	na	3314	-630	Eze 1:2	Ezekiel's vision in the 5th year	Zedekiah	Nebuchadnezzar
na	na	3315	-629	Eze 8:1	Ezekiel's vision in Babylonian captivity	Zedekiah	Nebuchadnezzar
na	na	3316	-628	Eze 20:1	God speaks to Ezekiel in captivity	Zedekiah	Nebuchadnezzar
na	na	3318	-626	Eze 24:1	Ezekiel prophesies siege of Jerusalem	Zedekiah	Nebuchadnezzar
3414	na	3318	-626	2Ki 25:1	Nebuchadnezzar beseiges Jerusalem	Zedekiah	Nebuchadnezzar
3414	na	3318	-626	Jer 52:4	Nebuchadnezzar beseiges Jerusalem	Zedekiah	Nebuchadnezzar
3414	na	3318	-626	Jer 39:1	Nebuchadnezzar beseiges Jerusalem	Zedekiah	Nebuchadnezzar
na	na	3319	-625	Eze 29:1	Ezekiel's prophecy against Egypt	Zedekiah	Nebuchadnezzar
3414	na	3319	-625	Jer 52:29	Nebuchadnezzar carries captives to Babylon	Zedekiah	Nebuchadnezzar
3414	na	3319	-625	Jer 32:1	Jeremiah's prophecy of the fall of Jerusalem	Zedekiah	Nebuchadnezzar
na	na	3320	-624	Eze 26:1	Ezekiel's prophecy against Tyre	Zedekiah	Nebuchadnezzar
na	na	3320	-624	Eze 30:20	Ezekiel's 2nd prophecy against Egypt	Zedekiah	Nebuchadnezzar
na	na	3320	-624	Eze 31:1	Ezekiel's 3rd prophecy against Egypt	Zedekiah	Nebuchadnezzar
3414	3328	3320	-624	Jer 52:28	Nebuchadnezzar takes Judah captive	Jehoiakim	Nebuchadnezzar
3416	na	3220	-724	Eze 40:1	Ezekiel's vision of measuring the city	Jehoiakim	Nebuchadnezzar
3416	3338	3320	-624	2Ki 25:2	Jerusalem falls to Nebuchadnezzar	Zedekiah	Nebuchadnezzar
3416	3338	3320	-624	Jer 52:5	Jerusalem falls to Nebuchadnezzar	Zedekiah	Nebuchadnezzar
3416	3338	3320	-624	Jer 39:2	Jerusalem falls to Nebuchadnezzar	Zedekiah	Nebuchadnezzar
3416	3338	3320	-624	2Chr 36:11	Jerusalem burned	Zedekiah	Nebuchadnezzar
3416	3338	3320	-624	Jer 1:3	The exile of Jerusalem	Zedekiah	Nebuchadnezzar
3416	3338	3320	-624	2Ki 25:8	Jerusalem burned		Nebuchadnezzar
3416	3338	3320	-624	Jer 52:12	Jerusalem burned		Nebuchadnezzar

Hidden in Genesis

Chronology from the Exile of Jerusalem to the Death of Alexander

Ussher	Seder Olam	Year AM	Year BC	Bk ch:v	Description of Event	Babylon	Persia
na	na	3321	-623	Eze 32:1	Ezekiel's 4th prophecy against Egypt	Nebuchadnezzar	
na	na	3321	-623	Eze 32:17	Ezekiel's 5th prophecy against Egypt	Nebuchadnezzar	
na	na	3321	-623	Eze 33:21	Ezekiel prophesies against Judah	Nebuchadnezzar	
3420	na	3324	-620	Jer 52:30	Nebuzaradan carries away 745 Jews	Nebuchadnezzar	
3442	na	3345	-599	2Ki 25:27	Jehoiachin released from prison	Evil-Merodach	
3442	na	3345	-599	Jer 52:31	Jehoiachin released from prison	Evil-Merodach	
3444	3364	3348	-596	na	End of reign of Evil-Merodach	Evil-Merodach/Neglissar	
3448	na	3352	-592	na	End of reign of Neglissar	Neglissar/Labosordacus	
3449	na	3353	-591	na	End of reign of Labosordacus	Labosordacus/Baltasar	
3449	3387	3353	-591	Dan 7:1	Belshazzar becomes king of Babylon	Belshazzar	
3451	3387	3355	-589	Dan 8:1	Daniel's vision of a ram and a goat	Belshazzar	
3465	3389	3370	-574	Dan 5:1	Babylon falls to Medo-Persian Empire	Belshazzar/Cyrus	Cyrus (29)
3466	3389	3370	-574	2Chr 36:21	70 years of desolation complete	Darius the Mede	Cyrus
3466	3389	3370	-574	Jer 25:12	70 years of desolation complete	Darius the Mede	Cyrus
3468	3389	3370	-574	2Chr 36:22	Decree of Cyrus to rebuild the Temple	Darius the Mede	Cyrus
3468	3389	3370	-574	Ezr 1:1	Decree of Cyrus to rebuild the Temple	Darius the Mede	Cyrus
3468	3389	3370	-574	Ezr 5:13	Decree of Cyrus to rebuild the Temple	Darius the Mede	Cyrus
3468	3389	3370	-574	Ezr 6:3	Decree of Cyrus to rebuild the Temple	Darius the Mede	Cyrus
3466	na	3370	-574	Dan 1:21	Daniel's favor in Babylon	Darius the Mede	Cyrus
na	na	3370	-574	Dan 11:1	Angel foretells of Alexander the Great	Darius the Mede	Cyrus
na	3390	3372	-572	Dan 10:1	Daniel's vision of a glorious man	Darius the Mede	Cyrus
3475	3394	3399	-545	na	End of Cyrus II's reign		Cyrus
3482	3402	3406	-538	na	End of Cambyses II's reign		Cambyses (Ahasuerus) (8)
3483	3402	3407	-537	na	End of Smerdis' reign; accession of Darius I		Smerdis (<1)
3483	na	3408	-536	Ezr 4:24	Restoration of the Temple halted		Darius I (36)
na	3390	3408	-536	Dan 9:2	Daniel understands Jeremiah's prophecy		Darius I
3485	na	3408	-536	Hag 1:1	God tells Haggai to rebuild the Temple		Darius I
3485	na	3408	-536	Ezr 3:8	Restoration of the Temple begins		Darius I
3485	na	3408	-536	Hag 1:15	God tells Zerubbabel to rebuild the Temple		Darius I
3485	na	3408	-536	Zec 1:1	God tells Zechariah that Israel must repent		Darius I
3485	na	3408	-536	Hag 2:10	Haggai's Prophecy that the Jews are defiled		Darius I
3485	na	3408	-536	Zec 1:7	Zechariah's vision of the four horsemen		Darius I
3487	na	3410	-534	Zec 7:1	Zechariah's prophecy on fasting		Darius I
3489	na	3412	-532	Ezr 6:15	Restoration of the Temple completed		Darius I
		3443	-501	na	Death of Darius I; Xerxes I becomes king		Darius I / Xerxes
3486	na	3445	-499	Est 1:3	Queen Vashti enrages King Xerxes I		Xerxes (21)
3490	na	3449	-495	Est 2:16	Ester crowned Queen of Persia		Xerxes
3491	na	3454	-490	Est 3:7	Haman conspires against the Jews		Xerxes
	3459	3464	-480	na	Death of Xeres I; accession of Artaxerxes I		Xerxes
	na	3470	-474	Ezr 7:7	Ezra goes to Jerusalem		Artaxerxes (41)
	na	3470	-474	Ezr 7:8	Ezra arrives in Jerusalem		Artaxerxes
	na	3483	-461	Neh 1:1	Nehemiah prays for Israel		Artaxerxes
	na	3483	-461	Neh 2:1	Artaxerxes frees Nehemiah to rebuild Jerusalem		Artaxerxes
	3521	3483	-461	Neh 5:14	Artaxerxes' decree to rebuild Jerusalem		Artaxerxes
	3533	3495	-449	Neh 13:6	Nehemiah is returned to Babylon		Artaxerxes
	3500	3511	-433	na	End of Artaxerxes' reign		Artaxerxes
	na	3511	-433	na	Xerxes II becomes King of Persia		Xerxes II (0.12)
	na	3512	-432	na	End of Sogdianus' reign in Persia		Sogdianus (0.5)
	na	3512	-432	na	Darius II becomes King of Persia		Darius II (19)
	na	3531	-413	na	End of Darius II's reign in Persia		Darius II
	na	3531	-413	na	Artaxerxes II becomes King of Persia		Artaxerxes II (46)
	na	3577	-367	na	End of Artaxerxes II's reign in Persia		Artaxerxes II
	na	3577	-367	na	Artaxerxes III becomes King of Persia		Artaxerxes III (20)
	na	3597	-347	na	End of Artaxerxes II's reign in Persia		Artaxerxes III
	na	3597	-347	na	Artexerxes IV becomes King of Persia		Arses (2)
	na	3599	-345	na	End of Artaxerxes IV's reign in Persia		Arses
	na	3599	-345	na	Darius III becomes King of Persia		Darius III (6)
	na	3605	-339	na	End of Darius III's reign in Persia		Darius III
	3598	3605	-339	1Mac 1:1	Alexander the Great conquers the Persian Empire		Alexander (13)
	3601	3618	-326	1Mac 1:7	Death of Alexander the Great		Alexander

Chronology from Antiochus Epiphanes to the Crucifixion

Ussher	Seder Olam	Year AM	Year BC	Bk ch:v	Description of Event	Judea	Empire
tbd		3764	-180	1Mac 1:10	Antiochus Epiphanes becomes king		
tbd		3770	-174	1Mac 1:10	Antiochus Epiphanes defeats Egypt & then invades Israel		
tbd		3772	-172	1Mac 1:54	Antiochus Epiphanes invades Jerusalem 2nd time		
tbd		3774	-170	1Mac 1:54	Antiochus Epiphanes invades Jerusalem 3rd time		
tbd		3775	-169	1Mac 4:52	Hannukah established to celebrate dedication of Temple		
tbd		3776	-168	1Mac 6:16	Antiochus Ephiphanes dies in Persia		
tbd		3776	-168	1Mac 6:49	A sabbath year - resets lines 380 to 386 by -3 years		
							Hasmonean
tbd		3881	-63				Roman
tbd		3907	-37		Herod becomes ruler of Judea	Herod the Great	Roman
						Herod the Great	Roman
tbd		3940	-4		Birth of Christ	Herod the Great	Roman
tbd		3970	26		Baptism of Christ		Roman
tbd		tbd	tbd	Isa 20:1			Roman
tbd		tbd	tbd	Eze 4:5			Roman
tbd		tbd	tbd	Eze 29:13			Roman
tbd		tbd	tbd	Isa 7:8			Roman
							Roman
tbd		3973	30 AD		Christ crucified		Roman

About the Author

Paul Knauber is a magna cum laude graduate of Villanova University with a Bachelor of Science Degree in Physics. He has also done MBA coursework at Temple University in Philadelphia and Gannon University in Erie, PA. Paul has worked in laboratory research and development environments doing work in fiber optics, magnetic switching, and laser isotope separation. While he has several years of Operations Management experience, the majority of his business career was in the field of electronic power conversion in Applications Engineering, Program Management, Marketing Management, and General Management. He has authored multiple articles for industry publications in power electronics. He retired in 2012 but continued to perform consulting work through 2019. Since then, having a passionate faith in Biblical historicity, *Hidden in Genesis* represents the summary of his investigations into the earliest parts of the Genesis account, addressing the implications and consequences of this commonly dismissed or avoided but intriguing span of our ancient history. He married his wife Neli (nee Wakulin) in 1977; she is also retired and they currently live in Green Valley, AZ.

www.ingramcontent.com/pod-product-compliance
Lightning Source LLC
Chambersburg PA
CBHW081232170426
43198CB00017B/2735